ODD PEOPLE

ODD PEOPLE

HUNTING SPIES IN THE FIRST WORLD WAR

BASIL THOMSON

Biteback Publishing

First published in Great Britain in 1922 by Hodder & Stoughton Ltd
This edition published in Great Britain in 2015 by
Biteback Publishing Ltd
Westminster Tower
3 Albert Embankment
London SE1 7SP
Copyright © Basil Thomson 1922, 2015

ISBN 978-1-84954-797-0

10 9 8 7 6 5 4 3 2 1

A CIP catalogue record for this book is available from the British Library.

Set in Bulmer

Printed and bound in Great Britain by
CPI Group (UK) Ltd, Croydon CR0 4YY

*To my colleagues, whose tact and unselfish
devotion averted many dangers*

CONTENTS

INTRODUCTION

BASIL THOMSON WAS an astonishing character and a dominant figure within the British intelligence community for a period that covered the First World War and the subsequent, and to a degree resultant, growth in support for left-wing ideas. As the head of Scotland Yard's Criminal Investigation Department, Thomson was in charge of hunting down German spies, in tandem with MI5, and, in the three years following the war, communist subversives within the trade unions. He dealt with some of the most interesting spies and traitors of that period, including the infamous female spy, Mata Hari, and Roger Casement, the Irish nationalist hanged for his attempt during the First World War to get the Germans to support a republican uprising.

Queer People, as this book was originally called (we have changed the title for obvious reasons), remains a rollicking read. Thomson provides a fascinating account of the main stories from that period. His dismissal of the various spy scares propagated by military intelligence and its successors in MI5 is entirely appropriate, albeit in part the result of an intense rivalry. Thomson held ambitions to take charge of a security and intelligence service which would absorb MI5 under his control. Although it was largely MI5 which uncovered the German spies sent to Britain ahead of, and during, the First World War, it was Thomson who arrested and interrogated them. His account here reflects a number of the common prejudices of the period, including Thomson's reference to Casement's homosexuality as 'obsessions' which could only have been induced by some form of madness. Thomson supposedly cannot bring himself to use the word 'homosexual', although he unscrupulously used Casement's diaries to smear him ahead of the trial. Similarly, Thomson's description of his interview with Mata Hari is underlain by what seems now to be an incomprehensible degree of misogyny in his dismissal of the effectiveness of women as spies, particularly given the fact that their effectiveness in that area is now generally accepted, and used, by the world's intelligence services. Nevertheless, it was a common view which Thomson shared with his rivals in MI5.

It is inevitably the stories of the spies he met which generate interest, but Thomson was an extraordinarily colourful character in his own right. The son of a future Archbishop of York, he was educated at Eton and then went up to New College, Oxford. Suffering from severe depression, he quit after two terms and went to America to find a new life, before joining the colonial service and working in Fiji first, then Tonga and finally New Guinea. Thomson returned to Tonga in 1899 to successfully fight off a German attempt to gain control of the islands.

After a spell as governor of a number of prisons, including Dartmoor and Wormwood Scrubs, he was appointed to the post of Assistant Commissioner in charge of criminal investigations at Scotland Yard, becoming Director of Intelligence in 1919. His ambitions to take over MI5 operations, and his thoroughly justified dismissal of their effectiveness during that period, ensured him many enemies, as did his efforts to root out left-wing elements within the post-war labour movement. This ultimately brought about his downfall. He was sacked in 1921 on the insistence of Prime Minister Lloyd George, ostensibly because of IRA graffiti daubed on the walls of Chequers (the Prime Minister's newly acquired country residence) and brought to public disgrace by an incident in Hyde Park in 1925 involving the well-known prostitute Thelma de Lava. His friends insisted it was a sting aimed at discrediting him and there remain good grounds for suspecting they were right. He died in March 1939.

Michael Smith
Editor of the Dialogue Espionage Classics series
October 2014

PREFACE

MY READERS WILL be divided between those who think that I have not told enough, that I have told too much and that I had better have told nothing at all. I bow my head to them all.

The list of those to whom my thanks are due is too long to set out in a preface. It would include the names of my admirable staff, of sailors, soldiers and civilians of many countries besides our own in almost every walk of life and even of a few of our late enemies. No drama, no film story yet written has been so enthralling as our daily repertory on the dimly lighted stage set in a corner of the granite building in Westminster. In a century after we, with our war-weariness, are dead and gone, the Great War will be a quarry for tales of adventure, of high endeavour and of splendid achievement; when that time comes even some of the humbler actors who play their part in these pages may be seen through a haze of romance.

My thanks are due to Mr Milward R. K. Burge for permission to use his verses on the Hotel Majestic during the Peace Conference.

Basil Thomson
London, 1922

CHAPTER 1

THE DETECTIVE IN REAL LIFE

I F I WERE asked what were the best qualifications for a detective I should say to be a jack-of-all-trades and a master of none. That, perhaps, is because I happen to be an indifferent jack-of-all-trades myself and I cannot remember any smattering that I acquired in distant corners of the earth that did not come in useful at Scotland Yard.

Other countries try to make specialists of their detectives. They would have them know chemistry, surgery and mineralogy; they would have them competent to appraise the value of jewels, to judge the time a corpse has been dead, or how long a footprint has been impressed upon damp earth. They forget that there is a specialist round every corner and that a detective who knows his work knows also where to find a jeweller or a doctor or skilled mechanic who will give him a far better opinion than his own. All that they succeed in doing is to furnish a very alluring laboratory for the edification of visitors and saddle themselves with a host of theorists who make a very poor show by the test of the statistics of discovered crime.

Real life is quite unlike detective fiction; in fact, in detective work fiction is stranger than truth. Mr Sherlock Holmes, to whom I take off my hat with a silent prayer that he may never appear in the flesh, worked by induction, but not, so far as I am able to judge, by the only method which gets home, namely, organisation and hard work. He consumed vast quantities of drugs and tobacco. I do not know how much his admirable achievements owed to these, but I do know that if we at Scotland Yard had faithfully copied his processes we should have ended by fastening upon a distinguished statesman or high dignitary of the Church the guilt of some revolting crime.

The detection of crime consists in good organisation, hard work and luck, in about equal proportions; when the third ingredient predominates the detective is very successful indeed. Among many hundred examples the Voisin murder at the end of 1917 may be cited. The murderer had cut off the head and hands of his victim in the hope that identification would be impossible and he chose the night of an air raid for his crime because the victim might be expected to have left London in a panic; but he had forgotten a little unobtrusive laundry mark on her clothing and by this he was found, convicted and executed. That was both luck and organisation. Scotland Yard has the enormous advantage over Mr Sherlock Holmes in that it has an organisation which can scour every pawnshop, every laundry, every public-house and even every lodging-house in the huge area of London within a couple of hours.

I took charge of the Criminal Investigation Department in June 1913. The late Sir Melville Macnaghten, my predecessor, who wrote his reminiscences, held the view that the proper function of the head of the CID was to help and encourage his men but not to hamper them with interference. He had an astonishing memory both for faces and for names: he could tell you every detail about a ten-year-old crime, the names of the victim, the perpetrator and every important witness and, what was more useful, the official career of every one of his 700 men and his qualifications and ability. Unlike my predecessors, I had already a wide acquaintance among criminals, chiefly those of the professional class. To read their records was to me like looking at crime through the big end of the telescope. At Dartmoor I had 1,200 of them, nearly all professionals with anything from one to thirty previous convictions. There were Scotsmen, Irishmen, Welshmen and Englishmen, with a good sprinkling of foreigners, some of whom had come to England when their own countries had become too hot to hold them. When you read of crime in the magazines or the detective novels it is nearly always murder. You have to be in charge of a prison in order to realise that the murderer is rarely a criminal by nature at all. But for the grace of God he is just you and I, only more unlucky. For the real criminal you have to go to the crimes against property. Most murders are committed without any deep-laid plot, whereas the professional thief or forger or fraud has carefully planned his depredations before he sets out to commit them: the murderer is repentant and is planning only how he can earn an honest living after he is discharged; the others are thinking out schemes for fresh adventures.

Criminal investigation was not quite what I expected to find it. The department was well organised, though perhaps a little rusty in the hinges. The danger of centralisation had been realised long before. London had been divided into twenty-one divisions, each with a criminal investigation staff whose business it was to know everything about its portion of the huge city. These divisional staffs dealt with all the ordinary crime that occurred in the division: it was only the graver crimes or those that were spread over several divisions that were taken up by the staff of the Central Office. In such cases it was usual to detach a Chief Inspector to take charge of the inquiry.

Every day we received a thick bundle of forms in which every crime, however small, committed in London during the previous twenty-four hours was reported. The graver of these formed the subject of a separate report and there was the excellent practice of making a detailed report upon every suspected crime as soon as it occurred, because one could never tell into what it might develop.

The Criminal Investigation Department at Scotland Yard is not responsible for the crimes committed out of London, but by an arrangement with the Home Office a chief constable may ask the department for help to unravel any serious crime committed in his area without any cost to the local authority. That this permission is not always acted on is due less to the very natural *amour propre* of the local force than to the difficulty in determining what difficulties lie ahead. The larger cities have, moreover, efficient detective organisations of their own: most of them have sent men to be trained in the Detective Classes at New Scotland Yard; these have greatly distinguished themselves in the examinations.

The training of detectives was almost entirely legal and, as far as it went, it was admirably done. It was essential that they should know the rudiments of the criminal law as well as the procedure of the criminal courts, otherwise they were bound, sooner or later, to commit some solecism that would incur the comments of the judge. But on its practical side their education was neglected. Very few were craftsmen and if it came to making an exhaustive search of a house they might be expected to look conscientiously in all the obvious places and make no search for such hiding-places as a short board in the floor or the space behind the wainscot; probably none of them had ever watched a house in the course of erection. It is only by experience and by failure that real proficiency in the matter of searching is acquired. Nor were they taught any uniform method of description.

The average police description was a very colourless document, for in any crowd one might find a dozen men with a 'fresh complexion, blue eyes, brown hair, oval face and medium height'. Such matters as peculiarities of gait and speech were very often omitted. They did not always know the trade names of articles of clothing or plate or jewellery, nor could they distinguish between real stones and pearls and their counterfeits. The more intelligent picked up these things by experience, but the others did not. Many of them seemed to me to be unimaginative in the matter of observation; at any rate, they seemed seldom to follow a man without his becoming aware of it. On the other hand, they were admirable when it came to dealing with the public. Their courtesy never failed and naturally it brought them much help from the people living in their locality.

I soon found that the London detectives were naturally divided into two classes, the detective and the 'thief-catcher'. The latter belonged to the class of honest, painstaking policeman without sufficient education to pass examinations for promotion, but who made up for this deficiency by his intimate knowledge of the rougher class of criminals, his habits and his haunts and by personal acquaintance with the pickpockets themselves, who had the same regard for him as a naughty little boy has for a strict and just schoolmaster.

The thief-catcher has no animus against the people he has to watch. He keeps his eye upon them warily, as the keeper at the zoo keeps his eye upon the polar bears and when it comes to business he arrests them impartially without rancour and without indulgence. This explained what I had never been able to understand in prison – how the convicted criminal seldom bears malice against the detective who brought him to justice provided he thinks that he was treated fairly. 'The man was only doing his dooty,' he says. The danger of over-educating your detective is that, little by little, you will eliminate the 'thief-catcher' for whom there is a very definite place in the scheme. I remember one whose zeal had communicated itself to his wife. At that time we were overwhelmed with complaints about pickpockets at the stopping-places of the buses in the crowded hours. They would take part in the rush to get in, crowding on with the other passengers and relieving them of the contents of their pockets; if they were disappointed of a place, they fell back and waited for the next bus to continue their business. If they saw any one eyeing them they would mount the bus until they came to a stopping-place where they thought they would be more free from observation. My 'thief-catcher' was a rather conspicuous person and when he appeared on the scene the pickpockets would melt away. He could not be everywhere at once, but he used to make a sort of 'busman's holiday' of his days off duty and go out with his wife. She mounted the bus with a gaping handbag, which was as effective a bait for a pickpocket as roast pork is for a shark; the pickpocket followed and just behind him went the husband to take him into custody in the very act. It must have been a quite exciting sport for both.

Every now and then the 'thief-catcher' would show a rare gleam of imagination. I remember the case of a man who was expected to pledge a stolen watch. It was impossible to search him until he did, because if he had not got the watch in his possession he would 'have the law on you'. The suspect vapoured about the railings of St Mary Abbot's church, watched from the kerbstone by John Barker's, where people are always waiting for the bus. There was a pawnshop at the corner. Suddenly he formed a resolution and walked quickly across the street to the pawnshop, but the 'thief-catcher' was too quick for him. Flinging off his coat as he went, he plunged into the shop, dashed behind the counter and received the suspect in his shirt sleeves, resting on his knuckles in the conventional style and asked him what he could do for him. 'What will you give me on this?' said the man, producing the watch.

'Come along to the police station and I'll tell you and I caution you that anything you say may be used in evidence against you at your trial.'

I have no doubt that the suspect said something which was not fit to use in evidence when he realised what a trap he had fallen into.

In one respect the Central Office was very much alive. Besides its admirable system of identification by finger prints, elaborated by Sir Edward Henry, the Commissioner, a system since adopted by the whole civilised world, it had a very complete and practical method of record-keeping.

The late Dr Mercier was responsible for the fallacy that there was an almost invariable tendency on the part of criminals to repeat the method in which they had been successful on a former enterprise. But a glance at criminal histories shows that Dr Mercier's theory was only partly true. Most of the practitioners vary their methods according to local conditions. You will find the blackmailer taking an occasional hand in a burglary; a pickpocket indulging in shop-lifting; an area thief boldly breaking in through the front door. All that can be said is that a man who has successfully poisoned a dog in one case is more likely than another man to do the same again. The only successful organisation in detecting crime must have method, industry and local knowledge and I found all these strongly culti-vated at New Scotland Yard.

The London thief is preternaturally quick in detecting that he is being followed. Even if he is not quite sure, he will adopt the expe-dient of turning sharp on his heel and walking for 50 yards in the opposite direction before resuming his journey and during that 50 yards his sharp eyes have taken a mental photograph of every person he has passed. In really big affairs he will pay a confederate to follow him at a distance, taking note of any other follower remotely resembling a policeman. The tubes are very useful to him. He books for a long journey, sits near the door and slips out at the next station just before the gates of the car are slammed and there is no time for the policeman to alight and having thus shaken him off, he sets off for his real destination. Four well-known thieves tried this device once with a pair of detectives in attendance. All went well up to the point of slamming the gate and then things began to go wrong. The detectives had the gate reopened. The lift was one of those that are operated by a liftman standing at the bottom and as it went aloft the detective explained the position to the liftman. Something went wrong with that lift: it stuck halfway for quite five minutes – time enough for the detectives to climb the stairs and summon uniformed policemen to man the gates on the level of the street. The feelings of the trapped rat who sees a group of terriers waiting for the wirework door of his cage to be opened must have descended upon the spirits of those four thieves when their cage rose at length to the surface.

Every now and then a detective would display real initiative in keeping observation. In quiet suburban roads a loitering man would at once bring a face to every window in the street. To keep watch upon a house there must be some excuse. In one case the detective became a jobbing gardener and undertook to clip the hedges and weed the paths of the house opposite and if he took a long time over the job, that is quite in accordance with the habits of jobbing gardeners; in another, attired in suitable clothing and armed with pick-axes, two detectives proceeded to dig up the roadway. Their leisurely method of work must have convinced the bystanders that they were genuine employees of the Borough Surveyor.

CHAPTER 2

THE IMAGINATIVE LIAR

URING THE WAR there was an outbreak of what the Americans call 'congenital lying', but which might better be termed 'adolescent lying' on the part of young persons. We all know the young girl who tells fibs and in normal times she would probably be spanked and sent to bed without her supper, but in wartime any story, however wild, was accepted.

One afternoon during the first year of the war I received an urgent request from a chief constable in the Midlands for help in a case of great difficulty. The family of a doctor in good practice had been upset by receiving a series of outrageous letters and postcards signed by a lady's maid who had lately gone to another situation. While she had been with them she was a quiet and respectable person and yet her letters could have been written only by a woman of vicious and depraved character. They came in all sorts of ways. Sometimes they were pushed under the front door; sometimes they were thrown in through an open window and, though the front door was put under police observation and no one was seen to come to it, they were dropped into the letter-box at intervals of three hours.

And then the house itself became bewitched. The mistress would put down her bunch of keys on the kitchen dresser for a moment and a wicked fairy whisked them away. The cook would put a pound of butter into the larder: it vanished. The housemaid lost her pen and ink, the doctor his comb and the whole house was ransacked from top to bottom without recovering any of these things. It is a most harassing thing for a doctor in a busy practice to come home to a house which has been bewitched by wicked fairies.

There was nothing to go upon except the bundle of letters, which certainly bore out the description which the chief constable had given of them. I suppose that Mr Sherlock Holmes would have taken another injection of cocaine and smoked three or four pipes over them before he sat himself down to analyse the ink and examine the paper under a powerful lens. The detective inspector to whom I entrusted the case did none of these things. He asked for the bundle of letters and took the next train. I thought that the case might take him a week, but it took him exactly two hours. When he returned next day he gave the following account of his proceedings.

On the way down in the train he read through the letters and made a note of every word that had been misspelt. There were seventeen. He then composed a piece of dictation which took in the seventeen words. It must have been like composing an acrostic. On his arrival at the house he summoned the entire household – the doctor, his wife, the children and the five servants – into the dining room and, adopting the businesslike procedure of the village schoolmaster, he served out paper and pens. When all were seated comfortably at the table he cleared his throat and gave them a piece of dictation. All entered into the spirit of the thing – all except one and she made no sign. At the end of twenty minutes the pens ceased to scratch and the copies were handed in. They did not take him long to run through. After a brief inspection he detained the mistress and the 'tweeny' and dismissed the others. He then said that he would like the mistress to take him up to the 'tweeny''s sleeping quarters with the girl herself. In her room was a locked box. The 'tweeny' had lost the key, but when he talked of breaking it open the key was suddenly discovered. In the box were writing materials identical with those of the incriminatory letters and then after a little pressing the girl burst into tears and made a clean breast of it. She did not like the ex-lady's maid; she did like to see the whole household in a flutter. She began with the letters and when she saw these beginning to lose their effect she became the wicked fairy with the keys and the butter-pats. Some people are surprised that children of sixteen can write horrible letters, but experience has shown that this is quite a common aspect of adolescent lying.

The spy mania was a godsend to the adolescent liar. A lady in a large house in Kensington came one day in great distress to say that her little maid had been kidnapped by masked men in a black car and carried off to some unknown destination in the suburbs, apparently with the intention of extorting information from her; but fortunately, with a resource of which her mistress had found no evidence in her domestic duties, she had escaped from them and returned the next morning. The mistress thought that we ought to lose no time in catching these masked miscreants and their black car. The girl's story was certainly arresting. It had been her evening out and while coming away from listening to the band in Hyde Park a tall, dark man (these men are always tall and dark) had stopped her and had said, 'You have got to come with me. You are wanted for the Cause.' She refused. He had then given a peculiar whistle (these men always give a peculiar whistle) and two other tall, dark men had emerged from the darkness and laid hold upon her.

'What were the policemen doing all this time? Didn't you cry out?'

'All the men wore masks and that frightened me so that I did not dare to cry out. Two of them took me, one on each side and led me out to the cab-stand. There I saw a dark car with the blinds down. They pushed me into it and shut the door and then the car started and drove at terrible speed with no lights.'

'No lights? But the police would have stopped it.'

'Well, I didn't see any lights. It all looked black.'

'Which way did you go?'

'Oh, we passed down Kensington High Street and away into the country, but I was too frightened to notice the direction.'

'And then?'

Then we got to a large house standing in a garden. It was all black. We stopped at the front door and I heard one of them say, 'Where shall we put her?' and the other said, 'Into the black room.' They took me out of the car and down a passage and pushed me into a black room with no light and locked the door. I heard them whispering and consulting and I thought they were going to kill me.

'Well, and then what happened?'

'Nothing, sir. I stayed on in the room for quite a long time and then I went to the window and found I could get out.'

'And then?'

'Well, then I got out and came home.'

'How did you find your way?'

'Oh, I met a lady not far from the house and she told me how to get home.'

'But it must have taken you hours.'

'It did, sir. I didn't get home till the morning.'

The inspector asked her whether the men had talked about spying. They had not. Why did she think they were spies? Because they wore masks and had a black car. Also, I suppose, because they were tall and dark. He then took the mistress aside and said that he would like an opportunity of searching her box, because something she had said led him to think that there was only one man and he was not tall or dark. The key was produced, the box opened and there on the top lay – a pair of soldier's gloves. And then the whole story was dragged out of her. He was in khaki, he had no confederates and no car, but he was soft-spoken and the poor fellow was just going off to the Front. That cleared up the mystery.

In 1915, when the spy mania was at its height, a little general servant, aged sixteen and fresh from the country, threw her master and mistress into an almost hysterical state by her revelations. One day the mistress found her in the kitchen writing cabalistic signs on a sheet of paper. The girl explained that this was part of a dreadful secret and when pressed a little, confided to her that she had become a sort of bondslave of a German master spy named 'E. M.', who had employed her to make a plan of the Bristol Channel and had taught her to operate an extraordinary signalling engine called the 'Maxione'. She said that she was in terror of her life, that the spy would come and tap at the kitchen window, that he had a powerful green car waiting round the corner in which he would whisk her off to operate the 'Maxione' and the red lights, without which the submarines lying in wait in the Bristol Channel would not be able to do their fell work. When she saw that her master and mistress swallowed her story she began to enlarge upon it. She introduced into it a mythical girl friend, a sort of Mrs Harris, in whose name she wrote to herself in a disguised handwriting and this girl friend gave her a great deal of good advice, such as: 'Trust in E. M. no longer. Really I believe he *is* a spy.'

This girl went on to say that in the course of a ride she had taken documents out of his pocket which she recognised as containing a plan for blowing up Tilbury Docks. She also produced letters from the spy himself – impassioned love-letters which contained gems like the following:

> *Herr von Scheuaquasha will pay you £50 for one tapping of the red light, the X signal of the seventh line, the universal plug and the signalling. The staff of the Kaiser Wilhelm will pay you greatly and you will be rewarded for the rest of your life. You will be mentioned in all the German head papers as the heroine of a brave act and heroic deed. I have a home in Germany and two servants awaiting your arrival. A valet shall wait on you, darling. You shall be driven in a smart car, you shall enjoy all the luxury possible for soul of man on the face of The Globe to bestow on a maid in the hand of marriage. I have an income of £500 a month. We shall live by Berlin honoured and welcomed through Germany and Germany's people. For the sake of those who love, which I am sure, you would sacrifice your country for my sake. Your excommunication of the language known in England will be brought before the Kaiser and for saving his people you shall be forgiven for your English blood. If I was certain that I had English blood in my veins I would go to the West Indies to be gnawed by a lion.*

From this it may be inferred that the German master spy was not a Fellow of the Zoological Society. In another letter E. M. reproached her for not keeping an appointment: 'You have ruined me and yourself by not coming out. There is yet plenty of time. Our men cannot get the messages through and even if it was switched halfway it would be well. Germany must have their report and I shall again try for you sooner or later.'

The letters from the spy were in code, but those from the girl friend were *en clair*. Gradually the volume of correspondence grew until it became a formidable bundle. The master and mistress confided in a sensible friend, who passed the whole matter over to the authorities. Some of the master spy's letters were amatory, but the love-making was indissolubly intertwined with strict business, only every now and then his admiration for her transcendent beauty would break loose – 'But your beauty may enchant us.'

The extraordinary part of this fraud was that the girl was quite uneducated and had never been out of her native village and yet she could fabricate different handwritings and make signs that distantly resembled Pitman's shorthand. She had dotted all over her map sham chemical and mathematical symbols and whenever she was cornered for an explanation she invented a new romance.

She had reduced her mistress to such distress that she did not dare to leave the house and therefore the police superintendent who was detailed to see her had to make a visit to the suburbs. There he found a simple, pleasant-faced country girl, the daughter of a labourer, who would have been supposed to have no knowledge of the world outside her native village. Her employers were in such a state of mind that it was decided to send her home to her mother. One of the curious points about her imagination was her power of inventing names upon the spot, which is a very rare quality even among practised liars. When pressed as to the name of the master spy, without a moment's thought she gave it as Eric Herfranz Mullard. When she was pressed to explain why the Germans were not able to operate their own machine, the 'Maxione', which she described as being a sort of collapsible framework of iron rods, quite portable, but 5 or 6 feet in height when extended, she said that the keys of the base, which flashed rays from the little lamps attached to the arms at the top, had to be worked with great speed with the fingers and the elbows as well and she gave a demonstration on the dining room table, which was so energetic that it must have left bruises on her elbows. The flashes were green and red and could be seen for a distance of 150 miles. That was why one had to strike the keys so hard and, naturally, a German's fingers were not likely to be so nimble as those of an English girl.

The ages of from fourteen to eighteen have been so productive of trouble to the police that I have sometimes regretted that all girls between those ages are not safely put to sleep by the state and allowed to grow quietly and harmlessly into womanhood unseen by the world. Perhaps the legend of the 'Sleeping Beauty' may have been suggested by the pranks of adolescent liars in the dawn of the Christian era. How many hay-stacks have been set on fire by little farm servants? How many ghosts have been conjured up? How much paraffin has been thrown on ceilings to attract photographers for the daily press, merely from an infantile desire to see the grown-ups buzzing about like a nest of disturbed wasps?

But to return to pre-war memories. At the moment when I took charge of the Criminal Investigation Department the Central Office was busy over the robbery of the pearl necklace. A necklace valued at about £110,000 had been dispatched from Paris to a London jeweller by registered post. The box was safely delivered with all the seals apparently intact, but the pearls were missing and lumps of coal had been substituted for them. At first suspicion fell upon the French postal servants. Elaborate inquiries were made on both sides of the Channel and it was established beyond a doubt that the wrapper and the seals were exactly in the condition in which the parcel was delivered for registration. There was no doubt whatever that they had been properly packed and therefore somewhere there existed a counterfeit seal of the firm, which consisted of the initials 'M. M.' within an oval border. My first contribution to the case was to establish by experiment that a counterfeit seal could be made and used on melted sealing-wax within four minutes and that therefore at some point in the parcel's journey it would have been possible to break the seals, undo the wrappings, remove the pearls and seal the parcel up again without the loss of a post. Gradually the police began to see daylight. Rumours fly in Hatton Garden and it was not long before the names of X and Y and one or two others were whispered in connection with the robbery.

Then began one of the most difficult cases of observation that I remember. No fox was ever more cunning in covering his tracks. The men had no reason to suspect that they were being followed and yet they never relaxed their precautions for a moment. If they took a taxi to any rendezvous they gave a false destination, paid off the taxi and took another, sometimes repeating this process of mystification two or three times. If they met in Oxford Street to lunch together at an ABC shop they would suddenly change their minds on the doorstep and go off to another and all the while they had an aged discharged convict in their pay to shadow them and call their attention to any suspicious follower. I shall not tell here what devices the police adopted, but I will say that at the last, when every other kind of observation failed, we did adopt a new device which was successful.

The object throughout had been to find a moment when one or other of the parties had the stolen pearls about his person and when the day came for making the arrest, just as the four thieves were entering a tube station the police failed, because on that particular day they had left the necklace at home. They were detained, nevertheless, in order that a thorough search might be made of all their hiding-places. As it then turned out, the necklace was in the possession of the wife of one of them and when the search became too hot and she feared a visit from the police she put the necklace into a Bryant & May matchbox and dropped it in the street. There it was found, without, however, its diamond clasp, which had been disposed of separately.

It did not take the police long to unravel the details of the crime. They found the engraver who had innocently cut the false seal and the office where the parcel had been opened. The thieves had arranged with the postman to bring the parcel to the office for three or four minutes before taking it on to deliver it. Whether the postman knew beforehand what they intended to do is uncertain. They expected to find diamonds, which were far more easily disposed of: when they found pearls, so large that in the trade each pearl had almost a history, they knew that they could not dispose of them and were at first tor throwing them into the Thames. It may be judged that I was not an expert in precious stones when I say that I had the matchbox and its contents laid out on my table for quite half an hour before I was sure that the pearls were genuine. They looked, to my untutored eye, so yellow. We telephoned to the owner and the insurance agent. The owner fell upon the pearls as a man might fall upon some beloved and long-lost child whom he had never expected to see again in this world. I then told him jocularly of my doubts. 'Yellow?' he said, with genuine amazement. 'Yellow? They are rose-colour.'

Every now and then there was a sensational seizure at the house of a receiver of stolen property. In October 1913 a certain jeweller's shop in Shaftesbury Avenue was raided and the contents were carried off to Bow Street, which resembled for some days an exhibition of wedding presents. It contained the proceeds of quite twenty known burglaries and even then only one-third of the plate had been identified because it has been found by experience that in these days, when people insure their jewellery against burglary and draw the insurance money, they take little interest in bringing the thieves to justice. There is also the fact that things are stolen from a house sometimes for many months before they are missed. Some of the objects in this exhibition belonged to a Lady H. and while she was going round she caught sight of a clock given to her by Lord Charles Beresford which she thought was still at home. Unclaimed stolen property is held by the police for a certain period and then disposed of by public auction.

In 1913 there was an epidemic of safe-breaking. The capacity of the oxyacetylene flame for cutting through steel plates appealed to the safe-breaker, who had long deplored the weight and inefficiency of the tools on which he had to rely for his livelihood. For years there has been a competition between the burglar and the safe-maker and so far I believe the safe-maker has won.

Two enterprising persons spent a Sunday afternoon in the summer of 1913 in a certain office in Regent Street cutting a great hole in the safe with an oxyacetylene apparatus, which they had transported to the house in a taxi-cab on the previous afternoon. Having secured their booty they left this very incriminating apparatus behind them.

Not many weeks later the police were forewarned that an attempt would be made on a safe in a certain much frequented cinema hall, but here the burglars received a nervous shock. All went according to plan that Sunday afternoon. The street and the hall had the deserted Sunday look when, on a sudden, just as operations were beginning, from every corner sprang truncheoned men and the burglars were caught in a trap.

CHAPTER 3

THE LURE OF SOMETHING FOR NOTHING

THE GREAT BUSINESS of transferring the contents of your neighbour's pocket to your own is what more than nine-tenths of the world live upon. Society draws the line between what is legitimate and what is dishonest rather low down in the scale. A grocer may rob you by high prices but not by giving you short weight; a moneylender may fleece you by usury but not by picking your pocket; but I confess to a sneaking preference for the rogue who, without any pretence of respectability, preys upon your vanity or your cupidity and cheats you quite openly.

The Spanish prisoner fraud has flourished for nearly half a century. It has the advantage over all other frauds in costing practically nothing for stock-in-trade and incurring no risk whatever to the practitioner. All he needs is a little stationery, a few postage stamps and the names and addresses of farmers in Scotland and England. The farmer receives a letter with the Valencia postmark from a Spanish colonel now languishing in prison on account of the part he played in a revolutionary conspiracy.

> *My dear sir and relative,*
>
> *Having not the honour to know you personally but only for the good references my deceased mother Mary Harris, your relative, did me about your family, I apply myself to you for the first and perhaps last time to implore your protection for my only daughter Amelia, child twelve years age.*

Here the writer is banking on the fact that very few of us are in a position positively to say that no one of the sisters or cousins of our parents was called Mary and that no one of that name married a Spaniard. The letter, which is beautifully written in halting English, goes on to say that the writer, a colonel named Alvaro de Espinosa, at the direction of the revolutionary committee, went to Berlin to buy arms, was betrayed and went to England, but that while in London he heard of the death of his wife. In the first shock of grief he converted all his property into English and French banknotes and with the proceeds cunningly concealed in the lining of his trunk he set out for Valencia.

> *Well disguised, I went out to Spain, arrived in this city. Arranged secretly some private business, took my leave from the martyr as was my noble wife and when I was very near coming in England again with my daughter but with my heart contrite by grief I was arrested. A wretch enemy had recognised and accused me. They proceeded me and after in a war court I was condemned by desertion and rebellion delinquency at one indemnification at twelve jail years and at the payment of the process outlays, a sentence I am undergoing now in these military jails, deprived of any intercourse.*

When I was arrested my equipage which is a trunk and two portman-teaux, was seized and sealed and folded before me and delivering me its keys without might be discovered the so well artful secret in which I hidden the said sum and it remained laid down in the same Court as a warranty for the outlays of process payment in the event of being condemned and as I am already unhappily sentenced it is indispensable to pay the court the amount of the expenses to be able to recover the luggage. Thereby necessary sum pay the tribunal by the process outlays since I would not see me in the debasing and shameful case to have to resort to my fellow countrymen; then I would be wretchedly betrayed again.

That is why he writes to Harris. But what is Harris to get out of all this? You shall hear. When the trunk reaches him,

you will see in its interior part and in its left side of Spain shield in its cen-tre you will set upon your forefinger so that when an electric bell is pushed and quickly the secret will appear in full view in which you will find my fortune … I will name you as tutor of my daughter and her fortune trus-tee until her full age and as a right reward for your noble aid I leave you the fourth part of all my fortune.

So there you have it – something for nothing – the bait which so few can resist; least of all when the something is £6,250 and a beautiful young Spanish ward.

The poor old revolutionary colonel is in a dying state, as you learn from a letter from the chaplain, the Reverend Adrian Rosado, which is enclosed. This devoted priest has letter paper headed with a cross and has a markedly feminine handwriting. He is not in the secret, as the cautious old colonel has been careful to warn you. He 'befriends me by his vocation and good feelings: he is a venerable priest and honest man and I do not think it necessary he knows the secret very extensively.' The honest man regrets very much 'that on the first time I write to you I may be herald of bad news, but the case so requires it and the truth must be said though it may be painful. Your relative's health state is very bad.'

Indeed, so bad that 'we must have patience to suffer with resignation what God dispose and beg his help to accomplish the last will of the unfortunate Sr Alvaro de Espinosa.'

The honest priest goes on to say that in a little while he will deposit Miss Amelia and the trunk at your door, always provided that the necessary expenses are defrayed.

> *By your relative charge I think convenient to beg your aid for getting out the seized equipage to which end I am making steps in order that the Tribunal tell me the exactly amount to pay the cost and process expenses.*
>
> *Awaiting anxiously your reply to accomplish the sacred mission your relative has commissioned me.*
>
> *I am, dear sir, your most affected servant and Chaplain,*
> *Adrian Rogado*

Strange that this holy and disinterested man should have a delicacy about receiving letters at his presbytery. He, no less than the poor prisoner, adds in a postscript – 'By greater security please answer to my brother-in-law, name and here as following: Mr Arturo Rivier, Maldonado 19, Entremets, Valencia, Spain.'

Is it because a letter addressed to the presbytery would be returned through the Dead Letter Office marked that no such person as Rogado exists?

The world may be divided into two classes – those who would reply to such letters and those who would consign them to the fire.

In spite of the picture drawn of Englishmen by envious foreigners, the Britisher is by nature an imaginative and romantic person. That is why you find him in every part of the globe: he goes abroad for adventure, to escape from the humdrum routine of his home surroundings. And the farther you go north the more romantic he becomes. That is why there are so few Scots left in Scotland. To judge from the correspondence filed by the police, nine out of every ten reply and because the Britisher is practical as well as romantic, the reply invariably asks how much money is required to pay the 'process outlays'. On this the dying Espinosa, whose handwriting is unusually firm for a stricken man so near his end, rises to fresh flights of eloquence:

'I will die peaceful,' he says, 'thinking of the good future welfare of my dear daughter near you.'

His 'health state is becoming grievous' and so he makes his will:

Here is my last will.

I name heiress of the three-fourths parts of my fortune my alone daughter Amelia de Espinosa.

I name you heir of the fourth part of my fortune and Tutor of my daughter and Manager of it until this one may reach her full age.

As soon as the equipage may be in the Chaplain's hands he shall go out to your home with my daughter and equipage in order that you may take away the money of my trunk secret to come immediately in possession of the sum.

From the part belonging to my daughter you will deliver to the Chaplain £200, for I will make a present to him. I beseech you to grant all your assistance to the Chaplain since he is poor and he does not reckon upon any resource to pay these outlays.

The equipage must be recovered immediately, for in the trunk is all my fortune.

You will place my daughter in a college until her full age … I shall die

peaceful thinking of her being happy near you and she will find on you
some warm-hearted parents and brothers.

Your unfortunate relative,
Alvaro de Espinosa

And still no mention of money: that was because the recipient was more than usually cautious and was, in fact, a wary fish that must be played. So wary was he that he took the letter to the police for advice. But I remember a case where a farmer in Norfolk was so much touched by the misfortunes of his Spanish cousin and so conscious of the sensation that would be caused among his neighbours when it became known that he was guardian to a beautiful young Spanish heiress, to say nothing of the things that might be bought with £6,250, that he sent £200 to the address indicated by Espinosa and sat down to wait. He waited so long that he became anxious about the safety of the chaplain and his ward and it was on their account and not from any doubt about the story, that he came to the police. He indignantly refused to believe that he had been a victim to the familiar Spanish prisoner fraud.

The war was unkind to Espinosa, who had been lingering upon his death-bed for over forty years and I hoped that it had killed him, but the ink was scarcely dry upon the Treaty of Versailles before he broke out again. From time to time the Spanish government has been furnished with the address to which victims are invited to reply, but hitherto to no purpose: the game is too profitable to be easily killed.

I can understand succumbing to the wiles of Espinosa better than I can understand the perennial success of the confidence trick, which is practised generally by Australians on American visitors to London. There are several variants because the tricksters are artists and are not above improving with practice. Here again the bait is 'something for nothing'. Though the commonest form has been described in the police court it may be well to repeat it here. An American walking in Hyde Park sees an elderly man drop a pocketbook. He overtakes him and restores it. The old man, whom we will call Ryan, is effusively grateful. He would not have lost that pocketbook for the world: it contained the evidence of his fortune: his benefactor must come and have a drink. He holds him with his glittering eye and while they imbibe whisky he tells his story – how an uncle of fabulous wealth but eccentric habits has left him a couple of million dollars on condition that he can find a really trustworthy person to distribute one-eighth of the sum among the poor of London. The dupe mentions the fact that he has a return ticket to New York and hails from Denver. So, as it now appears, does Ryan, who takes from his pocketbook a newspaper cutting setting forth the virtues and the enormous fortune of the uncle and at that very moment a third man, Ryan's confederate, drops in. Hearing the word 'Denver', he joins in the conversation, for he, too, is from Denver – George T. Davis, at their service. So there they are – three exiles from Denver – a little oasis in the vast waste of London. To George T. Davis Ryan relates his good fortune and the strange condition in the will.

'I know no one in this city. How am I to find a man in whom I have confidence to distribute all this money? Now I like your face, Mr Davis, but I don't know you – never saw you till this afternoon – how can I say I've confidence in you?'

'Confidence for confidence,' replies Davis. 'I've confidence in you anyway. I'd trust you with all I've got, and I've got more than what I stand up in. Why, see here! Here's what I drew from the bank this morning' – he thrusts a roll of bank (of engraving) notes into Ryan's unwilling hand – 'and here's my watch and chain! Take them all and just walk through that door. I know you'll bring them back because

I've confidence in you.' But Ryan still looks doubtful. 'No good,' whispers Davis. 'He don't take to me. Why don't you have a shot at the money? He takes to you.'

And so by appeals to the vanity of the man from Denver, by playing on his cupidity, under the softening influences of liquid refreshment, by the force of example, Davis succeeds at last. Into the still apparently unwilling hand of Ryan the victim presses all the money and valuables he possesses and out goes Ryan into the street. The two men continue drinking: George T. Davis is the first to betray anxiety.

'The old man ought to be back by now. Can't understand it – man I'd have trusted anywhere. Couldn't have been run over by a taxi? You stop here: I'll just step out and see where he's got to.' And that is the last that the victim sees of either of the rogues.

Before the war most of the confidence men lived in Ealing. Each pair have their own pitch and there was a tacit understanding that neither should poach on the ground of the other. Northumberland Avenue belonged to one; the Mall to another; a third worked Hyde Park. The essence of the trick is that the victim should be a bird of passage, for as soon as the trick is played the actors leave for Rome. Why Rome was chosen I never understood. There they stayed until a confederate reported that the victim had sailed for home and the coast was clear. During the war the poor confidence man fell on evil days: there were no American tourists to prey upon and if there had been any, one could not fly to Rome. The passport people saw to that. The absence of a prosecutor is a bar to police action, but occasionally one or other of the fraternity is run to ground.

I have sometimes doubted whether the police should be called upon to protect people so simple that they ought not to be allowed abroad without a nurse. I remember a prisoner making the same complaint to me. 'It's cruel hard on us chaps,' he said, 'when mugs like them are at large. It's a temptation: that's what it is.' But he was not doing his profession justice. Like all artistic callings – like the stage for instance – the reward lies not in the emoluments, but in the satisfaction of playing on the feelings of your audience until you hold them.

Given impudence and the artistic sense and a man may remove mountains – at any rate he may remove houses. At Dartmoor there was a man who boasted that he was 'the lad that stole a row of houses', and it was no idle boast. In the City there was a row of derelict eighteenth-century cottages which in these days would have been condemned as unfit for human habitation. Tenants must have come to a similar conclusion about them, for an agent's board, already weather-worn, announced that they were to let. One morning a young man called at the house agent's and got into conversation with the clerk. 'So those houses in Paradise Row are to let. I'd like to have a look at them and see whether it would suit my governor to make an offer.'

'Right,' said the clerk, 'come tomorrow and I'll take you round. I can't come now, I'm alone in the office.'

'Don't you worry, old man. Lend me the key and I'll be back with it in half an hour.'

The clerk was glad to be rid of him on such easy terms.

A week later an old client happened to look in. 'I see you're pulling down those old death-traps in Paradise Row. It was about time you did.'

'Pulling them down? What do you mean?'

'I mean what I say. I passed there just now and there's not much left.'

The clerk glanced hastily at the nail where the key was wont to hang. The key was gone and then he remembered how he came to part with it. He tore out of the office without his hat, risked a hundred deaths from buses and reached his goal breathless. He would have been breathless in any case at what he saw. The housebreakers had done their work thoroughly and at the moment were dealing with the ground floor. The lead, the guttering, tiles, cisterns, wood-work and bricks had all been carted away and gold to the order of the man 'who stole a row of houses.' He considered the months he had to spend in prison a cheap price to pay for the prestige he won in the only circles whose opinion he respected.

But his impudence paled beside that of the bogus doctor whose only claim to medical knowledge was the possession of a stethoscope. His method was to select a little artisan's house in a quiet street in south London on a Sunday morning, ring the bell and when the ten-ant opened the door ask for Mr Smith.

'I'm not Mr Smith. My name's Brown.'

'Then I must have got the number wrong. So sorry. You don't hap-pen to know which is Mr Smith's house? Never heard of him? Well, well!' And then, with great concern in his manner, 'Stop, don't shut the door. Do you know you are very ill?'

'Never felt better in my life,' growled Mr Brown.

'Excuse me, I'm a doctor and I know better. Phantasmagoria is a dreadful illness and you've got it badly. I can tell it from your eyes. Now, look here [pulling out a stethoscope and looking at his watch], I can just spare ten minutes. I'll examine you and it won't cost you a penny and if I'm wrong no one will be more pleased than I shall.'

Still talking, he would edge the now frightened Brown into the parlour, saying,

Don't make any sudden movement, my dear fellow. Just slip off your coat and trousers as gently as you can. Let me help you. That's right! Now lie down on that sofa. Gently now. That's right. Th-a-t's right. Now say 'A-a'. Now say 'O-o-o'. It's just what I thought. It's the worst case of

phantasmagoria that I ever came across. Not a word now. Move once and you may never move again. Now lie quite still while I run round to the chemist. I'll bring you round something that will put you right in two ticks. Not a word now: there's nothing to thank me for.

In this he was quite right. He clapped on his hat and ran out into the street and it was not by inadvertence that he carried over his arm all Mr Brown's Sunday clothes and whatever the pockets contained. And when it dawned upon Brown that he had been victimised, how was he to take up the pursuit on a Sunday morning in nothing but his shirt?

CHAPTER 4

THE FIRST DAYS

L IKE MOST ENGLISHMEN, I read of the murder at Sarajevo without a thought that it was to react upon the destiny of this country. It seemed to be an ordinary case of Balkan manners, out of which would proceed diplomatic correspondence, an arrest or two and a trial imperfectly reported in our newspapers. It did have the immediate effect of postponing a ball at Buckingham Palace on account of the court mourning, but that was all. During the postponed ball on 16 July, so petty were our preoccupations at this moment that when a message came in that Mrs Pankhurst had just been recaptured under the 'Cat and Mouse Act', I thought it worthwhile to find the Home Secretary and repeat it to him. A few days after the murder I met von Kuhlmann at luncheon. He can scarcely at that time have expected a rupture of relations, for in talking over Dr Solf, with whom I had been associated in the Pacific, he said, 'He has climbed high since you knew him and some think that he will go higher still [meaning that he would become Chancellor]. He is coming to London in August and I shall write to him to arrange a meeting with you.'

A few days later England began to feel uneasy. I overheard a certain Under-Secretary remark at luncheon of his constituency, 'Well, all I can say is that if this country enters the war there will be a rebellion in the north of England.' He left the ministry when the moment came and has now disappeared even from the House of Commons. I think that we all had at the back of our minds a feeling that a European war on the great scale was so unthinkable that a way would be found at the eleventh hour for avoiding it. A staff officer in whose judgement I believed remarked that if this were so he would emigrate, because he knew that the day was only postponed until Germany felt herself better prepared for the inevitable war. There were, in fact, no illusions at the War Office. Some day the story that will do justice to the services of Lord Haldane in those very critical weeks will be written. The plans that had been made during peace time were all ready; the names and addresses of the known German spies were recorded. We could only wait for midnight on 4 August. I was actually in the Tube lift at Gloucester Road on the stroke of midnight and I remarked to the liftman that we were now at war. 'Is that so?' he replied, with a yawn.

The credit of the discovery of the German spy organisation before the war was entirely due to a sub-department of the War Office, directed by officers of great skill. They had known for some time that one Karl Gustav Ernst, a barber in the Caledonian Road, who was technically a British subject because he was born in England, was the collecting centre for German espionage. All he had to do for his pittance of a month was to drop the letters he received from Germany ready stamped with English postage stamps into the nearest pillar-box and to transmit to Germany any replies which he received. Altogether, his correspondents numbered twenty-two. They were scattered all over the country at naval and military centres and all of them were German. The law in peace time was inadequate for dealing with them and there was the danger that if our action was precipitate the Germans would hear of it and send fresh agents about whom we might know nothing: it was decided to wait until a state of war existed before arresting them. On 5 August the orders went out. Twenty-one out of the twenty-two were arrested and interned simultaneously; one eluded arrest by embarking for Germany. Their acts of espionage had been committed in peace time and therefore they could not be dealt with on the capital charge. The result of this sudden action was to drop a curtain over England at the vital moment of mobilisation. The German Intelligence Service was paralysed. It could only guess at what was happening behind the curtain and it guessed wrong. Ernst was sentenced to seven years' penal servitude for his share in the business and, seeing that he was a British subject, the sentence cannot be called excessive.

The curtain had dropped not only for the enemy but even for ourselves. How many of us knew during those first few days that trains were discharging men, horses and material at the quays of certain southern ports without any confusion at intervals of ten minutes by day and night; that an Expeditionary Force of 150,000 men was actually in the field against the Germans before they knew anything about its existence? Von Kluck has recorded somewhere his surprise when he first found British troops in front of him. After the Armistice he is reported to have told a British officer that in his opinion the finest military force in history was the first British Army and that the greatest military feat in history was the raising of the second British Army.

Our great dread during that week was that a bridge or a railway arch might be blown up by the enemy and the smooth running of mobilisation be dislocated.

Most of the railway arches were let to private persons, of whom some were aliens. On 5 August I went myself to the War Office to find a general who could be vested with power to turn these people out. There was a good deal of confusion. Every head of a branch had left for the field that morning and their successors were quite new to their jobs. At last I found my general and while I was talking to him it grew dark and there was a sudden peal of thunder like an explosion. He said, quite gravely, 'A Zepp!' That was the state of mind we were all in. That same night my telephone became agitated; it reported the blowing up of a culvert near Aldershot and of a railway bridge in Kent. I had scarcely repeated the information to the proper authority when the bell rang again to tell me that both reports were the figments of some jumpy Reservist patrol.

Who now remembers those first feverish days of the war: the crowds about the recruiting stations, the recruits marching through the streets in mufti, the drafts going to the station without bands – the flower of our manhood, of whom so many were never to return – soldiers almost camping in Victoria Street, the flaring posters, the foolish cry 'Business as usual'; the unseemly rush to the stores for food until, under the lash of the newspapers, people grew ashamed of their selfishness; the silence in the buses, until any loud noise, like a motor back-fire, started a Zeppelin scare? Who now remembers the foolish prognostications of experts – how the war would result in unemployment and a revolution would follow; the assurance of certain bankers that the war would be over in six months because none of the belligerents could stand the financial strain for longer? We have even forgotten the food-hoarding scare that followed the spy scare during the height of the submarine activity, when elderly gentlemen, who had taken thought for the morrow, might have been seen burying biscuit tins in their gardens at midnight for fear that their neighbours should get wind of their hoard and hale them before the magistrate.

I began to think in those days that war hysteria was a pathological condition to which persons of mature age and generally normal intelligence were peculiarly susceptible. War work was evidently not a predisposing cause, for the readiest victims were those who were doing nothing in particular. In ante-bellum days there were a few mild cases. The sufferers would tell you gravely that at a public dinner they had turned suddenly to their German waiter and asked him what post he had orders to join when the German invaders arrived and that he, taken off his guard, had clicked his heels and replied, 'Portsmouth'; or they would whisper of secret visits of German aircraft to south Wales by night and mysterious rides undertaken by stiff guttural persons with square heads who would hire horses in the eastern counties and display an unhealthy curiosity about the stable accommodation in every farm that they passed. But in August 1914 the malady assumed a virulent epidemic form accompanied by delusions which defied treatment. It attacked all classes indiscriminately and seemed even to find its most fruitful soil in sober, stolid and otherwise truthful people. I remember Mr Asquith saying that, from a legal and evidential point of view, nothing was ever so completely proved as the arrival of the Russians. Their landing was described by eyewitnesses at Leith, Aberdeen and Glasgow; they stamped the snow out of their boots and called hoarsely for vodka at Carlisle and Berwick-on-Tweed; they jammed the penny-in-the-slot machines with a rouble at Durham; four of them were billeted on a lady at Crewe who herself described the difficulty of cooking for Slavonic appetites. There was nothing to be done but to let the delusion burn itself out. I have often wondered since whether some self-effacing patriot did not circulate this story in order to put heart into his fellow countrymen at a time when depression would have been most disastrous, or whether, as has since been said, it was merely the rather outlandish-looking equipment and Gaelic speech of the Lovat Scouts that set the story afloat.

The second phase of the malady attached itself to pigeons. London is full of pigeons – wood pigeons in the parks, blue rocks about the churches and public buildings – and a number of amiable people take pleasure in feeding them. In September 1914, when this phase was at its height, it was positively dangerous to be seen in conversation with a pigeon; it was not always safe to be seen in its vicinity. A foreigner walking in one of the parks was actually arrested and sentenced to imprisonment because a pigeon was seen to fly from the place where he was standing and it was supposed that he had liberated it.

During this phase a pigeon was caught in Essex which was actually carrying a message in the usual little aluminium box clipped to its leg. Moreover, the message was from Rotterdam, but it was merely to report the arrival of an innocuous cargo vessel, whose voyage we afterwards traced.

The delusion about illicit wireless ran the pigeons very hard. The pronouncement of a thoughtless expert that an aerial might be hidden in a chimney and that messages could be received through an open window even on an iron bedstead, gave a great impetus to this form of delusion. The high scientific authority of the popular play, *The Man Who Stayed at Home*, where a complete installation was concealed behind a fireplace, spread the delusion far and wide. It was idle to assure the sufferers that a Marconi transmitter needed a four-horsepower engine to generate the wave, that skilled operators were listening day and night for the pulsations of unauthorised messages, that the intermittent tickings they heard from the flat above them were probably the efforts of an amateur typist: the sufferers knew better.

At this period the disease attacked even naval and military officers and special constables. If a telegraphist was sent on a motorcycle to examine and test the telegraph poles, another cyclist was certain to be sent by some authority in pursuit. On one occasion the authorities dispatched to the eastern counties a car equipped with a Marconi apparatus and two skilled operators to intercept any illicit messages that might be passing over the North Sea. They left London at noon; at 3 they were under lock and key in Essex. After an exchange of telegrams they were set free, but at 7 p.m. they telegraphed from the police cells in another part of the county, imploring help. When again liberated they refused to move without the escort of a Territorial officer in uniform, but on the following morning the police of another county had got hold of them and telegraphed, 'Three German spies arrested with car and complete wireless installation, one in uniform of British officer.'

Next in order was the German governess, also perhaps the product of *The Man Who Stayed at Home*. There were several variants of this story, but a classic version was that the governess was missing from the midday meal and that when the family came to open her trunks they discovered under a false bottom a store of high explosive bombs. Every one who told this story knew the woman's employer; some had even seen the governess herself in happier days – 'Such a nice quiet person, so fond of the children; but now one comes to think of it, there was a something in her face, impossible to describe, but a something.'

During the German advance through Belgium an ingenious war correspondent gave a new turn to the hysteria. He alleged that the enamelled iron advertisements for Maggi soup, which were to be seen attached to every hoarding and telegraph post, were unscrewed by the German officers in order to read the information about the local resources, which was painted in German on the back. Screw-driver parties were formed in the London suburbs and in destroying this delusion they removed also many unsightly advertisements. The hallucination about gun platforms was not dispatched so easily. As soon as a correspondent had described the gun emplacements laid down by Germans in the guise of tennis courts at Mauberge there was scarcely a paved back-garden nor a flat concrete roof in London that did not come under the suspicion of some spy-maniac. The denunciations were not confined to Germans. Given a British householder with a concrete tennis-court and pigeons about the house and it was certain to be discovered that he had quite suddenly increased the scale of his expenditure, that heavy cases had been delivered at the house by night, that tapping had been overheard, mysterious lights seen in the windows and that on the night of the sinking of the *Lusitania* he had given a dinner-party to naturalised Germans. When artillery experts assured the patients that gun emplacements in the heart of London were in the wrong place and that even on the high lands of Sydenham or of Hampstead any tram road would better serve the purpose they wagged their heads. They were hot upon the scent and for many weeks denunciations poured in at the rate of many hundreds a day.

The next delusion was that of the grateful German and the Tubes. The commonest form of the story was that an English nurse had brought a German officer back from the door of death and that in a burst of gratitude he said at parting, 'I must not tell you more, but beware of the Tubes in April (1915).' As time wore on the date was shifted forward month by month, to September, when it died of expectation deferred. We took the trouble to trace this story from mouth to mouth until we reached the second mistress in a London Board School. She declared that she had had it from the charwoman who cleaned the school, but that lady stoutly denied that she had ever told so ridiculous a story.

A near kin to this was the tale that a German officer of rank had been seen in the Haymarket by an English friend; that he returned the salute involuntarily but then changed colour and jumped into a passing taxi, leaving his friend gaping on the pavement. A good many notable Prussians, from von Bissing, the Governor of Belgium downwards, figured in this story; a good many places, from Piccadilly to the Army and Navy Stores, have been the scene. The best attested version is that of the English girl who came suddenly upon her fiancé, an officer in the Prussian Guards, who shook hands with her, but as soon as he recovered from his surprise the callous ruffian froze her with a look and jumped into a passing omnibus. Another version was that on recognising her German fiancé the girl looked appealingly into his countenance and said, 'Oh, Fritz!', whereupon he gave one startled look and jumped into the nearest vehicle. This, it may be remarked, might have happened to any Englishman, for who would not, when accosted by a charming stranger under the name of 'Fritz', have jumped into anything that happened to be passing? In some of these cases inquiry showed that at the moment when they were said to have been seen in London these Germans were serving on the Continent and it is certain that all were hallucinations.

With the war, the Tower of London came into its own again. During the early months it began to be whispered at London tea-tables that the Crown Prince himself was languishing there (if languishing is the appropriate term for a person of his temperament). Later, when it became evident that he could not be in two places at once, the prisoners of distinction included several British peers and privy councillors. All these prisoners, who were at the moment adorning their several offices in free life, had been shot at dawn. These delusions may be traced to the fact that a few foreign spies were imprisoned in the Tower before execution.

A new phase of the malady was provoked by the suggestion that advertisements in the 'agony column' of newspapers were being used by spies to communicate information to Germany. It is uncertain who first called public attention to this danger, but since refugees did make use of the agony columns for communicating with their friends abroad, there was nothing inherently improbable in the idea. In order to allay public alarm it was necessary to check the insertion of apparently cryptic advertisements. Later in the war a gentleman who had acquired a considerable reputation as a code expert and was himself the author of commercial codes, began to read into these advertisements messages from German submarines to their base and vice versa. This he did with the aid of a Dutch–English dictionary on a principle of his own. As we had satisfied ourselves about the authors of the advertisements we treated his communications rather lightly. In most cases the movements he foretold failed to take place, but unfortunately once, by an accident, there did happen to be an air-raid on the night foretold by him. We then inserted an advertisement of our own. It was something like this: 'Will the lady with the fur boa who entered No. 14 bus at Hyde Park Corner yesterday communicate with box 29.' And upon this down came our expert hot-foot with the information that six submarines were under orders to attack the defences at Dover that very night. When we explained that we were the authors of the advertisement, all he said was that, by some extraordinary coincidence, we had hit upon the German code and that by inserting the advertisement we had betrayed a military secret. It required a committee to dispose of this delusion.

The longest-lived of the delusions was that of the night-signalling, for whenever the scare showed signs of dying down a Zeppelin raid was sure to give it a fresh start. As far as fixed lights were concerned, it was the best-founded of all the delusions, because the Germans might well have inaugurated a system of fixed lights to guide Zeppelins to their objective, but the sufferers went a great deal farther than a belief in fixed lights. Morse-signalling from a window in Bayswater, which could be seen only from a window on the opposite side of the street, was believed in some way to be conveyed to the commanders of German submarines in the North Sea, to whom one had to suppose news from Bayswater was of paramount importance. Sometimes the watcher – generally a lady – would call in a friend, a noted Morse expert, who in one case made out the letters 'P. K.' among a number of others that he could not distinguish. This phase of the malady was the most obstinate of all. It was useless to point out that a more sure and private method of conveying information across a street would be to go personally or send a note. It was not safe to ignore any of these complaints and all were investigated. In a few cases there were certainly intermittent flashes, but they proved to be caused by the flapping of a blind, the waving of branches across a window, persons passing across a room and, in two instances, the quick movements of a girl's hair-brush in front of the light. The beacons were passage lights left unshrouded. The Lighting Order did much to allay this phase of the disease. Out of many thousand denunciations I have been unable to hear of a single case in which signals to the enemy were made by lights during the war.

The self-appointed watcher was very apt to develop the delusion of persecution. She would notice a man in the opposite house whose habits seemed to be secretive and decide in her own mind that he was an enemy spy. A few days later he would chance to leave his house immediately after she had left hers. Looking round, she would recognise him and jump to the conclusion that he was following her.

Then she would come down to New Scotland Yard, generally with some officer friend who would assure me that she was a most unemotional person. One had to listen quite patiently to all she said and she could only be cured by a promise that the police would follow her themselves and detain any other follower if they encountered one.

Even serving officers were not immune. Near Woolwich a large house belonging to a naturalised foreigner attracted the attention of a non-commissioned officer, who began to fill the ears of his superiors with wonderful stories of lights, of signalling apparatus discovered in the grounds and of chasing spies along railway tracks in the best American film manner, until even his general believed in him. Acting on my advice the owner wisely offered his house as a hospital and the ghost was laid.

Sometimes the disease would attack public officials, who had to be handled sympathetically. One very worthy gentleman used to embarrass his colleagues by bringing in stories almost daily of suspicious persons who had been seen in every part of the country. All of them were German spies and the local authorities would do nothing. In order to calm him they invented a mythical personage named 'von Burstorph', and whenever he brought them a fresh case they would say, 'So von Burstorph has got to Arran,' or to Carlisle, or wherever the locality might be. He was assured that the whole forces of the realm were on the heels of 'von Burstorph', and that when he was caught he would suffer the extreme penalty in the Tower. That sent him away quite happy since he knew that the authorities were doing something. The incarnation of 'von Burstorph' reminded me of a similar incarnation in the Criminal Investigation Department many years ago. When one of my predecessors appeared to be blaming his subordinates for a lack of enterprise in the case of some undiscovered crime they would shake their heads and say, 'Yes, I recognise the hand. That is some of Bill the Boatman's work,' but 'Bill the Boatman' was a most elusive person and he has not been arrested to this day.

On one occasion a very staid couple came down to denounce a waiter in one of the large hotels and brought documentary evidence with them. It was a menu with a rough sketch plan in pencil made upon the back. They believed it to be a plan of Kensington Gardens with the Palace buildings roughly delineated by an oblong figure. They had seen the waiter in the act of drawing the plan at an unoccupied table. I sent for him and found before me a spruce little Swiss with his hair cut *en brosse* and a general air of extreme surprise. He gave me a frank account of all his movements and then I produced the plan. He gazed at it a moment and then burst out laughing.

So that is where my plan went! Yes, monsieur, I made it and then I lost it. You see, I am new to the hotel and, in order to satisfy the head waiter, I made for myself privately a plan of the tables and marked a cross against those I had to look after.

The Germans, as we now know, had the spy-mania even more acutely. It became dangerous for Americans in Berlin to speak their own language: gamekeepers roamed the country armed to deal with spy cars and Princess Ratibor and several other innocent persons were shot at and wounded. Our own anti-German riots in which the shops of bakers with German names were damaged had their counterpart in the mob attacks upon the British embassy in Berlin.

CHAPTER 5

THE SPECIAL BRANCH

T HROUGHOUT THE WAR the Special Branch was combined with the Criminal Investigation Department. There is a dividing line between ordinary and political crime. In normal times the function of the Criminal Investigation Department is to unravel crimes that have been committed and of the Special Branch to foresee and to prevent political agitators from committing crime in order to terrorise the community into granting them what they want. At that time there were about 700 criminal investigation officers, of whom rather over a hundred belonged to the Special Branch.

The Special Branch was instituted in the early '80s to cope with the Irish dynamite outrages in London and elsewhere. Scarcely had these been put down when foreign anarchists began to follow the Irish example. The lives of ministers were threatened, public buildings were attacked and legislation in the shape of the Explosives Act was passed through both Houses at panic speed. The arrest and sentence of the Italian anarchists, Farnara and Polti, both caught red-handed with bombs in their possession, the fate of the anarchist who blew himself to pieces when attacking Greenwich Observatory and, even more, the hostility of the crowd when the anarchists under the protection of a strong escort of police attempted to give the man a public funeral, were so depressing to criminal aliens that this form of outrage ceased. Shortly afterwards one of the popular weekly newspapers offered a reward to the man who would suggest the most effective form of advertisement and some bright spirit conceived the plan of sending the Home Secretary a bomb containing a copy of the newspaper in question. From the point of view of advertisement it achieved more than he had counted upon. The parcel containing the bomb was opened by the private secretary, who immediately summoned the Inspector of Explosives. When he entered the room he found the bomb lying on the hearth-rug before a bright fire with an office chair standing over it and a group of Home Office officials in a respectful semicircle round it. He asked what the chair was for. They explained that if the bomb went off they thought it would be some protection. It reminded the inspector of an episode at Shoeburyness, when a live shell fell in the mud in the middle of a class of young gunners. 'Lie down, gentlemen,' shouted the instructor and no one moved. When the shell had been rendered harmless he asked why they had not obeyed orders: they might all have been blown to pieces. One of them faltered, 'Well, sir, it was so muddy.'

To return to the advertisement competition. When the bomb was opened and the newspaper was disclosed it was found that it was not an offence to scare the wits out of a Cabinet minister. But the young gentleman had neglected one precaution: he had not removed from the bomb a percussion cap and this was his undoing, for under the Postal Act it was unlawful to send explosives by post. When he appeared at the police court upon this heinous charge he had all the advertisement that he wanted.

If there was any disposition to reduce or disband the Special Branch at that time, the criminal activities of Indian students, which culminated later in the assassination of Sir Curzon Wyllie, showed that the branch could not be dispensed with and while the Indian students were still active the suffragettes took to crime. I am not sure that these ladies were not a more troublesome problem than all the rest put together. They steered clear of assassination, but they burned down churches, blew up the Coronation Chair in Westminster Abbey, damaged priceless pictures, set valuable property on fire, smashed half the plate-glass windows in Regent Street and attempted to throw the King's horse at the Derby. Most of them had quite forgotten the vote and were intent only upon the excitement. Many of them lived in studios where they could plot and contrive street pageants uninterrupted by their elders to their hearts' content. When they were caught they used to scream down the witnesses or the magistrate and when they were committed to prison they went on hunger-strike. The so-called 'Cat and Mouse' Act was devised to meet this contingency, but many of them eluded re-arrest by a large expenditure of money on cars and by an ingenuity that might have been employed upon a better cause. In official circles I was stigmatised as an incurable optimist when I said that the violent tactics of the suffragettes would end as suddenly as they had begun and perhaps they were right, because neither I nor anyone else had foreseen the war. On 5 August 1914 there were actually three women in custody for an assault upon Downing Street. On that morning a deputation of suffragettes called at the Home Office to demand their release. It was felt that these women quite probably would throw all their misdirected energies into the national cause. The three culprits were released and from that moment the militants undertook war work and in not a few cases gave conspicuous service to the country. Sometimes their enthusiasm was embarrassing, as when they began to denounce the wrong people as being traitors to their country, but on the whole they did more good than harm.

With the outbreak of the war the work of the Special Branch became more exacting than that of the Criminal Investigation Department. It was maid-of-all-work to every public office, for, being the only department with a trained outdoor staff, it was called upon for every kind of duty, from the regulation of carrier pigeons to investigating the strange behaviour of a Swiss waiter. Ordinary crime decreased progressively with every month of the war. The very qualities of enterprise and adventure that swept so many youngsters into crime during peace time took the same men to the recruiting office and when conscription came in our prisons were more than half empty.

Looking back over the eight years in which the branch was responsible under my control for the safety of ministers and distinguished foreign visitors, it is natural to take satisfaction in the fact that there has never been a mishap. Apart from the obvious danger run by the Viceroy and the Chief Secretary of Ireland, there have been anxious moments, especially during the Prime Minister's travels abroad; and if it had not been for the network of information of the plans of international assassins, against which precautions could be taken beforehand, there might have been incidents that would have left their mark upon history.

In 1915, 1,100 habitual criminals were known to be fighting; more than seventy had been killed. One of these had stood his trial for murder and had been condemned to death, but his sentence was commuted to penal servitude for life and in due course he had been set at liberty on licence. He was one of the first to answer the call. In one case an ex-warder serving as a private recognised in his sergeant a former prisoner who had been in his ward, but, like a wise man, he held his tongue. One 'old lag' did give a comrade away. The colonel of a certain battalion had chosen as his sergeant-major an old soldier who had rejoined, who feared nobody and was a strict disciplinarian. All went well until one day a corporal asked for a private interview with the colonel and imparted to him the news that the sergeant-major was an ex-convict. It turned out that he had attempted to trade upon this knowledge with the sergeant-major himself but had failed and now he was having his revenge. Having made his revelation the corporal deserted, knowing that his sergeant-major was no less redoubtable with his fists than he was with his tongue.

The police who had the duty of supervision over ex-convicts drew the line only at the Royal Army Medical Corps. It was their duty to prevent crime wherever possible and it was not considered fair to men of these antecedents to place them in the way of temptation in the shape of the kit and valuables of the dead and wounded. There were, of course, a few backsliders. Many of the men gravitated to the lines of communication rather than to the trenches and there were cases of the purloining of stores and rations and comrades' property. Generally, however, the punishment awarded by court-martial was suspended and the men were given another chance in the trenches.

In one case a man who had been convicted for burglary won the Victoria Cross. He volunteered on a night of heavy rain to crawl to the enemy's trenches alone and silence a machine-gun post. He told the officer before he left that if he did not return in half an hour the company was free to open fire, 'and never mind me'. Just before the interval expired he dropped back into his own trench, plastered with mud from head to foot. Returning again to the Front after the award of the VC, he was killed in action. I knew the man – a rough, silent, Lancashire lad, who had come to grief, I believe, through a love of adventure and who was as free from egotism, pose and self-consciousness as any of the men I knew. When the Great Book is opened his crimes, such as they were, will, I think, be found erased on the debit side of his account and the Recording Angel will have set down virtues which had but a tardy recognition while he walked this earth.

The Criminal Investigation Department was called upon to provide trained men for the personnel of the Intelligence Corps in France. They were the nucleus of what afterwards became an important body – the Intelligence Police, who took control of the passenger traffic at the ports and of counter-espionage on the lines of communication. Several of them who obtained commissions reverted quite cheerfully to the rank of sergeant of police after the Armistice. One of them whose work in London had been the detection of white slave traffickers was detailed to protect the Commander-in-Chief, Lord French. In the street of GHQ he recognised a man whose deportation from England had been due to his investigations. He followed the man, who went straight to Lord French's quarters. He stopped him on the doorstep and taxed him with his identity. There, at least, one would have said that the capture was important, but no! It turned out that the man had been engaged by someone who knew nothing of his unsavoury character, to assist in the kitchen.

It may be imagined that the enormous rush of correspondence in those first days of the war dislocated the smooth-running machinery of the Special Branch. There was likely to be a shortage of trained police officers and we took on a number of pensioners to cope with the correspondence. I remember the hopeless expression on their faces when I visited them about a week after they had started. Piles of unopened letters lay on the floor, great stacks of docketed letters stood on every table. They were working I do not know how many hours overtime and still the flood of correspondence was threatening to submerge them. In those first few months I do not think that any of us left the office before midnight. If all the angry people who poured in their complaints had realised that everyone had to suffer some inconvenience in the war we might have done better work.

I really think that at this time the American tourist was the most difficult. Not content with besieging his own embassy, he would sometimes come to demand satisfaction from me for the outrage of having had questions put to him at the port of arrival. These ladies and gentlemen had never seen a war before and they could not understand why it should be allowed to interfere with the elementary comfort of a neutral who was ready to pay liberally for everything. Sometimes I am afraid that my subordinates paltered with the sacred truth, for they had discovered that the quickest way to smooth the ruffled feelings of these tourists was to say, 'Do you know that you are the first American who has ever complained of such inconveniences? We have always found Americans so quick to realise our difficulties and to make allowances for them.' That never seems to have failed to put the angriest of them on their good behaviour. It made them, in a sense, custodians of their country's reputation. But when the first tourist rush had been seen safely off to the other side of the Atlantic I began to find the Americans, both official and unofficial, a very great help and I made many permanent friends among them. The temptation to win affection in this country by displaying unneutral feelings must in some cases have been very great and yet, though I knew many official Americans intimately, I never heard one of them go outside the reserve which every official neutral was expected to entail. The announcement that America had entered the war must have been to some of them like removing the top from a boiling saucepan.

I knew that not a few Englishmen thought that when America began to send over staff officers to Europe they would not want to learn from our experience but would be more inclined to put us under instruction. They were quite wrong. The whole attitude of the American officer was exactly what good sense would prescribe. We had been buying our experience at great cost for nearly four years and we were prepared to give it all freely to our new allies. They, on their part, came over to learn and when they had learned all that we were able to teach them they began to make discoveries for themselves. Never during the whole course of the war or afterwards was there any difference between my American friends and myself. We worked as one organisation and when they had had time to extend theirs until it reached all over Europe I thought sometimes that it was the better of the two. Nor must I forget the American journalist. It had been a tradition in some British official circles to be afraid of the journalist, probably lest his trained persuasiveness might have induced them to open their mouths when they meant to keep them shut. I have always found it best to be perfectly open with them; to tell them as much as they ought to know for the proper understanding of the question and then to settle with them what they shall publish. I have never known an American journalist exceed the limits within which he has promised to keep. Sometimes when it was essential that a matter should be made public they have gone out of their way to publish it. No doubt the European representatives of the great American newspapers are very carefully chosen: I have been surprised at their wide knowledge of international affairs and the excellent forecasts they have made.

In those early days weird people would swim into my horizon. One morning information came to me that a gigantic American had arrived at the Carlton Hotel and had declared his intention of buying a yacht in order to pay a visit to the Kaiser. He thought that a few minutes' straight talk between them would finish the war. I invited him to call and there walked into my room a very menacing figure. He was well over 6 feet and must have weighed quite eighteen stone. He stood there glaring at me with his hat on, chewing the stump of a cigar.

'Won't you take off your hat and sit down?' I began.

'I'd rather stand.'

'We don't usually smoke in this office.'

'I am not smoking.' (The cigar was unlighted.)

'I hear that you are going to buy a yacht.'

'That's my business.'

At this, my assistant, who was almost equally powerful, rose to his full height. I think he expected that my visitor intended mischief. After this unpromising beginning it was useless to question him further and we parted. Throughout the interview he had not relaxed his scowl. Later in the afternoon the American embassy received a cable to the effect that a gentleman of large means, who was mentally unstable and was being looked after by his friends privately, had eluded them and embarked for Liverpool. The name corresponded with that of my friend of the hat and the cigar. I was asked whether I saw any way of restoring the gentleman to his relations. They were ready to wait on the other side with their arms open to receive him if only he could be persuaded to go. It was a desperate venture, but I tried it. I sent a courtly inspector to the hotel with instructions to be mysterious but urgent in an invitation to come down at once to another interview. He came and this time I did not trouble him with preliminaries. I looked round to see that all the doors were closed and then addressed him. 'I want to give you a word of advice,' I said.

Ask me no questions, but if you are wise you will do exactly as I say. There is a boat leaving for New York tomorrow morning. Don't stop to think; just go by it. If the matter had not been so urgent in your own interests I would not have sent for you. Now waste no time.

He looked at me blankly for a moment and left the room without a word. Two hours later inquiries were made at the hotel. He had looked in for a moment to pay his bill and had left without his luggage. A telegram to Liverpool produced the reply that he had gone on board the steamer, booked his passage and had locked himself in his cabin. We heard later that he was met by his friends and that the luggage had been sent on after him.

On one other occasion my companion felt called upon to intervene. A middle-aged man had been asked to call on some quite unimportant matter. He was of fierce and truculent mien. When I asked him a question he glared at me and was silent. I put the question again, whereupon he clapped his hand to some mysterious pocket about his person and began to draw out what my companion thought must be a revolver. He was about to fall upon the visitor when the object was disclosed. He was pulling out a curious little telephonic apparatus which he planted on my table in front of me and connected with his ear. The man was stone deaf. The faintest ghost of a smile flickered across his rugged countenance when he realised our mistake.

Very soon after the declaration of war every public man whose speech was reported in the newspapers received a letter in a foreign handwriting, filled with abuse of the English and extravagant praise of the Germans, who, according to the writer, were chosen by God to sweep us into the sea. The brutality and vainglory of these compositions were tempered with scholarship: the man was an omnivorous reader and had a quotation in support of every boast. The letters were posted from every district in London and bore an address in Loughton which did not exist. Apart from the work entailed in the laboriously ornamental handwriting, the man must have expended time and money in travelling from one part of London to another. Abusive letters injure nobody, but that a truculent Hun should be at large in London in wartime, in the opinion of those who received his letters, reflected little credit on the efficiency of the police. In order to cut this troublesome inquiry short I induced *The Globe* to publish a facsimile of one of the letters and immediately several people wrote to say that they identified the handwriting as that of their former German tutor living in Dalston. I was curious to see this fire-eating Hun: I pictured him as a heavy, florid, square-headed Prussian. Square-headed he was, but he proved to be a rather diminutive abject person with the wide-staring eyes of a wild animal brought to bay. He was mentally deranged, but in the choice of his pseudonym, in the precautions he had taken in posting his letters, he had shown the cunning of a monomaniac. He had a son serving in the British Army and a very loyal wife who undertook to keep him out of mischief for the future.

As the German tide poured over Belgium we received our daily flood of refugees. The arrangements improvised by the Belgian Relief Committee were a high tribute to the power of organisation which is latent in our people. Naturally there was a little confusion at first because the rush of refugees far exceeded the room for accommodation during the first few days. Considering that the refugees included all the unemployable and most of the disreputable part of the Belgian population, as well as the industrious and the intellectual, it is remarkable, on the whole, how well they behaved. There were one or two amusing incidents. I remember hearing that at one of the receiving stations in London a couple who spoke Flemish but no other language were received late in the evening. The woman was shown into her room and shortly afterwards the supposed husband was conducted to the same apartment. Immediately a fearful uproar arose and the interpreter had to be telephoned for. It then appeared that neither of the couple had ever seen the other before.

Antwerp was being threatened, the Naval Division was pouring in for its defence and I was asked to send a police officer to the city because my officer at Ostend could not possibly leave his post. No officer was available at the time except a middle-aged man with a large family who had done excellent service in advising upon doubtful literature. In fact, he was the greatest living authority upon the kind of literature on which a successful prosecution could be founded. At the call of duty he said 'goodbye' to his family and departed. A few days later, when the German siege guns were in position, there came a telegram from him, suggesting that he should be recalled. Events were moving fast and before I could reply to the telegram his arrival at Scotland Yard was announced. I sent for him and said gravely, 'I had your telegram, inspector, but you left your post without waiting for a reply.'

He bowed in his usual courtly manner and replied, 'Yes, sir, but a 15-inch shell took the corner off my bedroom, sir and I don't know how it is, but I think I am getting too old for sieges.'

'Too old for sieges' became a byword in my office throughout the war when any one was asked to undertake a job that he did not relish.

There were two sides to the question of interning enemy aliens who were kept in the country. When war broke out there were no internment camps, but there were many Germans who were known to be dangerous. Some place of internment had to be improvised forthwith and for London the obvious place was Olympia. Bedding and blankets were hastily gathered in and a guard was provided from Wellington Barracks. I used to go there daily for a time because some useful information might be gleaned from the civilian prisoners. They were a most unprepossessing lot. During the first fortnight two Austrian ships put into the Thames before they knew that war had been declared. The crews were all marched to Olympia and interned with the Germans.

When I arrived the next morning the Austrians had been relegated to the annexe and were roped off from the others. It appeared that they had not been more than an hour with the Germans before a violent quarrel broke out and the Austrian officers formed a deputation to the commandant to request that they might be separated from 'those German riff-raff'. Among them were four young Austrian students who had apparently taken a voyage for the enlargement of their minds. These young men had very definite and uncomplimentary views regarding their brothers-in-arms, the Prussians. On the whole, the prisoners in Olympia gave very little trouble. On one occasion a German waiter became insolent to a guardsman, but the Irish corporal, who had a sense of humour, approached the two while they were in mid-dispute and said to the private in pretended seriousness, 'Why stop to argue with him? Shoot him,' whereupon the German waiter dived under a table and was quite polite for the remainder of his stay.

The cry, 'Intern them all,' which was taken up by certain newspapers, was very embarrassing. Though, no doubt, it did interpret the public feeling and allayed public alarm, it was the cause of thousands of complaints and investigations. My own view at the time was that we had so full a knowledge of the dangerous Germans that we should confine internment to that class and leave the innocent ones at liberty. Many of them were doing good work for us in munitions and manufactures, some were definitely ranged in their sympathies with the Allies, such as the Poles and Czechs. To 'intern them all' would be to invite the enemy countries to intern all our nationals, which, of course, they did, but the real argument against indiscriminate internment was that we had no place ready to receive such vast numbers. This meant that until camps were ready it would be impossible to give the prisoners the accommodation prescribed by the Hague Convention. Complaints would reach the enemy, who would then feel themselves justified in maltreating our prisoners. Nevertheless, it had to be done and every day one might see furniture vans packed with Germans proceeding through the streets to Olympia before being drafted off to such camps as could be improvised.

Some of the Germans brought this fate upon themselves. There was a well-known café in Oxford Street in which the staff – even the manager and the bookkeeper – were all registered enemy aliens. On the afternoon when the news of de Wet's rebellion in South Africa reached London the waiters and some of the guests began to cheer. I had news of this by telephone and in half an hour the entire staff was rounded up, put into a furniture van and driven off to Olympia. There was an indignant protest from the British directors of the company that evening, but my case was quite unanswerable.

CHAPTER 6

WAR CRIMES

URING THE EARLY months of 1915 the war spirit seized upon all classes. New Scotland Yard was often mistaken for the recruiting office in Scotland Yard and the policeman at the door was kept busy directing callers to their proper destination. All day long the flower of the nation might be seen marching down Whitehall in mufti on their way to the station. The saddest part of the business was that in those early days we were sacrificing in the trenches what would have been magnificent material for officers of the conscripted army later on, but the sacrifice was not in vain if example counts for anything.

My old friend, Sir Schomberg M'Donnell, was working at this time as Intelligence Officer to the Home Forces. He was past fifty. I found out quite by chance that he was spending his spare time at Wellington Barracks learning his drill and one morning he came to say 'goodbye'. He had taken a commission and was going to the Front. Not many weeks afterwards came the news that he had been killed in action.

They tell a story of a certain artistic dilettante well known in London who, when he was offered a commission, said, 'Look at me. Could I lead men? I have never done anything yet but sit and sew.' (He excelled at embroidery.) He insisted upon going out as a private and when the commissariat broke down in bad weather and the nerves of his comrades were all on edge, he kept them cheerful and contented by a never-failing flow of good spirits. He said he had enlisted because, being 'the greatest rotter in London', he thought that if he went others less rotten would have to go too. They relate that when an ill-conditioned NCO, addressing him with ill-disguised contempt, said, 'And what was your line?' he replied, 'Well, they say that I was best at embroidery.' He returned badly wounded in the hand and when a sympathetic old lady saw him at his own door fumbling with his latchkey, she fluttered up to help, saying, 'Oh, you are wounded!'

He replied, 'Oh no, madam, I fell off a bus when I was drunk.'

It is strange now to think that in March 1915 Russia was thought in England to be breathing a new inspiration to the West. It was said that the Crusader spirit was alive again; that the whole Russian nation was inspired with a determination to rescue Constantinople for Christianity and to win again the Holy Sepulchre; that when she came into the war Russia was busy with her own evolution, not revolution and that vodka was prohibited with the unanimous approval of the nation, who had tried prohibition for a month and then approved it as a permanency; that crime had almost disappeared among the peasants, who were now investing in the savings bank the money which they used to spend upon liquor. If they were successful in the war they were told that there would come a struggle between their religious idealism and their high ethical instincts and the monster of western materialism from which, so far, they had kept themselves clean. All this was honestly believed by persons who thought they knew Russia: now, after a short six years, their voices are heard no more.

In the early days of May 1915 the Germans torpedoed an American oil-tanker called the *Gulflight* and killed the captain. The body was landed in the Scilly Islands. It occurred to a person gifted with imagination that if the body were embalmed and sent over to the United States for burial the effect might be far-reaching, because as long as the submarine attacks upon harmless merchant vessels resulted in the death of Englishmen the real horrors of submarine warfare would never come home to the great mass of Americans. I was asked to find out a man who would consent to go down to the Scilly Islands to embalm the body, but on the very day when the arrangements were completed – 7 May 1915 – at about three o'clock I received a telephone message announcing that the *Lusitania* had been sunk. After that, of course, the sinking of the *Gulflight* became insignificant. Of all the many mistakes made by the Germans, the sinking of the *Lusitania* was the greatest. It split the German-American sympathies from top to bottom and ranged the native American very strongly upon the side of the Allies. I could scarcely believe that the Germans had struck a medal in commemoration of this outrage until I received an actual specimen of it. From that moment every person in England with a German name who entertained his friends was accused of drinking to the sinking of the *Lusitania*. I can never ascertain that any such accusation was well founded; on the contrary, I believe that many persons of German origin definitely cast off all sympathy with their country from that date. After that they were ready to believe any infamy of which the Germans were accused.

I remember very well the Zeppelin raid on London on 31 May 1915. I was dining with a certain Cabinet minister to meet the new Home Secretary and the new Lord Chancellor, together with Sir

Edward Henry, the Commissioner of Police, and several Heads of Departments. I was discussing with Sir John Simon a question that was exercising us very much at the time, namely, the denaturalisation of former aliens who were believed to be hostile to this country, but against whom there was no definite evidence of acts of espionage.

Our conversation was interrupted dramatically. Our host came in from the telephone room, crying, 'Zeppelins!' He had been rung up from the Admiralty and told that Zeppelins were coming up the Thames. Our hostess's first thought was for her small children. Were they to be taken to the cellar? The whole party trooped into the telephone room and grouped itself round the instrument in a wide circle. As one of the guests remarked, it was exactly like the second act of a melodrama. A secretary sat impassive at the instrument and, having got through to Scotland Yard, handed the receiver to Sir Edward Henry, who said very quietly, 'Dropped bombs at Whitechapel, four or five killed, many injured; then turned north, now dropping bombs on Stoke Newington. Any fires? Oh, a good many fires. Thank you,' and he rang off. We stood no longer on ceremony. Our hostess and one of the guests ran upstairs to bring the children down and the rest of us trooped off to Scotland Yard, where the telephone room would give us information at first hand. I walked home across the park. It was a lovely, clear night, but there was not a sign or sound of Zeppelins and the police in Kensington had not even heard of the raid at 11.30. So huge a city is London! I learned afterwards that no one in London saw the airships. Altogether, ninety-two bombs were found, of which thirty were high explosive, generally of small size, with a little propeller attached which turned during the descent and un-screwed the fuse. Attached to each of these was a piece of stuff like a stocking-leg. A good many had failed to explode, but two of them had killed children. Three very large high-explosive bombs had been dropped. One had made a huge crater in Kingsland Road, one was found in a garden unexploded at a depth of 8 feet and another had gone through the roof and floor of a stable and was found embedded at a depth of 7 feet. This one weighed 150 pounds, it was 36 inches in circumference and would have done great damage had it exploded. It appeared that the Zeppelin had followed the Great Eastern line as far as Bishopsgate Station, where it dropped a bomb and had then followed the branch line towards Waltham Abbey. From Waltham Abbey it turned east towards the coast and was not heard of again, until we learned long afterwards that she was the LZ 38 and that a few days after her return to her hangar near Brussels she was destroyed in her shed by an English airman. She could climb 10,000 feet with a cargo of 1.5 tons of bombs.

The business of the police was now to organise bomb shelters, a very difficult business in a city such as London. It was unfortunate that the East End, where the houses are small and unprovided with cellars, should always be the first to suffer from Zeppelin attacks and the danger of improvising shelters was that unless the roof was absolutely proof against penetration the shelter might well become a death-trap. This actually happened in Dunkirk, where a house was demolished by a high-explosive shell fired from a distance of 25 miles, when the cellar was packed with people. The cellars in Dunkirk were covered with a skin-thick brick arch, which would scarcely resist the impact even of a small bomb. Though people worked heroically far into the night to dig put those entombed in the cellar, when they reached them, all, to the number of more than forty, were found dead of suffocation.

The object of the Germans in making Zeppelin raids on London was to produce panic and a cry for peace. It did neither. Even in the East End, though there was great alarm, there was no panic. A few months ago, when discussing the war with a highly placed German, he said, 'No one but a person who knew nothing about national psychology would have thought that one could terrorise a northern nation like the British by Zeppelin raids. If you had retaliated by air raids on Berlin you would only have succeeded in stiffening our war spirit. It may be different with the Latin races. There we might have produced panic, but with a northern race the idea was so futile that no one but a Prussian general would have conceived it.'

But while there was no panic there were great hardships, as a visit to any of the Tube stations in the east of London on the night of an air-raid would have shown – the stairs crowded with half-awakened and hungry children, the platforms so packed with humanity that there was not a vacant square foot. I used to wonder how many of these children would feel the permanent effects. On the whole, however, young children between five and thirteen really seemed to enjoy air raid nights. They were full of excitement and you would take them out of bed wrapped in blankets and give them unexpected meals. It was a little grim when one knew the reality to hear from infant lips, 'Oh, Daddy, I do hope there'll be an air raid tonight.'

One incident in connection with the Zeppelin that was brought down at Cuffley was never quite cleared up. As the airship approached the ground the crew began to tear up their papers and throw them out of the car and two fields were so littered with the fragments that they looked as if there had been a local snow-storm. As soon as the news spread spectators in every kind of vehicle overran the place and among the fragments of paper collected by the Air Service with a view to piecing them together was found the name of a Belgian woman with an address in London. The woman was sent for and it was found that she had moved to that address only ten days before. It transpired, however, that she was in the habit of giving her name and address to strangers in the street. On the face of it, an address obtained during the last ten days and found among the papers of a German Zeppelin was disturbing, for it implied that a German officer had been in London a few days before the attack. I think the explanation was that one of the spectators had brought the address with him and had dropped it in the field with the other fragments.

It was a humorist who commanded the aircraft that came over on 8 September 1915. When over Wrotham Park, Barnet, he dropped a hambone attached to a small parachute inscribed with a fancy portrait of Sir Edward Grey, on whose devoted head a bomb is in the act of falling. It was inscribed in German, 'Edwert Grey, poor devil, what am I to do?', and on the reverse, 'In remembrance of starved-out Germany.'

There were many jokes about the anti-aircraft defences in the early days. It was alleged, for example, that one of the guns posted near the Admiralty was in charge of a librarian and that one of the first executive orders of the new First Lord had been, 'Stop the librarian from firing off that gun.'

Early in 1916 there were curious stories about the German foreknowledge of the weather conditions in this country which they could have acquired only from spies. It was said that after the raid in October a conversation was overheard in a café in Rotterdam, in which a full description of the damage done by bombs in London the night before was given and that of three places named as having been hit by bombs two were correct. This conversation took place about noon and the news could have reached Rotterdam only by cable or wireless. It was suggested that the wireless operators on some of the neutral boats began sending messages as soon as they cleared from England, but though most careful investigations were made we were never able to discover that there was any leakage of this kind.

General von Hoeppner has told us the German side of the air-raids. At first the enemy hoped to cause panic; then to keep our airmen away from the Western Front, which they think was accomplished. But by the end of 1916 they recognised that the Zeppelin attacks were a failure. The Allied airmen were so successful in bombing the hangars in Belgium that the Zeppelins were withdrawn to the Rhine stations and the distance they had to cover was then too great even for the newest airships. They were then turned over to the navy for scouting purposes. The daylight air raid on London on 13 June 1917, under Captain Brandenburg, filled them with joy because all the machines returned safely owing to our shells bursting too high and our machines never really having got into touch. The attacks on favourable nights in the winter of 1917–18 were maintained, he says, with the object of keeping our airmen away from the Western Front.

In January 1915 the Germans produced a propaganda film for the edification of neutral countries. An American who was carrying it to the United States consented to show it to diplomatists and officials at the Ambassadors' Theatre. The film displayed the usual German ignorance of the psychology of other peoples. Part of it was not 'faked.' We had the Kaiser standing beside a road with his staff, while picked troops marched past. His hair was quite grey and there was a hollow shadow in his cheek. His movements were nervous and jerky. At one point he had been told to look at the camera, which he did stiffly and gravely before getting into a car and driving off. There were pictures of engineers carrying out sapper operations at high speed; reviews before the Kings of Saxony and Bavaria; the huge monument erected to Hindenburg in Berlin; a mass meeting; diplomatic presentations to the Sultan, with Enver Pasha in the foreground; the Sultan sitting under an awning receiving Balkan diplomatists; several spools of the Danish Army and navy manoeuvres intended to give the impression that Denmark was on the German side and was mobilising. Then came the 'fake' spools. You saw German soldiers feeding hordes of Belgian and French children under the title, 'Barbarians feeding the Hungry' and there were rows of colossal grinning German soldiers, with the title, '*Sehen Barbaren so aus?*' (Do Barbarians look like this?), which provoked the comment that no barbarian had ever looked quite so unattractive. Then there were English prisoners grinning all over with delight while they worked for the Germans under the stern eye of Prussian soldiers. It was propaganda laid on with a trowel.

One of the great dangers at the beginning of the war was the form of the first Treasury notes. It was recognised that if these were forged in any quantities public confidence in the currency would be shaken and people might refuse to accept our paper money as legal tender. In 1915 the expected forgeries began to appear. It was reported that a considerable quantity of the 'G' series of £1 and 10s. Treasury notes was being circulated in London. The method was that a man would go down a street calling at small shops, buying some inexpensive trifle and tendering a note, for which he took the change in silver. Specimens of the notes showed the forgery to be remarkably good. No one but an expert could have detected the imposition, especially at dusk, which was the time of day usually chosen for passing the notes. We felt that we were on our mettle. After a week or two information reached us, no matter how, that an ex-convict E— was the distributor, though not the printer, of the notes, for which his price was half the face value. At this price he was prepared to sell any number to persons whom he could trust. It was his practice to make the sales on Saturdays, for on Fridays he disappeared to some mysterious rendezvous whence he obtained the notes.

Now E— could have been arrested at any moment, but it was no good arresting him while the printer remained undiscovered, for a man who could reproduce a watermark that would almost pass muster by daylight would most certainly not discontinue his operations because a minor confederate had been arrested. All our efforts, therefore, were turned towards the discovery of the printer. One of our own men bought some of the counterfeits and, in order to convince the forgers of his good faith, it was necessary that he should pass them. It was impossible, of course, that he should pass counterfeits and therefore the counterfeits had to be exchanged for genuine notes, a very expensive proceeding when it extended over several weeks. But the matter was growing serious. It was computed that at least £60,000 worth of false Treasury notes had been put into circulation and it was necessary to spend a considerable sum in unearthing the conspiracy. A free hand was given to me and then events began to go a little quicker. It was found that E— used to meet a few other choice spirits for card-playing at a little office in Jermyn Street. He had been traced one Friday to a paper merchant, where he bought the very best kind of typewriting paper and the samples we obtained showed that such paper had been used in the forgeries after the false watermark had been impressed upon it. We knew also when he had left his flat in a taxi with the paper, but further inquiries showed that this taxi did not carry him to any particular destination: it was stopped in mid-street and paid off, and from that moment all trace of E— was lost. But that evening there he was at the card-party and there, too, was our man. As the evening wore on, a few friends dropped in and among them a young man who lost his stakes and always paid in little sums that suggested change for a 10s. note; it was also noticed when he was staking his money that his fingers were stained with printer's ink. When he had left the place in disgust our man drew a bow at a venture. 'I used to know that young fellow,' he said. 'He used to be a clerk in your old registry office in Leicester Square.'

'No, he was not,' replied E— shortly. 'You are mistaken.'

But our man persisted. 'I remember him quite well now; his name was Brown.'

'You are mistaken. He was never a clerk. He is a printer and his name is W—.'

With this slender clue the police proceeded to scour London for a printer named W— and at last, on a wooden gate in an unpretentious street in north London, they discovered the almost obliterated inscription, 'W—, Printer'. The gateway led into a yard, and from it ran a little carriage road through a tunnel under the house to a stable and coach-house in the rear. But this gate seemed permanently to be locked. The police now rented a window on the other side of the street and sat down to wait. Three days passed; Friday approached and as the dusk fell the watchers saw E— come down the street and kick on the door.

A few seconds later it was opened from inside and he disappeared. Then Chief Inspector Fowler, who was in charge of the case, marshalled his men about the door and waited until it should open again. The delay seemed interminable, but at last, long after dark, the door did open and E— was in their midst.

Never in its history had that quiet street been startled by such an uproar. E— was wheeling round, spouting streams of notes from his pockets like some sort of centrifugal machine and emitting wild beast howls, which were intended to alarm his partner in the stable. The whole neighbourhood was raised. The street was carpeted with notes like autumn leaves and E—'s resistance had resulted only in a modification of his features that would have puzzled his nearest friends. The police, too, had not gone unscathed.

When E— had been secured they vaulted the gate, went through the tunnel and knocked on the stable door. It was opened by a young man in his shirt-sleeves who, on seeing the police, fell flat on the floor in a faint. The place was crammed with machinery; notes still damp were lying on the press and it was observed that the forger had gone one better than the legitimate printer by introducing into his die a numbering device. You had only to turn the handle of the press to forge £1 notes until your arms tired. There was, besides, a very ingenious device for watermarking which must not be divulged. Nor was this all. When this forger's den came to be searched there were found the lithographic stones on which had been printed certain forged postage stamps that had formed the subject of a criminal action some years before. In fact, this expert printer had been making a fine art of forgery for some years. The next morning I visited the place with the Chancellor of the Exchequer and Sir John Bradbury, whose signature was on every treasury note and then and there, while Sir John fed in the paper, the Chancellor of the Exchequer turned the handle. It was the first instance in history in which the Chancellor has been guilty of forging the currency. The notes were so good that when they took specimens from the press they thought it well to write 'Forged' in large letters across each note for fear they should get mixed up with genuine notes. Steps were at once taken to issue a new note which would be proof against fabrication.

CHAPTER 7

THE GERMANS AND THE IRISH

A S SOON AS war broke out, the veteran John Devoy, together with Judge Cohalan and other sympathisers, put themselves into communication with Bernstorff, the German ambassador, von Papen, the military attaché and Boy-Ed, the naval attaché in Washington. The war with Germany was to be made the supreme opportunity for establishing a Republic in Ireland. Naturally, the Germans were ready to make use of any means that might embarrass their enemy and they were as ready to help the Irish revolutionaries as they were the Indian. Devoy was in no lack of funds, for besides the money which he could always collect from Irish-Americans, he could draw upon the German Secret Service funds. The Germans described him as one of their 'agents'.

During the early months of the war James Larkin, of the Irish Transport Workers, appeared in America on platforms decorated with the German and Irish flags intertwined and no pains were spared to make it clear to Americans that German and Irish interests were identical.

During the autumn of 1914 Sir Roger Casement was in New York. At that time all that was known in England was that he was in clandestine communication with Bernstorff. It was not until many months afterwards that his real scheme was disclosed. His proposals to the Germans were that he should go over to Berlin and form an Irish Brigade out of the Irish prisoners of war and that his brigade, with the assistance of a German military force, should effect a landing in Ireland when the time was ripe, but that in the meantime the German government should furnish the Irish volunteers with great supplies of arms and munitions in order that, when the time came, they should be able to take the field and welcome the invaders. A document (Casement called it a 'Treaty') was negotiated and signed between 23 and 28 December 1914.

I do not believe that any disloyal thought had entered into Casement's head before the war. He had been for many years in the service of the Foreign Office as a consular officer in west and east Africa and Brazil; he had published accounts of atrocities by the Belgians on the Congo and by certain Peruvians in Putumayo; he had been knighted for his services in 1911. In view of his subsequent conduct, it may be well to bear in mind that he wrote to the Foreign Secretary on 19 June 1911, in terms somewhat extravagant for the moderate honour of a Knight Bachelor which had been conferred upon him. This letter was read at his trial.

Casement sailed for Norway in October with a Norwegian servant who afterwards gave some information about the voyage. The vessel was stopped by one of our auxiliary cruisers, but Casement was not recognised. While he was in Norway he circulated a fabricated story which, however, he himself may have believed, that the British minister was concerned in a plot against his life; but when Bernstorff was urged to make public capital of this he replied that it would be better to wait for confirmation. In fact, in adopting this cautious attitude he was doing no more than Casement's former official colleagues had always done.

Casement arrived in Berlin on 2 November. Soon after his arrival he had an interview with Zimmermann, of the Foreign Office.

He asked Devoy to send over an Irish-speaking priest and in due course the Rev. John T. Nicholson was dispatched from America via Italy and Switzerland to become Roman Catholic chaplain at the internment camp in which the Irish prisoners were being collected. The expenses of Casement's journey are believed to have been furnished by John Devoy.

Throughout 1915 the real direction of Irish affairs was in the hands of John Devoy and Bernstorff, who was acting through him. The process of arming the Irish rebels was not proceeding quite smoothly. Von Papen had purchased for use in India or in Ireland 11,000 rifles, 4,000,000 cartridges and a number of revolvers, but the Germans were quite firm in their view that these could not safely be landed in Ireland. Instructions and information were carried to and fro by Devoy's messengers who, as American citizens, could travel about Ireland very much as they liked. But early in February 1916 Devoy began to change his waiting policy. The Irish volunteers had become increasingly active. There was the threat of conscription, for though Ireland had been exempt from compulsory service Devoy expected that the leaders in Ireland would be arrested and that then, when everything was in confusion, conscription would be enforced. He decided, therefore, that there must be a rising on Easter Saturday, 1916, on the occasion of a review of the Irish Volunteers and that the Germans must land munitions in or near Limerick at some time between Good Friday and Saturday. He was also counting upon German military help as soon as a rising had begun.

It may be wondered why the arrest of the leaders, so much dreaded by Devoy, was not carried out. According to rumour, Mr Birrell, the Chief Secretary, was much swayed by the opinions of the Nationalist leaders, who counselled tolerance under every provocation for fear of precipitating a disastrous conflict.

On 4 March the Germans promised to send two or three trawlers containing 20,000 rifles and ten machine guns to Tralee Bay between 20 and 23 April and a messenger was dispatched to Ireland from America with full instructions. The Irish leaders were very anxious that a submarine should enter the Liffey and go right up to the Pigeon House at the same time.

These preparations on the part of the Germans were not a military or naval enterprise, they were directed by the German Foreign Office. On 26 March Devoy was informed that three trawlers and a cargo steamer would arrive with 1,400 tons of cargo and that lighters must be ready to unload them. These instructions were transmitted to Ireland. The Germans had agreed to arrange a demonstration by airship and naval attack to divert attention from the landing of the munitions and these took place; but the Germans would not consent to the landing of troops, which had been urged so strongly by both Casement and Devoy, nor would they send a submarine up the Liffey, because the naval authorities foresaw technical difficulties.

We must now return to Casement in Germany. Evidence was given at his trial about the manner in which he carried out the first part of his scheme – the formation of an Irish Brigade. His reception by the Irish prisoners of war was not all that he had expected. Many of the men were inclined to give him a hostile reception, but he did succeed in seducing fifty-six men from their oath of allegiance. How far they were impressed by his appeal to patriotism for Ireland or how far by their desire to obtain more liberty and better treatment from the Germans there are no means of knowing. These men were put under the command of Monteith, who obtained a commission as lieutenant and were removed to a camp at Lossen. Rumour says that their behaviour, especially when not entirely under the influence of sobriety, was embarrassing to the Germans, who were compelled to limit their bounds and to impose certain other restrictions. They provided them with a handsome green uniform but not with arms.

A highly placed personage in Germany has since told me that towards the end of 1915 the attitude of the German authorities towards Casement had cooled; so much so that a very strong hint was conveyed to him to leave the capital. However this may be, in January 1916 he went to Munich and from there to Kuranstalt for a health cure. While he was undergoing this cure and was still in bed he received on 3 March a letter from Monteith, asking him to come to Berlin at once. He replied that he could not move and that Monteith should come to him. On 7 March Monteith arrived and told him that on 1 March Lieutenant Frey, of the General Staff, Political Section, had sent for him and told him that they had received a message from Devoy to the effect that something was about to happen and asking for the dispatch of munitions, which the Germans were now ready to supply. Upon this, Casement drew up a memorandum setting out the best means of landing arms in Ireland and Monteith returned with it to Berlin. In the memorandum Casement suggested that he and two picked men should be conveyed to Ireland in a submarine to concert measures with the Irish leaders for landing the arms. On 16 March he went himself to Berlin and had an interview with Captain Nadolny and two other officers of the Political Section of the General Staff, who told him that the Admiralty had declined to furnish a submarine; that Devoy had asked for trained gunners; that instead of 100,000 rifles only 20,000 could be sent, together with ten machine guns and 5,000,000 cartridges. Captain Nadolny asked whether Casement would be prepared to take over with him the fifty-six members of the Irish Brigade from Lossen. To this Casement objected that it was highly improbable that the whole body could equally be trusted.

This news was most disturbing to Casement, who had never dreamed of an armed rebellion taking place so soon. All he wanted was that the Germans should pour arms into Ireland and follow later with a military expedition. After thinking things over, he called at the German Admiralty on 17 March to ask why it was impossible to send a submarine and on learning that the objections were technical he suggested sending a messenger over to Ireland to bring back accurate particulars of the local plans and the scheme for landing the arms. It happened that in the previous November one John M'Govey had come over from the United States as a volunteer. The German Admiralty approved of the suggestion and on Sunday 19 March, M'Govey was sent into Denmark with instructions to reach Dublin without delay. Monteith, meanwhile, was to obtain from the German military authorities an experimental gun with which to train the Irish Brigade at Lossen.

Having made these arrangements Casement returned to Bavaria. As he said afterwards, he felt himself under no obligation to the German government. He thought that the munitions should have been offered much earlier, 'since the political services of Irishmen in America to the German cause far transcended the value of any possible gift of arms Germany might make to Ireland'. He had always been opposed to any armed revolt in Ireland unless it was backed up by strong German military help. He said that in the 'Treaty' of 23 to 28 December 1914 it was stipulated that 'should the Irish Brigade be sent to Ireland, the German government would support its dispatch with adequate military support of men, arms and supplies'. On

29 March he returned to Berlin very much concerned about his responsibility towards the Irish soldiers whom he had seduced from their loyalty. As he expressed it, 'They had committed treason under a distinct and formal promise, sealed and delivered, by the German imperial government, that, in the event of their being dispatched to Ireland, they should be supported by an ample German force, a part of an Army of Deliverance.' He had also an uneasy feeling that if any of them should chance to be captured on the high seas they might, with perfect justice, turn King's Evidence and establish a very damaging case against himself, who would be regarded as a paid tool of the German government.

With his mind filled with these disturbing thoughts, he called again upon Captain Nadolny, who, to his surprise, addressed him in terms of great discourtesy and accused him of a breach of faith in having sent M'Govey to Ireland without consulting him. Probably the traditional jealousy between the naval and military departments was at the bottom of this outburst. Nadolny further threatened that unless Casement submitted to the conditions a telegram would be sent to Devoy that though Germany was quite ready to send the help she had promised, the whole plan had been frustrated by Casement himself and he would then appear as a traitor to the Irish cause. The next day he was asked to call again and on this occasion he was treated with conventional politeness. Captain Nadolny pointed out that it was the Irish who had decided upon a revolt; the Germans were in no way responsible: they were merely fulfilling their promise to furnish arms to the fullest possible extent at the request of the Irish. He made the aims of the German government quite clear: they were not idealistic but severely practical. They would supply the arms, but they expected them to be used without delay and if Casement opposed the plan he would stop the arms and throw the entire responsibility upon him.

Casement replied that the German government was entirely ignoring the agreement it had made with him in December 1914; that he felt sure that at the most the Irish would be able to put 12,000 men into the field and that the rebellion must fail. He said that a firing party of twelve machine gunners ought to be furnished by the Germans to cover the disembarkation of the arms. In view of all that Captain Nadolny had said, he thought that the arms must be sent on the date fixed, but he still pressed for a submarine in which he would go by himself without the Irish soldiers and, to impress Nadolny still further, he declared that he would take poison with him for use if the steamer conveying him were stopped by a British warship, in order to escape the indignities reserved for him 'should I fall into the hands of the government I have dared so unwisely to defy'.

Casement had written a letter to von Wedell. A man of this name was captured by a patrol boat off the north of Scotland in 1915. On the way to the coast the patrol boat struck a mine and foundered and von Wedell, with most of the crew, was drowned. A few weeks later the German government began to inquire about him through the American embassy. Where was he? Was he interned? Did the British government know where he was and was he in a position where he could communicate with his friends? We could say with perfect truth that the British government did know where he was and believed he could communicate with his friends. Great importance must have been attached to this man, for as late as 1917 among the instructions given to a spy was a direction that he should ascertain the fate of von Wedell.

On 1 April, Casement was ill in bed and on that date he read in the *Irish World* Devoy's speech at the Irish Convention on 4 and 5 March. On this he modified his views about the rebellion and thought that Devoy's contention that the British government was determined to destroy the Irish Volunteers and arrest the leaders and that conscription would be applied to Ireland, altered the whole situation. A rising did seem to be necessary and he decided to go. The Germans met him halfway and furnished the submarine, in which he, Monteith and Corporal Bailey arrived in Tralee Bay on Good Friday, 21 April.

Has there ever been a time in history when Irish rebels appealing for foreign aid have not wrecked all by their hopeless incapacity for organisation and administration? For mark what happened. The Germans were true to their promise. They had loaded a small steamer, the *Aud*, with 1,400 tons of munitions concealed under a deck-load of timber. She had Norwegian papers and professed to be bound for the west coast of Africa and her naval crew were cleverly disguised in the ordinary kit of a Norwegian tramp.

There was ample time for the rebels to prepare for unloading the cargo. They had done nothing. The ship proceeded round the north of Scotland unobserved and anchored in Tralee Bay on Good Friday. Almost immediately a small patrol boat ranged up alongside, went through her papers and made a cursory inspection of the deck, though the Germans alleged that one of the hatches was actually open at the time of the visit and the arms were thus exposed to view. The Germans thought that their presence in Tralee Bay had excited no suspicion, but the captain thought it prudent, as there was no sign from the shore, to put to sea and come in again with his cargo when the coast was clear. But fortune was against him. His ship was sighted by the *Blue Bell*, who signalled her to stop and then ordered her to follow to Queenstown. For a short time she obeyed the order and then the signalman on the *Blue Bell* reported that her engines had stopped and that they had run up a flag to the fore. At the same moment there was a dull explosion. The German war flag broke at the top-mast and the ship's crew were seen leaving in the boats. The

Aud was sinking by the head. When the crew were received on board the *Blue Bell* they were in German naval uniform, but they refused to give any account of themselves and they were sent over to Scotland Yard for examination.

This incident was tinged with romance. There was nothing actually to show what the *Aud* had on board and why she had put into Tralee. The first step was for the Admiralty to dispatch a diver to the scene of the sinking. Fortunately the sea was calm. I saw the diver on his return. He was a very spruce, intelligent and observant young man. He described to me the sandy bottom of the bay on which the *Aud* was lying with a great rent in her side and the floor of the Atlantic littered with broken rifles, six of which he had brought back with him. There were Russian marks on the rifles. We sent for the Russian military attaché and then it was found that even this grudging service to the cause of Ireland had been done on the cheap, for the rifles were all Russian, captured at Tannenberg and very much the worse for wear.

CHAPTER 8
THE CASEMENT CASE

T HERE WAS A sensation at New Scotland Yard when the entire crew of the *Aud*, including the officers, were marched over one evening for interrogation. They blocked the passages and a crowd assembled outside. I always found that when German naval prisoners are examined it is better to take the juniors first, for they frequently make admissions which are useful when the time comes for examining the officers, but in this case we reversed the order.

All had agreed to tell the same story – that they were carrying pit-props with a few arms for the Cameroons and that, having delivered their cargo, they were to become an auxiliary cruiser. The limited coal capacity and the slow speed of the boat (in knots) showed this version to be absurd. They said that they had anchored off the Irish coast to re-stow their cargo, but on this their stories differed. No doubt they were actually engaged in preparing the cargo for landing when the patrol boat came up and signalled by wireless for a cruiser. On this the captain of the *Aud* had taken alarm and steamed away.

The captain was one of the most unpleasant Germans I have ever met, besides being entirely lacking in a sense of humour. He has since written a book about his experiences which, for that reason, is dull reading. During the course of his examination I observed to him that a naval crew who sunk their ship after capture was guilty of piracy. He looked uncomfortable and said that the orders of his Emperor had to be obeyed. 'We were not a naval crew, we were a civilian crew.'

I said, 'You cannot be both.'

'But we were both,' he persisted. 'When we wore uniform we were a warship; when we wore civilian clothes we were a merchant ship. I kept the uniforms hanging on a line and when we broke the war flag the men jumped into them and we became a warship.' He was seriously annoyed when we laughed.

And now to return to Casement. The submarine on which he was originally to cross had broken down and had had to signal for another, commanded, as it turned out, by a less agreeable captain, to take over the passengers. This captain declined to approach the shore, but put his passengers into a flat-bottomed canvas boat without a rudder and, as Casement described it, 'left them to their fate'. At the last moment the captain asked Casement what clothes he wanted and Casement, describing the conversation, waved his hand with a theatrical gesture and said, 'Only my shroud.' The boat upset in landing and they were all wet through. They buried their belongings in the sand and Casement sent his two companions into the country to obtain help. Monteith did find friends, was driven off in a car and eventually made his way to the United States. Bailey, less fortunate, was arrested. Meanwhile, Casement was sheltering in an old ruin called M'Kenna's Fort, where, on being arrested, he gave the name of a friend with whom he used to stay in England.

On Saturday, I was taking my turn of night 'Zeppelin duty' at New

Scotland Yard. At 10.30 p.m. my telephone rang and a voice said, 'You know that stranger who arrived in the collapsible boat at Currahane – do you know who he is?'

I said, 'You're joking?'

'I am not,' said the voice, 'and he will be over early tomorrow morning for you to take him in hand.' It was not necessary for either of us to give a name. We had been expecting Casement's arrival for many weeks.

At ten o'clock on Easter Sunday I had my first interview with Sir Roger Casement. He walked into the room rather theatrically – a tall, thin, cadaverous man with thick black hair turning grey, a pointed beard and thin, nervous hands, mahogany-coloured from long tropical service. His forehead was a network of wrinkles, his complexion deeply sunburnt. I told him to sit down and asked him his name.

'Surely you know it.'

'I have to guard against the possibility of personation.'

'Well, I am Sir Roger Casement.'

I administered the usual caution that anything he said might be used against him. At first he was reticent, his great fear being that he might say something that would betray other people, or make him appear a traitor to the Germans, whose guest he had been. As long as the shorthand-writer remained he said little beyond admitting acts of high treason, but when we were alone he became far more communicative. He rose from the armchair and sat easily on the corner of my table. The rising in Ireland, he said, was to have been on Easter Sunday; he was to have landed a week earlier. He professed to know nothing of the intrigues in America which had fixed the date for the rising. He said that he was lying ill in Munich when 'a trusted friend' asked him to go to Berlin, for the time had now come to act. When he found that the Germans intended to send only one ship with munitions and not a single German officer, he said that he charged them with criminal folly and that the officer blushed and said, 'Well, this is all that the government intends to do. You must go with them, because if you refuse your countrymen shall know that you betrayed them.' They wanted him to go in the *Aud* herself, but he stipulated for a submarine, in order, so he said, to warn the rebels that they had no chance of success. The breaking down of the submarine prevented this. He was very insistent that the news of his capture should be published, as it would prevent bloodshed. We felt pretty sure that the Irish rebels knew all about his capture from his companion who escaped, quite apart from the fact that the arrest had appeared in the newspapers on the Saturday. When commenting some weeks afterwards upon the Rebellion, the Germans remarked that Casement had credited himself with possessing superhuman powers; that he imagined that his personality among the Irish would carry all before it, but that, in fact, they could not discover that his personal influence was great. They seem to have read him pretty well. The negotiations had really been carried on over his head and there is nothing to show that any of the leaders thought it necessary to consult him before they came to a decision.

I told him that we were aware of his efforts to recruit Irish soldiers from internment camps to fight for the Germans and he said that he had not recruited them for the German but for the Irish Army; that the Kaiser's proclamation to the Irish was conditional on an Irish Army being enrolled and, as to the oath of allegiance, many great Englishmen had had to break their oath for the sake of their country. He himself had never taken an oath of allegiance, but if he had it would not have weighed with him.

He returned again to his object in coming to Ireland. It was to stop, not to lead, a rising which could only fail with the paltry aid that the

Germans had sent. He wanted to prevent 'the boys' from throwing away their lives. He went on to say that in the early part of the war the Germans really believed that a rising in Ireland might be successful, but as they grew weaker this belief had begun to fade and now they had only the desire for bloodshed in Ireland as an embarrassment to the British government. He said that Germans would do things to serve the state which they would never do as private individuals and that in all the General Staff he had only met one gentleman. He seemed to regard the German cause as already lost. At the end of the interview he was sent to Brixton Prison to be placed under special observation for fear of an attempt at suicide. There was no staff at the Tower to guard suicidal cases.

Some months earlier, when we first had evidence of Casement's treachery, his London lodgings had been visited and his locked trunks removed to New Scotland Yard. Towards the end of the interview a policeman entered the room and whispered to me that Casement might have the key of the trunks. I asked him and with a magnificent gesture he said, 'Break them open; there is nothing in them but clothing and I shall not want them again.' But something besides clothing was found in one of the trunks – a diary and a cash-book from the year 1903 with considerable gaps. A few days later Casement must have remembered these volumes, for his solicitor demanded the surrender of his personal effects. Everything except these books was sent to him and there came a second letter, pointing out that the police must still be retaining some property. It is enough to say of the diaries that they could not be printed in any age or in any language.

During a subsequent conversation Casement said, 'You failed to win the hearts of the people when you had your chance.'

I replied, 'You are speaking for a minority of the Irish people. You must have had a rude awakening when you went to the internment camp to recruit men for the Irish Brigade.'

He said, 'I never expected to get many. I could have had them all if I had given them money, but though the Germans offered me as much money as I wanted I refused it. Besides, you were competing.'

'How?' I asked.

'By sending the Irish prisoners more money and larger parcels than the English prisoners had.'

Nothing would persuade him that this was not intentionally arranged by the British government: as a matter of fact, the parcels were supplied by a committee of Irish ladies.

Casement struck me as one of those men who are born with a strong strain of the feminine in their character. He was greedy for approbation and he had the quick intuition of a woman as to the effect he was making on the people around him. He had a strong histrionic instinct. I have read many of his early letters. They are full of high ideals that ring quite true and his sympathy with the down-trodden and his indignation against injustice were instinctive; but, like a woman, he was guided by instinct and not by reason and where his sympathies were strongly moved it is very doubtful whether any reliance could be placed upon his accuracy. I have often wondered since how much exaggeration there was in his revelations about the Congo and Putumayo. Colleagues who served with him in his official days have told me that they never took his statements quite literally. They always allowed for an imaginative colouring.

A few days before his execution he received a telegram from the person who had been most injured by his statement about Putumayo, imploring him at that solemn moment to retract his unjust charges. As far as I know, he did not reply to this telegram. I have made special inquiry with a view to ascertaining how long Casement had been under the obsessions disclosed in the pages of his diary and I feel certain that they were of comparatively recent growth, probably not much before the year 1910. This would seem to show that some mental disintegration had begun to set in, though it was not sufficient to impair his judgement or his knowledge of right and wrong.

His success with the Germans was due to his curious power of investing others with his overweening belief in his own powers. During the Boer War, according to one of his colleagues, he persuaded the Foreign Office that he could counteract the Boer influence in Delagoa Bay and obtain full information about their activities. Accordingly, he was sent to Delagoa Bay from west Africa, but though he worked there for many months he accomplished nothing. His colleagues could never decide whether the curious swagger in his walk was due to self-satisfaction or to a physical peculiarity. When he visited their offices he preferred to walk about the room, but when he could be induced to sit down he had a way of laying his palms together with the fingers pointing upward that reminded them of the attitude of the praying mantis. In Delagoa Bay he showed no sympathy with the Boers or with the Germans, nor did he discourse upon the wrongs of Ireland, though the Foreign Office had to intervene once when he began to use stationery headed, 'Consulate of Great Britain and Ireland'. He was excellent company and his colleagues were always glad to see him, though inwardly they were amused by the airs he assumed and the importance he attached to his sayings and doings. He was a good pioneer, a great walker, indifferent of his appearance and his dress and to the hardships he underwent when travelling on duty. He had a way of wearing his coat without putting his arms into the sleeves and he had his overcoat made without sleeves, possibly with an eye to the picturesque. He was a clear and forcible writer and was quite indifferent to money, though he kept his private accounts meticulously.

Casement's trial for high treason at the High Court will take its place among the most notable of state trials. Certain legal questions arising out of the fact that the acts of high treason had been committed abroad were argued at length. The Lord Chief Justice (Lord Reading), Sir F. E. Smith, the Attorney-General (now Lord Birkenhead) and Mr Serjeant Sullivan played their parts with great distinction. I was sitting just below the witness-box throughout the proceedings. At the luncheon adjournment, when the judge had left the bench, one of the Irish soldier witnesses who had been in the German camp on the occasion of Casement's visit was left in the witness-box. Casement had just left the dock above his head. He was thirsting for a confidant and I was the only person within earshot. He jerked his thumb at the retreating figure and in a thick brogue made a very opprobrious remark about him.

It is a curious fact that one of the revolvers brought over by Casement practically saved Dublin Castle. An officer of the Royal Irish Constabulary happened to be showing it to the Under-Secretary in the Castle on Easter Monday when he heard a shot fired and, looking out, he saw the sentry writhing on the ground and a ragged crowd rushing in at the gate. He had some cartridges in his pocket, with which he opened fire, keeping the rebels at bay for an hour and twenty minutes. Casement also brought with him a banner, which he intended to hoist over Dublin Castle. It was of green bunting made in Germany. It was last, I believe, in the possession of the headquarters of the Royal Irish Constabulary.

It has never been quite clear to me why the Irish Rebellion was postponed from Easter Saturday to Easter Monday. There was a conflict of authority, as there usually is, in the Irish ranks. The failure to land the arms can scarcely have been responsible for the postponement because, as it proved, there was no lack of arms in Dublin. Since there was no rising on Easter Saturday, we thought it possible that the sinking of the *Aud* and the arrest of Casement might have had the effect of postponing it altogether. After midday on Monday the question of the arrest of the leaders was still under discussion, though at noon all telegraphic communication with Ireland had been interrupted. It was not until three o'clock that we learned that the Dublin Post Office had been in possession of the rebels since noon, that another party had entrenched themselves in St Stephen's Green and that there was heavy firing in the city. The rebels had hoped for simultaneous risings all over Ireland, but these failed to take place. It is significant that a police officer who went over to Tralee Bay to bring over witnesses for Casement's trial had an ovation from the local farmers, who were delighted that the Rebellion had been put down.

It is curious that among the things picked up in Tralee Bay was a document in German giving an account of the enemy losses at Verdun, a strange thing to find on a lonely Irish beach so long after the event.

To Devoy in America came the Irish version of the Rebellion. The rebels put a bold face upon their failure. They said that Casement had sent a message to Dublin, begging them to defer the rising until he arrived. They admitted their bad staff work. They had counted upon 5,000 men in Dublin and secured only 1,500 and they were mostly men belonging to the Transport Workers rather than Sinn Feiners. In fact, there was a strong revolutionary element in the business. The reason why M'Neill had put off the rising from Saturday to Monday was the non-arrival of the munitions. Their main complaint was against the rebels in the south and west, who, though sufficiently armed to have done a good deal, did nothing. They did not even obey orders as regards the landing of munitions. They professed, however, to be pleased with the result of the Rebellion, because they said that for every man in favour of a rebellion before the rising there were now ten.

Two months had scarcely elapsed when they were again planning rebellion. They felt sure of success if only they had sufficient arms and they demanded from the Germans an adequate supply under a strong military escort. On their side they undertook to supply 250,000 men after an initial success. They held out as an inducement to the Germans a Zeppelin base for operations upon England. On 17 June the Germans said they were ready 'in principle' to give further aid, but they wanted full particulars. Like other foreign invaders of Ireland, they had learned to distrust the organising ability of the Irish. On 31 December 1916 they promised a new supply of 30,000 rifles and ten machine guns, but this offer was declined by the Irish rebels unless the Germans would undertake to land a military force. The entry of America into the war prevented any further negotiations.

CHAPTER 9

STRANGE SIDESHOWS

ALL THIS TIME we were living in the atmosphere of a 'Shilling Shocker' or, as the Americans call it, the 'Dime Novel'. When one started work in the morning one could never tell what the day was to bring forth, what curious personage would be ushered into the room, what high adventure or what squalid little tragedy would be unfolded by some occupant of the low armchair. Vivid impressions trod close upon the heels of one another. It was like fragments of melodramatic films pieced together at random: all had to be carried in the mind until the case might be considered closed. Most of the actors in these dramas disappeared into outer space and then months later they would drift in again in some new drama, only to disappear finally after the Armistice.

What has become of them all? What are all those spies and pseudo-spies now doing for a living? Where are all the temporary officers who were living riotously at the Savoy like butterflies that emerge untimely into the winter sunshine? Where are the girls that shared their revels during those purple weeks? Are they serving behind some counter? Have they pawned their jewellery and their furs? Or are they safely married in some suburban lodging and finding life a little flat? What has become of the young men who tore about the country in high-powered cars, who loved to use their cut-out while racing up the Mall? Do they now drive buses, or are they chicken-farming in Canada? The whole drama and all the actors have vanished, as they do in the real theatre ten minutes after the curtain has fallen. And where are the young women who used to take us elderly gentle-men by the elbow and help us into buses? Do they miss the toes of the passengers on which they used to tread; the uniform, the excite-ment of doing men's work; or are they glad to be quit of it all and settle down to some less exciting occupation? These young people thought that there was to be a new heaven and a new earth in which the young would toil not nor spin but would have purses like the widow's cruse. And the rest of us thought that there would certainly be a new earth – mostly made up of revolutions. As the war went on we began to realise that the real England – all the England that really mattered – was in northern France, in Gallipoli, in Salonika, Egypt and Mesopotamia.

All the exciting events, from the point of view of police action, seem to have been crowded into 1915 and the early part of 1916. September was a notable month because we had at the same time the great for-geries of the 'G' series of Treasury notes, the seizure of the Austrian dispatches from the United States which were being carried by an American journalist and the Indian murder conspiracy.

It had been reported to the police that the little active band of Indian revolutionaries who were working with the Germans in Berlin were running to and from Switzerland in connection with an extensive assassination plot. A seizure of documents late in August corroborated this. Whether the plot was devised by certain Indian revolutionaries or by the Germans themselves is not clear. The plan was to bring about the simultaneous assassination of the leading men in Entente countries. The names of the King of Italy, Lord Grey, Lord Kitchener, Mons. Poincaré, Mons. Viviani and Sr Salandro were specially mentioned. The bombs had been manufactured in Italy and were tested by the German military authorities at the military testing ground near Berlin. At the English end of the conspiracy were certain British Indians, one of whom was living with a German woman whom he declared to be his wife. An Englishwoman was known to be privy to their plans and a Swiss girl was the messenger between Switzerland and the English group. The case was one of extraordinary difficulty, because the real culprit, Chattopadhya, an Indian well known in Berlin, made only flying visits to Switzerland and was careful never to set foot on the soil of an Entente country. As soon as the available evidence was complete steps were taken simultaneously to detain all the persons who were in British jurisdiction. They were interned as persons dangerous to the safety of the realm and kept in internment until the Armistice, despite repeated appeals to the committee set up to revise internment orders made by the Home Secretary.

About the examinations in my room there was never anything in the nature of what the Americans call the 'Third Degree', which, I understand, consists in startling or wearying the suspect into a confession. If they preferred not to answer questions they were detained until further inquiry could be made about them. In many cases it was the detention that influenced them. They were not sent to prison unless it was clear that their detention would have to be prolonged. There was a range of cells in the adjacent building of Cannon Row Police Station: one of these was furnished as a bed-sitting room and was known as 'the extradition cell': the others were the ordinary cells in which remand prisoners are placed after arrest. One has to put oneself into the suspect's position in order to realise what this change of circumstances meant to him. He had been full of the excitement and interest of foreign travel, fresh from a voyage in a liner, where he was unsuspected and liked. Suddenly he found himself within four narrow walls, in silence and without the amenities of comfortable arm-chairs and tables. If he wished to write he might do so, but everything he wrote would be subject to scrutiny. He had, however, ample time for reflection and now that the first move must come from his side it was not long before he would send a request for another interview. If he did not he would, in course of time, be sent for, but the period of waiting without any fixed date usually had its effect.

In the middle of October 1915 very definite evidence reached us of the extent of the German-Indian conspiracy and the length the conspirators were prepared to go. The Indian Committee in Berlin was established quite early in the war. After his expulsion from the United States Har Dayal, who had been conducting the *Ghadr* (*Mutiny*) newspaper in California, went to Switzerland and on the outbreak of war he, Chattopadhya and some other Indian revolutionaries who were living in Switzerland went to Berlin. At first the Germans, feeling that they had them quite in their power, treated them with some contempt, but this attitude changed when one or two Germans who posed as Indian experts persuaded the government to found an Indian Committee to concert measures for starting a revolution in India under a German President. They had a press bureau and a regular working scheme for corrupting the loyalty of Indian prisoners of war. Still, though tons of paper and lakes of ink were consumed, no headway was being made until March 1915, when an Indian land-owner named Pertabr conceived the plan of going over to the Germans in the character of an Indian prince. He had some slight claim to this self-assumed title since he was the son of a deposed ruler of a small native state. Having obtained a passport from the Indian government on the backing of a man whose loyalty was unquestioned, he arrived in Switzerland from Marseilles and lost no time in communicating with Har Dayal, who took him to see the German Consul. Now it does not take much to deceive a German official about oriental matters. Pertabr wore native dress and was aloof and condescending. In fact, his haughtiness was exactly what the German Consul would have expected from a Rajah. When pressed to enter the Fatherland Pertabr declared firmly that he would not cross the German frontier until he had a promise that the Kaiser would receive him in person. This arrangement suited Har Dayal admirably, for he would become the intermediary between the two potentates and the springs of money would begin again to flow. After several journeys to and from Berlin an audience was arranged. It was characteristic of the German Consul that he besought Pertabr in all humility to say a good word for him to the All Highest when he should enter the Presence.

No doubt Pertabr had daydreams of himself mounted on a fiery white steed at the head of conquering bands as the new liberator of India. At Delhi he would receive the homage of the native princes. He may have imbued the Kaiser with some of these ideas, though one cannot imagine that the imperial mind had any daydreams of oriental conquests in which some other man was to prance on a white horse; but however this may be, a mission did start for Kabul, headed by 'Prince' Pertabr with three German officers and several released Indian prisoners of war, to raise the Amir against India. They passed through Constantinople during the first week of September and then they disappeared into space. It was learned afterwards that they got no farther than Afghanistan and that the fragments of the mission were reported many months later to be wandering as homeless out-casts about Central Asia.

That was not the end of the German attempts upon India. Some few months later there came into our hands an autograph letter addressed by the Kaiser to the ruling princes in India, which had been photographed down to a size little exceeding that of a postage stamp and enclosed in a tiny tube to be concealed about the body. The belief in German circles was that Persia was about to rise on the side of Germany and that that would be the signal for the invasion of India by the Afghans.

The headquarters of the Indian conspirators who were being manipulated by the Germans in America were at Berkeley, California. It was there that the *Ghadr* newspaper was printed in the vernacu-lar and arrangements were made for shipping arms to India at the German expense. It took many months to convince the Californian police authorities that there were ample grounds for taking action under the neutrality laws, but when they did move they moved to some purpose. The two Indian leaders were arrested. When they were brought to trial one of them, convinced from the intimate knowledge of his secret activities disclosed by the prosecution that the other had turned informer, slipped a pistol from his pocket and shot his companion in open court. But in the western states such incidents do not disturb the presence of mind of Assize Court officials: the deputy-sheriff whipped an automatic from his pocket and from his elevated place at the back of the court, aiming above and between the intervening heads, shot the murderer dead. And so, in less than ten seconds the sentence which the judge was about to pronounce was more than executed.

The Germans are not naturally fitted to acquire an influence over Orientals, though they have tried hard to do it. The Kaiser, who was a master of pantomimic display, rode into Jerusalem properly clad as a new Crusader. He conformed to such oriental customs as were considered compatible with his dignity and he was getting on quite well until some vulgar-minded non-German Europeans set the natives laughing at him. Ridicule kills more surely than the assassin's knife.

I remember a rather pompous proconsul who was determined to impress the natives of the Pacific Islands by stage-management. He happened to be a Doctor of Law at Cambridge and, in addition to his gilded Civil Service uniform, he arrayed himself in the scarlet robe of a Doctor of Law and stalked solemnly under the palm-trees with two little native boys carrying his train. The natives had never seen anything quite so gorgeous and all went well until the procession had to pass a store kept by a certain ribald Englishman with an extensive knowledge of the vernacular. It was enough for him to utter one phrase in the native language to scatter all the official pomp to the four winds. The comment ran down the whispering gallery to the farthest recesses of the island and, instead of the awed hush on which the proconsul had counted, he was received with broad and rather pitying smiles. That finished any prestige that he might have had in this particular group.

It was so once with a French naval post-captain who determined to overawe the natives with a display of naval force. To this end he landed a considerable force of bluejackets and began to drill them on shore. He had a peculiar strut in his walk which fired the imagination of a small native boy who had been born lacking in a sense of reverence. As the captain marched proudly at the head of his men he became conscious that there was something about him which was provoking roars of merriment among the spectators. He began furtively to pat various parts of his anatomy to see whether there had been a mishap to his clothing and it was not for some time that he realised that just behind him was a small boy caricaturing his every movement. That little episode settled the French question.

But I am wandering far from my subject, which was German intrigues in the Orient. Some little time before the war German agents had made great play with the tribes in the hinterland of Tripoli and when war was declared they did succeed in producing in the Senussi a hostile spirit against the Allies. In 1916 an English ship of war, the *Tara*, was sunk by a submarine off the north African coast. As usual, the German commander made no attempt to save the crew, but officers and men to the number of about a hundred did succeed in getting ashore. They found themselves in an inhospitable sandy desert, with nothing but what they stood up in and with no means of communicating with the outside world. For all that was known, the ship had been sunk with all hands.

The first step, of course, was to get something to eat and drink. A little way inland they found a well, but there was a dead camel in it. At first they thought that the death of the camel might have been recent and they hauled him up with the idea of eating him, but the first cut with a knife was enough and they left him where he was and yet forty-eight hours later some of them were glad to eat of this loathsome food, or go under.

Very soon after their landing they fell into the hands of Senussi Arabs, who gave them almost nothing to eat and insisted upon their marching inland under the pitiless sun half dead with hunger and thirst. At last they reached a little village presided over by what they took to be a Mohammedan priest, but the bluejackets nicknamed him 'Holy Joe'.

'Holy Joe' was a holy terror. He drove these wretched men out in the morning under the lash to till his fields and he gave them next to nothing to eat. Fortunately, the desert in these parts grew snails

– great grey-shelled monsters – in prodigious numbers and it was part of the routine to bring in from the fields a quota of these snails for the evening meal. The cook became quite expert in the management of snails. There was no lid to the pot and there was not enough fuel to bring the water to the boil before putting in his snails, so he put them in cold and poured water upon them, or what passed for water in these parts and lighted the fire. As the pot warmed up, the snails, not unnaturally, tried to get out and the cook had to spend his time in heading them back again. When the evening meal was ready the snails had left their shells and lay in a muddy and unappetising mass at the bottom of the soup. That is what our wretched men had to live upon for months and as time wore on the hunting-grounds were farther afield. They had eaten all the snails for furlongs round the plantations.

Once the commander made an attempt to escape in order to report the existence of the prisoners to someone who would communicate with Egypt, but he failed. He had, however, written appeals to the Turkish authorities for more food and it was through one of these appeals that deliverance came.

Everyone remembers the fine exploit of the Duke of Westminster with his fleet of armoured cars – how he scattered a Turkish Army and how he carried terror into the hearts of the tribesmen. Now it chanced that on the evening of the action some of his men discovered a derelict car and searched it and that, in the course of the search, they lighted upon a dirty piece of paper and brought it in to the Duke. It was actually one of the commander's appeals and it gave the name of the village. Thus, for the first time certain rumours that British prisoners were detained by the Senussi were confirmed. But now came a fresh difficulty. No one knew where the village was. It was not marked in any of the maps and one could not scour the desert in every direction to find what might be a mythical village. Inquiries were made of the Turkish prisoners and at last one was found who had heard of the village. In fact, his father had once taken him there when he was a little boy, but all he remembered of it was that on the hill above it there was a single date-tree and under the date-tree an ancient stone well. He thought that it lay in the direction to which he pointed.

This prisoner was taken up on one of the light cars as a guide. For many hours they ploughed the sand and then there was a council of war. They had petrol not much more than sufficient for the return journey.

If they went any farther they might have to leave the car behind them, but the Duke would not turn back. Whatever happened, he meant to find this village and to rescue the prisoners and so they went on and a very few minutes later the guide uttered a loud cry, sprang from the car and lay grovelling in the sand. 'An ambush!' every one said and they covered him with their rifles in order that, if any had to die, he should be the first, but it was no ambush. With keener sight than theirs he had spied the single date-palm. They took him up again and drove to the palm. He jumped down and dug at the sand like a dog, until he disclosed the coping of an ancient well and a few yards farther on they came in sight of the village.

The company of prisoners were just sitting down to discuss their evening snails when a bluejacket came in breathless to say that he had seen a 'blinking motorcar'. Either he was pulling their legs or he had a touch of the sun and in either case the best treatment was to throw stones at him, which they did, but he persisted and at last a few of them broke away from the circle to reconnoitre. There, sure enough, in the slanting rays of the sun was a car. They ran towards it hailing it as loudly as they could and those in the car itself, seeing a party of gaunt and vociferous natives almost naked in their rags, were for keeping them at a safe distance. It was not until they recognised the English language that they knew they were fellow countrymen.

Normally, the story stops there, but a bluejacket who was one of the party added a little postscript of his own. Before they left the village there was a little account to settle – a little matter of account with 'Holy Joe', who had wielded the whip over them all these months. He winked and he nodded and he would say no more, but it was gathered that 'Holy Joe' did not go out of this world with a smile upon his face.

The Germans were as busy with the Moors as they were with the Arabs and their efforts were quite as ineffective. It must have been uphill work in Morocco for the German agent. There was one who had brought the Sus tribes almost up to the point of rising, but they stipulated for arms. Otherwise they would throw in their lot against Germany. There was nothing for it but to tell them that arms had been written for and that they might be expected by ship at any moment. With such promises the Germans managed to keep up the spirit of expectation until one day the lights of a steamer were seen approaching. Evidently this was the long-promised vessel. The whole tribe turned out upon the beach to assist in landing the cargo, but suddenly a dazzling beam shot out from the vessel, illuminating the whole of the foreshore. It was a French warship and in another moment a shell from one of the guns landed right in the middle of the village. So that was the kind of lie on which the German agent was feeding them! There were whispered consultations. No one knows except the German agent, who is not now in a position to tell us, exactly what happened. One must always make subtractions from native stories, but the tale that reached Tangier was that the German was bidden to a meal at which he ate certain viands which disagreed with him, so that in the end, being a very fat man, he burst asunder and gave up his life.

The war work of women made many friendships and a few implacable enmities. The husband of a lady of high degree came to consult me about an anonymous letter that had reached her. No threats, either actual or implied, brought it within the criminal law and, as he pointed out, the handwriting and the notepaper, as well as an obviously intimate knowledge of the lady, marked it as being the production of a person of the same class, not improbably a 'friend'. To say that it contained home-truths would be a reckless understatement. It was the outpouring of a spirit that can endure no more. 'You are well known,' it said, 'as the most disagreeable and vulgar woman in London,' and it went on to tell her why. I could almost hear the sigh of relief as she signed herself, 'A well-wisher'.

No question here of a German spy nor of criminal proceedings, but mysterious documents are always fascinating and by the time the husband called again I had identified the writer beyond possibility of error as a lady of the same War Committee revolving in the same social circle as the recipient of the letter. I told the husband that the mystery was cleared up. 'But what we want to know,' he said, 'is who wrote it.' On that point I said I could not enlighten him: it was against the rules. The next day he returned with a list of his wife's friends whose attachment to her was doubtful and asked me to say whether the list did or did not include the anonymous writer. I fear he has never forgiven me for remaining firm.

They have curious ideas abroad about the way in which the British conduct a war. A Bulgarian who was taking leave of an English official when returning to Bulgaria said, 'Remember, I have nothing to say about this plan of assassinating Ferdinand.'

'What plan?' asked the astonished Englishman.

'Your plan. You are clearly within your rights, but I think as time goes on you will find out that Ferdinand will be more useful to you alive than dead.'

Before Romania came into the war, a Romanian met a general of the Prussian Staff at dinner in Berlin. After dinner the general said, 'I knew your late King. He was a fine man. What a pity the English murdered him.' The Romanian replied that there must be some mistake: the King died in his bed. But the general brushed this aside and gave him a list of the notables in various countries who had been murdered by the English. One of them was Jaurès, the French socialist!

In July 1915 officers returning from the Front noticed a wave of pessimism as unreasonable as the former optimism. People were just recovering from the shock of learning that Lord Kitchener had foretold that the war would last three years instead of the six months that so many had been counting upon. The cry of 'Look at the map' was in the mouth of constitutional pessimists in high places and if one had looked at the map instead of at the men there would have been no spirit left in any one. Fortunately, geography is not efficiently taught us at school. All we knew was that, man for man, our soldiers were better than the Germans and that if, as we were sometimes told, the winning of the war depended upon killing Germans we should win through in the end; or if, as the Germans were never tired of telling each other, it was to be a war of endurance, we felt sure that we could hold out longer than they. When a party was criticising the conduct of the war in November 1915, I remember a naval officer retorting, 'If our Admiralty and our War Office and all our government departments had been perfect we should have lost the war long ago.'

A little later in the war the same naval officer was examining a captured German submarine officer. The German said bitterly, 'I cannot understand you English. If you had joined hands with us we should have dominated the world between us.'

'But,' replied the British sailor, 'we did not want to dominate the world.' The German appeared to feel that he understood the English less than ever.

In the autumn of 1915 the horde of young Irishmen who were emigrating to escape military service became a scandal. The number of Irish emigrants of military age during October 1915 was 4,000. Even so, it is to be doubted whether a new regulation prescribing that no passport was to be granted to men of military age would have been passed but for the fact that the Irish stokers on a White Star liner refused to carry such emigrants and one company after another, including even two American lines, refused to allow them to come on board their ships.

The suppression of a daily newspaper was resorted to only once during the war. On 5 November 1915, *The Globe*, which had helped the police more than once, published a statement that Lord Kitchener had tendered his resignation to the King, whereas, in fact, he was leaving the country on an important mission which could not at the moment be made public. On the following day a warrant was drawn up, empowering officers of the Special Branch to suppress the paper. As no newspaper had been suppressed in England for about a century there were no precedents on which we could work, nor was I sufficiently acquainted with the mechanical details of newspaper production to be able to instruct the officers off-hand what part of the machinery should be seized and removed. We entered the premises between five and six that evening. The machines were in full blast in the basement. Newspaper boys were hurrying in and out. The inspector showed the warrant to the manager and the machines were stopped. Going downstairs, I found a very obliging man who must have thought that I was a more or less distinguished visitor who was to be shown over the plant. I said to him, 'Supposing that you wanted to take away some part of this machinery which would make it impossible to run the machines again until it was restored and yet do no damage to the plant, what would you take?'

'Oh, that's easy,' he said and he led me to a certain engine, from which he took a portion which I could carry away in my hand. I thanked him and carried it away. That was how *The Globe* was suppressed until such time as the directors of the newspaper had come to an arrangement with the government.

The restrictions on the liberty of the press were really imposed by the press itself. Proprietors and editors measured all their criticisms by one test – whether what they wished to publish would be turned to account by the enemy. Their patriotism throughout the war was whole-hearted and unquestioned.

In 1916 an Austrian submarine stopped a steamer in the Mediterranean on which Colonel Napier and Captain Wilson were passengers. They were carrying the diplomatic bags from the legation in Athens. All but one of the bags were immediately thrown overboard, but as they contained buoyant packages insufficiently compensated by weights, one at least failed to sink and was picked up by the submarine. From the fact that the Austrians hailed the steamer and demanded the surrender of Colonel Napier by name it was clear that a spy, probably at Corfu, had given them information. Naturally there was some confusion: a lady concealed the bag that had not been thrown overboard; Colonel Napier went on board the submarine and was interned in Austria; the steamer continued her voyage to Italy.

Now it chanced that on the steamer was a very tall, lanky currant merchant who spoke no tongue but his native Greek, but was brimming over with geniality, particularly towards English people, on whom he was dying to practise the few words of English that he knew. Another British officer who was on board undertook to carry the bag to England and for this purpose the steamer called at an Italian port specially to land him. The irrepressible Greek, seeing an opportunity of making the journey to England with a companion who would interpret for him, hastily collected his modest luggage and, wreathed in ingratiating smiles, attempted to board the boat. He was sternly repelled from the gangway; the steamer continued on her voyage and landed her passengers.

The officer had gained no time by his detour: the other passengers arrived in Rome in time to take the same train for Paris; he was just taking his seat with the precious bag when the currant merchant recognised him and rushed upon him with outstretched hand, as if to say, 'My deliverer! We will travel in the same compartment.' Probably he ascribed the rebuff he received to the well-known eccentricity of the British character, for at the Gare du Nord the same comedy was enacted, as well as on the Havre–Southampton boat. Long before this he had been classed as a German spy and at Southampton he was handed over to the police and brought to me in custody.

In a seedy frock-coat, unshaved, speechless, except in voluble Greek and bewildered by British eccentricity, he certainly seemed to justify all the suspicions that had been attached to him. I was about to send for a Greek interpreter when I was informed that his brother, a currant merchant of Mincing Lane, was asking leave to come in and there walked into the room his double – a man so like him in stature, attenuation and feature that when dressed alike they could never have been distinguished. But the brother spoke fluent English and the motive for all this misplaced geniality was explained. I hope that this currant merchant has not lost his love for the English nation, but I have my doubts.

At a time when the spy-mania was at its highest we found ourselves involved in a ghost story. A certain titled foreigner, a devout

Catholic, had taken and enlarged an early Tudor farm in one of the southern counties in which, according to local tradition, a Spanish friar named Don Diego had been found concealed during one of the Recusant persecutions and murdered. To the simple villagers any foreigner, disembodied or otherwise, was almost certain to be engaged in intrigues against the Allied cause and if he had been a priest in these troublous times he could have had no love for this Protestant country. Moreover, the farm had been filled with strange furniture and was full of dark corners, mysterious doorways and galleries. Strangers came down from London for weekends and it was whispered in the village that there were strange doings behind the oaken shutters after nightfall. In this rumour was for once correct. Don Diego made no corporeal appearance: he was a voice and nothing more, but a voice of such a musical and thrilling quality that, in the opinion of those who listened, it could have proceeded from no earthly throat. Don Diego was more concerned with mundane than with spiritual matters and his chief concern was matchmaking, which was unusual in disembodied spirits and not altogether becoming in a murdered priest. He wanted his host to make an advantageous marriage.

The manifestations began generally at dinner. A singularly sweet voice of the quality which in ghost stories is called sepulchral would be heard calling the name of a guest: the family professed not to hear the voice. The guest would leave the table and follow the voice to the hall, where she would commune with it in private and return to her dinner filled with its mysterious injunctions. She had heard it, now from the gallery, now from the staircase, for the shade of Don Diego was amazingly agile in its movements and to prove that it was no human voice there was the fact that whichever lady happened to be called the ghost could always tell her something of her past life, or some family secret that was known only to herself. These, however, were mere conversational by-paths; the burden of the sing-song voice was that people must be up and doing if the Count (for that was the host's title) was to make an advantageous marriage.

The rumours of espionage became so persistent that I invited the gentleman to an interview. He was nervous and evasive; he admitted the supernatural manifestations, but remarked that he could not be held responsible for having taken a haunted house. I felt certain, nevertheless, that he knew all about it and I told him plainly that Don Diego must thenceforth lie quiet in his grave. It was a peculiarity of the murdered priest that he became vocal when the Count was present in the room. Sometimes the butler and one at least of the two footmen were there too; at others the Count would be absent and the servants be clearing the dinner table.

The fame of Don Diego spread very rapidly and a small party of gentlemen interested in psychic phenomena took the matter up. What they represented themselves to be in order to gain admission to the haunted house I do not know, but I can conjecture. They found the poor Count in a state of nervous prostration from a disturbing anonymous letter that had reached him and he was prepared for a visit of some kind; in fact, he was in a condition very favourable to their designs. What passed at an interview in which there was consummate acting on both sides has not transpired, but it resulted in a full written confession and Don Diego has since appeared no more. The Count himself, aided by his Irish butler and two other menservants, had been the voice in turns, the duty falling upon him who happened to be disengaged at the moment and the confession was countersigned by them all. The supposed apparitions of Don Diego, it said, were produced by purely natural means for the purpose of practical joking and an undertaking was given that no more phenomena would occur.

CHAPTER 10

THE GERMAN SPY

MY READERS MAY now be asking themselves how soon I am going to write about German spies. There are obvious reasons why it is impossible to divulge secrets. I shall tell, therefore, as much as the military authorities have already allowed to be divulged and nothing more, but I shall tell most of it at first hand.

There is much confused thinking about the ethics of spying on movements of an enemy. The very word 'spy' has acquired so ugly a significance that we prefer to disguise our own spies as 'Intelligence' or 'Secret Service Officers' and to regard them as necessary evils; but any government that accepted the standards set up by certain censorious newspapers and declined to ask Parliament for a vote for Secret Service on the grounds that it was dishonourable would be guilty of treason against its own countrymen. To be forewarned about the intentions of an enemy, whether internal or external, may be to save the lives and property of many hundreds and to allow the enemy to make all his preparations unheeded would be criminal negligence of the worst kind. The cost of a good system of intelligence is like the premium paid for insurance against fire.

Whether an individual degrades himself by engaging in espionage depends on how and why he does it. If his motives are purely patriotic and he performs this dangerous duty at the risk of his life, without thought of personal gain; if in carrying out the duty he does not stoop to form friendships in order to betray them, but comes out with clean hands, what is there degrading in his service? But if he spies upon a nation with which his country is not at war merely for the money he can make and lives riotously, as nearly all such hirelings do, he should be treated like the vermin that he is and nailed to the barn-door as a warning to others. Nevertheless, there is something pitiful even about such men when they have played their stake and lost and they feel the cold hand laid upon them and all their profitless debaucheries sour upon the palate. It is as if they ran unheeding round a corner and came suddenly upon Death standing in the path. Then all honour to them if they can meet him with a smile, for not all of us, feeling that cold breath on our cheek and the grip of the bony fingers closing on us, can be sure that we should pass through the ordeal with credit.

During the first few days of the war I remember a staff officer remarking that we should repeat the experience of the Napoleonic Wars: we should begin the war with the worst Intelligence Service in Europe and end with the best. I was inclined to think that he was right about the first part of his prediction and I now think that he was right about the second. But then if he had gone on to say that the Germans started the war with the most elaborate Secret Service organisation in Europe and ended it with the worst he would have been equally right. I have already related how at the vital moment of mobilisation the whole of the German organisation in the United

Kingdom was broken up; how it was possible for us to dispatch our Expeditionary Force to France without the loss of a single man or a single horse and without the knowledge of the Germans. It was, of course, not long before they attempted to make good. They had established espionage centres at Antwerp and Brussels, they had branch offices in connection with the German Consulate at Rotterdam. Unfortunately for them, there was great jealousy between the navy and the army and each had been entrusted with a certain amount of Secret Service money, on which they entered into a sort of civil war of competition. Anything reported by a spy employed by the German naval authorities was at once ridiculed by the military Intelligence and vice versa. This keen competition made them very easy prey. On one occasion an adventurous Englishman actually passed into Belgium to take service in one of these intelligence offices and came back with useful information. They were prone also to engage quite unsuitable people – the sort of people who in wartime at once become what the French call *agents doubles*; that is to say, they attempt to serve both sides, either with the object of obtaining double pay or of making their lives safe in the event of detection. What these men do for a living in peace time is hard to guess. I can imagine them running cheap gambling-hells, frequenting the docks to pick up some dishonest profit, resorting to a little blackmail and performing the humbler offices for the white slave trafficker. In wartime you will find them swarming in every capital, for war is their brief summer. The money they get by their complicated villainies is spent with both hands. They live like princes and dress like bookmakers' touts. The Germans were so easy to manipulate that quite early in the war some of these men came over and offered their services to us. They felt sure that any story, however improbable, would be swallowed. Certainly the Germans got more interesting information from the *agents doubles* than they ever got from their own spies in England. Sometimes they acted upon it and they paid quite liberally. When you come to think of it, not many private Englishmen were in a position to give naval or military information of importance and still less a foreigner who dared not ask questions.

There was in my office an armchair in which every spy, real or fancied, sat while he was accounting for his movements. It was realised during the first weeks of the war by the judges and the law officers, as well as by the laity, that the ordinary criminal procedure was of no avail against spies. If no questions could be asked of a person under arrest, how were you to piece together the documents in his possession – marked dictionaries, memoranda of addresses, code telegrams and the like. The only way and, to the innocent, the fairest way was to adopt something like the French criminal procedure. As I have said, there was never anything approaching what is called in America 'the Third Degree'. The suspects were cautioned that they need not answer any questions, but that what they said might be used in evidence against them, a caution which almost invariably induced loquacity and questions and answers were recorded in shorthand. I suppose that on the average four persons a day sat in that chair throughout the war. At the least, nine out of every ten who might otherwise have been detained under suspicion for an indefinite period were entirely cleared by the examination. It used to be a joke among my staff that no single person, however angry he was when he came in, left the room without thanking me profusely, though one, and he was a Mexican, did afterwards make a claim of £10,000 for moral and intellectual damages. One man was so grateful that he asked leave to make a contribution to the fund of the Police Orphanage. This I had not the face to allow, perhaps because his arrest had been the result of a mistake and I felt that, if money had to pass, it should be going the other way.

I made a discovery about that low armchair. For some time I had noticed that whenever a particularly disconcerting question was put the suspect instinctively raised himself by the arms to reply to it. My assistant, in peace time an eminent KC, suggested one day that I should sit in it and be interrogated by him. I felt at once an irresistible impulse to raise my face to the level of his. The fact is that if you want to get the truth out of a witness the worst way is to put him in a box above the level of the cross-examining counsel; if our law courts were intelligently constructed the cross-examiner should take his stand in a kind of lift and be suddenly elevated to the proper position just before his cross-examination begins. Primitive races have found this out, for their chiefs stand erect while their inferiors squat on the ground when they are being questioned.

During the first few days of the war I detained a curious person who arrived in the country on an American passport and who claimed to be a major in the Mexican Army. He was a typical international spy – mysterious, wheedling and apprehensive. He pretended to be eager to enter our service. I told him that we would make use of his services – as a prisoner of war in Brixton Prison. It was not until early in 1916 that the capture of von Papen's chequebooks disclosed his real activities. He had been engaged in the United States in sabotage and probably he had come to this country for the same purpose, but he took alarm, imagining that his every movement was being watched and he came to us with offers of service to save his own skin. When we found his name among the cheques I sent for him from prison to ask him to explain. He then made a statement about his activities in America, which was considered so important that on 18 March 1916 he was sent over to the United States to give evidence against two of the German Consuls, one of whom was Krupps's agent, for attempted outrage and breach of neutrality. The American government was quite ready to send us back our prisoner at the end of the case, but I assured them that we were altruistic and had no desire to deprive them of so interesting a personality. Afterwards he published in America his own version of his adventures.

The first serious spy to be arrested was Lody. Carl Lody was a good example of the patriotic spy. He had been one of those Germans who had lived long enough in the United States to acquire what he believed to be fluent English with an American accent. He had held a commission in the German Navy and was a Reserve officer. He then entered the employment of the Hamburg-America Steamship Line as a guide for tourists. In that capacity he had travelled all over England and had even attempted, though unsuccessfully, to obtain employment under Messrs Thomas Cook & Son. A few days before 4 August 1914 Lody returned to Berlin from Norway and got into touch with the German Intelligence. It happened that there was staying in Berlin at that time an American named Charles A. Inglis, who had applied to the American embassy for a visa to his passport, enabling him to continue his travels in Europe. His passport was passed by the embassy to the German Foreign Office for the visa, but there it was 'mislaid' and the Foreign Office promised an exhaustive search. This passport was used by Lody. Mr Inglis's photograph was removed from it and Lody's substituted. Mr Inglis obtained a new American passport from his embassy.

As Mr Charles Inglis, Lody presented himself at the North British Station Hotel in Edinburgh and from Edinburgh he sent a telegram to one Adolf Burchard, in Stockholm. Telegrams had to pass the Censor and there were matters in Inglis's telegram that called for close scrutiny. Meanwhile, Lody took private lodgings, realising, no doubt, that hotels are not very safe places for spies. He hired a bicycle and spent a fortnight in exploring the neighbourhood of Edinburgh, looking into Rosyth Harbour and asking too many questions for the ordinary sightseer. From Edinburgh he came to London and put up at a hotel in Bloomsbury. Here he interested himself in our anti-aircraft defences. He was back in Edinburgh two days later and on 26 September he went to Liverpool, where ocean liners were being fitted out as auxiliary cruisers. From Liverpool he went to Holyhead and thence to Ireland and here his nerve was a little shaken by the close questioning that he underwent. From the Gresham Hotel in Dublin, where other Americans were staying, he wrote to his Swedish correspondent that he was becoming nervous. He wrote all his letters both in English and German in ordinary ink, without any disguise. His information would have been of comparatively little value even if it had reached the Germans, which it did not. The only report that was allowed to go through was the famous story of the Russian troops passing through England.

From Dublin Lody travelled to Killarney, no doubt on his way to Queenstown, but on 2 October he was detained by the Royal Irish Constabulary to await the arrival of the detectives from Scotland Yard. They found among his luggage the forged passport, about £175 in English notes and gold, a notebook with particulars of the naval fight in the North Sea of a few weeks earlier, addresses in Berlin, Stockholm, Bergen and Hamburg and copies of the four letters that he had written to Stockholm. He was tried by court-martial at the Guildhall, Westminster, on 30 and 31 October. His counsel made no defence except that Lody was a man who, having done his duty, left the consequences in the hands of the court. His grandfather had a military reputation; he had held a fortress against Napoleon and the grandson wished to stand before his judges in that spirit. He was not ashamed of anything that he had done, he would not cringe for mercy, he would accept the decision of righteous men. He was found guilty and sentenced to death and was executed in the Tower five days later. A letter that he wrote to his relations in Stuttgart before his execution was as follows:

My dear ones,

I have trusted in God and He has decided. My hour has come and I must start on the journey through the Dark Valley like so many of my comrades in this terrible war of nations. May my life be offered as a humble offering on the altar of the fatherland.

A hero's death on the battlefield is certainly finer, but such is not to be my lot and I die here in the Enemy's country silent and unknown, but the consciousness that I die in the service of the Fatherland makes death easy.

The Supreme Court-Martial of London has sentenced me to death for Military Conspiracy. Tomorrow I shall be shot here in the Tower. I have had just Judges and I shall die as an Officer, not as a spy.

Farewell. God bless you,

Hans

He wrote a letter also to the officer commanding at Wellington Barracks:

London, 5 November 1914

Sir,

I feel it my duty as a German Officer to express my sincere thanks and appreciation towards the staff of Officers and men who were in charge of my person during my confinement.

Their kind and considered treatment has called my highest esteem and admiration as regards good-fellowship even towards the Enemy and if I may be permitted I would thank you for make this known to them.

I am, sir, with profound respect,

Carl Hans Lody, Senior Lieutenant Imperial, German Naval Res. 11. D.

He left a ring to be forwarded to a lady in America and this was done. It was believed that the German government had insured his life for £3,000 in favour of his relations and that when, after some months, his death became known in Germany, the people of his native village planted an oak to be known evermore by his name. He met his death unflinchingly and on the morning of his execution it is related that he said to the Assistant Provost Marshal, 'I suppose you will not shake hands with a spy?' and that the officer replied, 'No, but I will shake hands with a brave man.' Lody made a favourable impression on all who came into contact with him. In the quiet heroism with which he faced his trial and his death there was no suspicion of histrionic effect. He never flinched, he never cringed, but he died as one would wish all Englishmen to die – quietly and undramatically, supported in his courage by the proud consciousness of having done his duty.

In those early days there was some difference of opinion as to whether it was sound policy to execute spies and to begin with a patriotic spy like Lody. We came to wish later on that a distinction could have been made between the patriotic spy and the hireling who pestered us through the ensuing years, but on the whole I think that the military authorities were right. It is an international tradition that spies in time of war must die and if we had departed from the tradition the Germans would not. While the risk of death may appeal to the courageous national, it was certainly a deterrent to the scum of neutral spies who were ready to offer their services to either belligerent.

On 14 February 1915 there arrived in Liverpool another spy not less courageous and patriotic than Lody, but grotesque in his inefficiency and forbidding in his personal appearance. This was Anton Kupp-ferle, who was believed to have been a non-commissioned officer in the German Army. How von Papen, who had financed him, could have sent a man so obviously German, so ignorant of the English language and the American accent, into an enemy country is incomprehensible. He pretended to be a commercial traveller in woollen goods, of Dutch extraction and there was some slight colour for this in the fact that he had once traded as a woollen merchant in Brooklyn under the name of Kuppferle & Co. On the voyage over he was profuse in his conversations with strangers, to whom he represented himself as an American citizen with business in England. From Liverpool he wrote a letter to a certain address in Holland, which was probably the first letter that contained writing in invisible ink. In this he conveyed information about the war vessels he had seen when crossing the Atlantic. From Liverpool he went to Dublin and from Dublin to London, where he was arrested with all his belongings and brought to New Scotland Yard. In his luggage was found letter paper corresponding with that which contained the invisible writing, together with the materials for communications in secret ink.

He proved to be a typical German non-commissioned officer, stiff, abrupt and uncouth. He made little attempt to explain his movements and fell back upon monosyllables. By this time the machinery for substituting civil trials for the military courts-martial was complete and when the case was ready he was arraigned at the Old Bailey before the Lord Chief Justice of England and two other judges, with all the trappings that belong to that historic court, even to the herbs that are scattered about the court in the ancient belief that they averted the infection of jail fever, though modern science knows that there is now no jail fever to avert and that herbs would not avert it if there were. Sir John Simon, the Attorney-General, prosecuted and Sir Ernest Wild defended. The evidence produced on the first day left little doubt of the result of the trial and the court rose with the practical certainty that it would meet again the following morning. But it never met. During the night in Brixton Prison the chief warder heard a muffled rapping from Kuppferle's cell. He dressed himself hastily and came out into the passage, where he was met by the night warder, who announced that he could not see Kuppferle in his cell. With the aid of the master key the door was thrown open and there they found the man hanging dead from the cell ventilator. He had tied his silk handkerchief tightly round his neck and, taking his stand on a heavy book, had kicked it away from under him. Every effort was made to restore life by artificial respiration, but in vain. On his cell slate was found the following message:

> *To whom it may concern:*
>
> *My name is Kuppferle, née to (born in) Sollingen, Rastatt I. B. (Baden). I am a soldier with rank I do not desire to mention. In regard to my behalf lately I can say that I have had a fair trial of the U. Kingdom, but I am unable to stand the strain any longer and take the law in my own hands. I fought many a battles and death is only a saviour for me.*
>
> *I would have preferred the death to be shot, but do not wish to ascend the scaffold as (a Masonic sign). I hope the almighty architect of this universe will lead me into the unknown land in the East. I am not dying as a spy but as a soldier; my fate I stood as a man, but cannot be a liar and perjur myself. Kindly I wish permit to ask to notify my uncle, Ambros Broil, Sollingen, Rastatt, Germany and all my estates shall go to him.*
>
> *What I done I have done for my country. I shall express my thanks and may the Lord bless you all.*
>
> *Yours,*
> *Anton Kuppferle*

On the back of the slate was written: 'My age is thirty-one and I am born 11 June 1883.'

While in Brixton Prison he wrote a letter to another spy awaiting trial which was confiscated by the authorities:

Dear friend,

After my study today I cannot refrain from writing a few words again. Here is the true appearance of that deceitful friendship. (He referred to our declaration that Belgian paper money was worthless.) The English refuse credit to her so-called best friend; so I suppose the fact that Belgium is now in our hands has nothing to do with the state of things.

I believe Ypres and neighbourhood have now fallen. If I could only see the day when the whole British trickery is exposed; England's shame must be made known, otherwise there can be no justice. Oh, if I could only be at the Front again for half an hour!

That is my sole remaining wish. I shall not admit or say I am a soldier, or that I know anything about Military matters.

Our Cavalry has been heard of in Russia for the first time. Of course, the Cavalry has been used by Infantry Service. Reports have been made by cycle and telephone and the latter is of greater importance. The gas must have a great effect and be distasteful to the English. In any case, it is a stupefying death and makes them first vomit, like sea-sickness It is an easy death and if the war lasts for some time many more will be killed by it.

This letter shows Kuppferle in a less amiable light. He had the true Prussian mentality. It was believed that in the early days of the war he had fought on the Western Front: he bore on his face the marks of a blow which may have been caused by the butt end of a rifle. He was buried in Streatham Park Cemetery.

CHAPTER 11

MULLER AND OTHERS

EARLY IN 1915 the Germans began to organise spy-receiving offices in Holland. Usually they pretended to be legitimate commercial agencies. Sometimes one member of a not too prosperous firm of commission agents would lend his offices for the purpose; sometimes a 'business' was opened in some upper room, where a few samples of cheap cigars and other goods were on view. Quite early in the year it was discovered that some foreigner who could write fluent English was sending regular communications to one of these addresses in a simple secret ink and it was evident that he was the sort of person who would find out something which might at any time be of great use to the enemy. The letters were posted at various places in London and there was no clue at all to the sender's address. Like all spies, he was continually demanding money and it was hoped for some time that a remittance from Holland would disclose his identity, but in the end the denouement came about in quite another way. A letter was intercepted in the censorship which disclosed secret writing. It was not in the usual hand and the incriminatory words said that 'C' had gone to Newcastle and that the writer was sending the communication 'from 201' instead. I remember very well the morning when this sentence was shown to me. The postmark was Deptford. '201' might or might not be the number of a house. We rang up Deptford Police Station and asked for a list of the streets in their area which ran to 201 houses. There was only one – Deptford High Street – and the occupant of that house had a German name, 'Peter Hahn, Baker and Confectioner'.

No one was more surprised than the stout little baker when a taxi deposited a number of police officers at his door. He proved to be a British subject and to have been resident in Deptford for some years. While he was being put into the cab a search was made of his premises and in a back room the police found a complete outfit for secret writing neatly stowed away in a cardboard box.

When seated in my armchair Hahn was not at all communicative. He professed to know nothing of 'C', and when further pressed he refused to answer any questions, but patient inquiry among his neighbours produced a witness who remembered that a tall Russian gentleman had been visiting Hahn at frequent intervals. His name was believed to be Müller and his address a boarding-house in Bloomsbury. This limited the field of search. The register of every boarding-house was scrutinised and within a few hours the police found the name of Müller; the landlady of the boarding-house confirmed the suggestion that he was a Russian and said that he had lately gone to Newcastle to see some friends. The search was then transferred to Newcastle and within a few hours Müller was found, arrested and brought to London. He was a tall, spare, worried-looking person, anxious only to have an opportunity of clearing himself. He had never seen Hahn; had never been in Germany and could not even speak the language. For some time he adhered to the story that he was a Russian. An inquiry into his past showed that he was one of those cosmopolitan, roving Germans who are hotel-keepers in one place, commercial travellers in another. At some time they have all been car agents and touts. He spoke English with scarcely any trace of a foreign accent. With his glib tongue he had gone through the usual spy routine of making love to impressionable young women and winning acquaintance by the promise of partnership in profitable speculations. He had some claim for registering himself as a Russian, for he had been born in Libau and spoke Russian as well as Flemish, Dutch, French, German and English. Hahn, on the other hand, was merely a tool. He had been born in Battersea and was therefore a British subject. In 1913 he was a bankrupt with assets of £3 to meet liabilities of £1,800. His object, no doubt, was purely mercenary. As a British subject he had the right to be tried by civil court and therefore, as it was not desirable to have two trials, both he and Müller were indicted at the Old Bailey in May 1915. Both were found guilty of espionage. Müller was sentenced to death and Hahn to seven years' penal servitude on the ground that he had been acting under Muller's influence. Müller appealed unsuccessfully against his sentence.

On 22 June 1915 Müller was removed from Brixton Prison to the Tower in a taxi-cab and by a curious fatality the cab broke down in Upper Thames Street. It was the luncheon hour and a crowd formed immediately. A foreigner seated between two military policemen and going up the street towards the Tower was not lost on the crowd, which raised a cry of 'German spy!' Another taxi was quickly found and the journey was resumed without further accident. The condemned man was highly strung and he broke down on the night before his execution. On the following morning he pulled himself together and insisted on passing gravely down the firing-party and shaking hands with each man. The Germans did not hear of his death for some time, for letters containing remittances continued to be received.

About the middle of 1915 we learned that on a steamer bound from Rotterdam to Buenos Aires was an Argentine citizen named Conrad Leyter, who was believed to be carrying dispatches from Berlin to the German embassy in Madrid. Leyter was removed from the steamer and brought to London. He said he was a shipping clerk, that he had come to Europe for a holiday and was now on his way back to Buenos Aires. He gave a long and rather wearisome account of his holiday adventures in Germany and Holland and nothing could be done until the clockwork had run down. Then we said, 'But why were you going to Spain?' There was another burst of eloquence, but no reply to that particular question. Whenever he paused for breath he was asked, 'Why were you going to Spain?' At last he could bear it no more. He jumped from his chair and said, 'Well, if you will know, I am going to Spain and if you want to know why, I am carrying a dispatch to Prince Ratibor, the German ambassador in Madrid.'

'Thank you. And where is the dispatch?'

'I have not got it. It is sewn up in the life-belt in my cabin.'

That was all we wanted to know. Leyter went to an internment camp, the wireless was got to work and in due course the dispatch was found in the life-belt, as he said. It was quite useful.

Every now and then doubtful persons captured at sea came to us from far afield. In October 1915 a boarding officer in the Mediterranean, who was examining passengers on board the blue-funnel liner *Anchises*, found a man who was carrying a false passport believed to be forged. He was detained and sent to Egypt. In Cairo the luck was against him. While he was being interrogated and his imagination was soaring in full flight, a British officer who had known him in former years chanced to pass through the room and recognised him. 'Hullo, von Gumpenberg!' he cried, slapping him on the back. After that it was useless to dissemble and he gave his name as Baron Otto von Gumpenberg and said that he had been squadron commander in the Death's Head Hussars and had been involved in a scandal for which he was arrested and imprisoned for seven months. On his release he became a vagabond adventurer. In Constantinople he was aide-de-camp to Enver Pasha; later he attached himself to Prince Wilhelm of Wied in his futile attempt to govern Albania. When war broke out he was called back to Germany to serve as a trooper and, according to his own account, he served for eighteen months on the Russian Front with such distinction that when he returned wounded to Germany his commission was restored to him and he was posted to the command of a troop at the Front; but at this moment there happened to be a scheme for stirring up the tribes in north Africa and he was dispatched to see what he could do with the Senussi. About that time the Senussi had captured a number of Italian prisoners and von Gumpenberg accounted for being on the Anchises by saying that he was being sent to the Senussi to obtain the release of these prisoners. We were impolite enough to express entire disbelief in this story. Unfortunately, in return for his confession made in Egypt he had been promised that he would be treated as an officer prisoner of war and he had to be interned at Donington Hall. His real object, no doubt, was to direct the hostile movements of the Senussi and other tribes against the Allies.

The Germans now adopted commerce as the best cover for their agents. England was to be flooded with commercial travellers, especially travellers in cigars. The Censor began to pick up messages containing orders for enormous quantities of cigars for naval ports such as Portsmouth, Chatham, Devonport and Dover. The senders turned out to be furnished with Dutch passports, though their nationality was doubtful. Now something happened to be known about their supposed employers in Holland, who kept one little back office in which a few mouldy samples were exposed and yet here they were with a traveller in the southern counties and another sending orders from Newcastle. Naval ratings are not abstainers from tobacco, but they are not known to be in the habit of consuming large quantities of Havana cigars. One of the travellers named Haicke Petrus Marinus Janssen and the other named Wilhelm Johannes Roos were found doing the sights of London. Janssen was questioned first. He was a self-possessed person of about thirty years of age and he claimed to be a sailor. He knew no German, in fact he had never been in Germany and, being a Dutchman, he had a dislike for Germans. Why, he was asked, did his employers, Dierks & Co., engage a sailor to travel in cigars? To that he had no answer except that he had been unsuccessful in obtaining a berth as officer on a steamer. A friend had introduced him to Mr Dierks because he could speak English and was looking for work. He said that he was the only traveller that Dierks had in England. We asked him whether he knew a man named Roos. 'No,' he said, he had never heard of him. He was then sent to another room while Roos was brought in. He, too, was a seaman, a big, powerful man with the cut of a German seaman. He, too, said that he was a traveller for Dierks & Co.; that Dierks had two travellers, himself and Janssen. Would he know Janssen if he saw him? Certainly he would. Janssen was brought again into the room. He made a faint sign with his eyes and lips to Roos, but of course it was too late. 'Is this the man you say you know?' he was asked. He nodded and Janssen was silent. On the way over to Cannon Row Roos suddenly dashed at a glass door which opened into the yard, smashed the panes and jabbed his naked wrists on the jagged fragments of glass in the hope of cutting an artery. He was taken to Westminster

Hospital to be bandaged and later was removed to Brixton Prison, where he was put under observation as a potential suicide.

The code used by these men was simple enough. They would send telegrams for 10,000 Cabanas, 4,000 Rothschilds, 3,000 Coronas and so on. A message telegraphed from Portsmouth of this kind would mean that there were three battleships, four cruisers and ten destroyers in the harbour and these messages, so interpreted, corresponded with the actual facts on the dates of the telegrams. Neither man could produce any evidence that he had transacted bona fide business with his cigars. They could not produce one genuine order. They were brought to trial for espionage and were convicted. A few days later both made confessions. Janssen actually gave some useful information about the German spy organisation in Holland. He said that his sympathies were really with us and he could not understand how he had been tempted to serve the other side. It appeared that in 1913 he had actually been granted a silver medal by the Board of Trade for life-saving on the immigrant steamer *Volturno*, which was burnt at sea with the loss of 400 lives. Her wireless call for help was responded to by the vessel in which Janssen was serving and he, among others, was instrumental in saving 500 lives. Roos feigned insanity in prison and it was one of the pleas put forward by his counsel. There was, however, no medical support for this plea and it was arranged that on 30 July both men should be executed in the Tower. They met their end stoically. Janssen was shot first. Roos asked as a last favour to be allowed to finish his cigarette. That done, he threw it away with a gesture as though that represented all the vanities of this world and then he sat down in the chair with quiet unconcern. The news of the execution soon reached Holland and the Germans began to find it very difficult to obtain recruits from neutral countries.

During May and June 1915, in about a fortnight, no less than seven enemy spies were arrested. The most spectacular were Reginald Roland, whose real name was Georg T. Breeckow and Mrs Lizzie Wertheim.

Breeckow was the son of a pianoforte manufacturer in Stettin and he was himself a pianist. It is curious to reflect that professional musicians should have formed a respectable proportion of the detected spies. One would have thought that it was the last class that would be able to report intelligently on naval and military matters. Breeckow spoke English fluently and knew enough Americanisms to pose plausibly as a rich American travelling in England for his health. Before he left Holland he was furnished with the address of Lizzie Wertheim, a German woman who had married a naturalised German and had thus acquired British nationality. She was a stout and rather flashy-looking person of the boarding-house type and she had been in England for some years. She was separated from her husband, but on terms that made her independent. She was equally at home in Berlin, the Hague and London.

Breeckow, who appeared to be possessed of a considerable sum of money, was at once accorded a warm welcome. The pair hired horses from a riding-school and rode in the Park during the mornings. They took their luncheon at expensive restaurants and Lizzie Wertheim became intoxicated with this kind of life and waxed so extravagant that Breeckow had to expostulate and report the matter to his employers. She would no longer travel without a maid.

It was decided between the two that the best working arrangement would be for the woman to do the field work and for Breeckow to work up her reports in London and dispatch them to Holland. Mrs Wertheim went to Scotland, hired a car and drove about the country picking up gossip about the Grand Fleet. Her questions to naval officers were, however, so imprudent that special measures were taken;

Breeckow's address was discovered and in due course the two were brought to New Scotland Yard for interrogation. The artistic temperament of Breeckow was not equal to the ordeal. His pretence of being a rich American broke down immediately and he was aghast to find out how much the police knew about his secret movements. Though he made no confession, he returned to Cannon Row in a state of great nervous tension. Lizzie Wertheim, on the other hand, was tough, brazen and impudent, claiming that as a British subject she had a right to travel where she would. She declined to sit still in her chair, but walked up and down the room, flirting a large silk handkerchief as if she was practising a new dancing step. Further inquiries showed that, unlike the previous American passports carried by spies, which were genuine documents stolen by the German Foreign Office, this passport was a forgery right through. The American Eagle on the official seal had his claws turned round the wrong way and his tail lacked a feather or two. The very red paper on which the seal was impressed did not behave like the paper on genuine documents when touched with acid, nor was the texture of the passport paper itself quite the same. It also transpired that Breeckow had been in America continuously from 1908, that he had got into touch with von Papen's organisation, which had sent him back to Germany for service in this country. For this purpose he became an inmate of the Espionage School in Antwerp, where he was taught the tricks of the trade, which were quite familiar to us. He had also a commercial code for use when telegrams had to be sent.

Breeckow had maintained throughout that he knew no German, but his assurance began to break down in the loneliness of a prison cell. He had a strong imagination and no doubt the thought that his female accomplice might be betraying him worked strongly on his feelings. One morning I went over with a naval officer to see how he was. There was a question about signing for his property and he was sent into the room for the purpose. When he found himself alone with us he said suddenly, 'Am I to be tried for my life?'

'I understand that you are to be tried.'

'What is the penalty for what I have done?' (Up to this point he had made no confession.) 'Is it death?'

'I do not know,' I said. 'You have not yet been tried.'

'I can tell from your face that it is death. I must know. I have to think of my old mother in Stettin. I want to write a full confession.'

I told him that of course he was free to write what he pleased, but that anything he did write would almost certainly be used against him at his trial.

'Never mind,' he said. 'I have carried the secret long enough. Now I want to tell the whole truth.'

So paper and ink were supplied to him and he wrote his confession.

As Mrs Wertheim was a British subject and could claim trial by civil court the two were tried together at the Old Bailey on 20 September before three Judges of the High Court and were found guilty. Breeckow was sentenced to death and Mrs Wertheim to ten years' penal servitude, as it was considered that she had acted under the man's influence. Breeckow appealed unsuccessfully and his execution was fixed for 26 October at the Tower. The five weeks that elapsed between the sentence and the execution were extremely trying to the persons responsible for his safety. He had broken down completely and was demented by fear. On the morning of his execution he was almost in a state of collapse. At the last moment he produced a lady's handkerchief, probably the relic of some past love affair and asked that it might be tied over his eyes instead of the usual bandage, but it was too small. It had to be knotted to the bandage and then tied. He was shivering with agitation and just before the shots were fired there was a sudden spasm. It was believed afterwards that he had actually died of heart failure before the bullets reached him.

Lizzie Wertheim was removed to Aylesbury Convict Prison to undergo her sentence and there she died some two years after the Armistice.

Of all the spies that were convicted and executed the man for whom I felt most sorry was Fernando Buschman. He was a gentleman by birth, he had no need of money, for he was married to the daughter of a rich soap manufacturer in Dresden, who had kept him liberally supplied with funds for his studies in aviation. He was quite a good violinist and he had all the instincts of a cultivated musician. He was of German origin, but his father had become a naturalised Brazilian and he himself had Latin blood in his veins. He was born in Paris, but his boyhood was spent in Brazil, where he attended a German school. He had invented an aeroplane and in 1911 the French government allowed him to use the aerodrome at Issy for experimental purposes. For the three years before the war he had been travelling all over Europe and when hostilities broke out the German Secret Service got hold of him. He had been to Spain, to Genoa and to Hamburg and in 1915 he was in Barcelona and Madrid and then in Flushing, Antwerp and Rotterdam. It speaks volumes for the stupidity of the directors of the German Espionage School in Antwerp that they should have selected as a disguise for such a man as Buschman the role of commercial traveller. The imposture was bound to be discovered at once. He was far too well dressed and well spoken and he knew nothing whatever about trade. He arrived in London with a forged passport and put up at a good hotel with his violin, not usually part of the luggage of a commercial traveller. After a few days he moved to lodgings in Loughborough Road, Brixton and thence to lodgings in South Kensington. This he thought was enough to fit him for moving about in England. He visited Portsmouth and Southampton and from certain minute notes found among his papers it became evident that his one qualification – his knowledge of aeronautics – was not to be turned to account: he was to be employed as a naval spy. Unfortunately for him he ran short of money and was compelled to write to Holland for fresh supplies. He was arrested at his lodgings in South Kensington and was found to be quite penniless. When the detective arrived he said, 'What have you against me? I will show you everything.' Then he reeled off his lesson. He was in England for the purpose of selling cheese, bananas, potatoes, safety razors and odds and ends and in France he had sold picric acid, cloth and rifles. He implied that his employers did a miscellaneous business almost unrivalled in commercial annals, but when he said that they were Dierks & Co., of the Hague, we pointed out that they occupied one room and were cigar merchants. Moreover, it was found that his passport was written in the well-known handwriting of Flores, who used to instruct German spies in Rotterdam. This man had been a schoolmaster and his characteristic handwriting was well known. There was also a letter from Gneist, the German Consul-General in Rotterdam, from Colonel Ostertag, the German Military Attaché in Holland and from two persons who were known to be active in recruiting for the German Secret Service. He was tried at the Westminster Guildhall on 20 September 1915, the day of the trial of Breeckow and Mrs Wertheim at the Old Bailey and was sentenced to death. I know that persons who were present at the trial were impressed by his manly bearing and his frankness. After his sentence he was not separated from his violin. It was his great solace through the long hours of waiting. He asked for it again on his removal to the Tower on the night before his execution and played till a late hour. When they came for him in the morning he picked it up and kissed it, saying, 'Goodbye, I shall not want you anymore.' He refused to have his eyes bandaged and faced the rifles with a courageous smile. How differently the artistic temperament works in men and women!

CHAPTER 12

THE HIRELING SPY

AVING FAILED WITH Germans, the enemy now turned to South America for their spies. The large German colony in Central and South America was an excellent recruiting-ground. In June 1915, a few days after the capture of Fernando Buschman, two postcards addressed to Rotterdam attracted the attention of the Postal Censor. They announced merely that the writer had arrived in England and was ready to begin work. The postmark was Edinburgh. The police in Scotland were set to work and a few days later they detained at Loch Lomond a native of Uruguay, who gave his name as Agusto Alfredo Roggin. He was a neat, dark little man, not at all like a German, though he admitted that his father was a German naturalised in Uruguay in 1885 and that he himself was married to a German woman. Unlike many of the spies, he did not pretend that his sympathies were with the Allies. His account of himself was that he had come to England to buy agricultural implements and stock; that his health was not very good and that Loch Lomond had been recommended to him as a health resort. He spoke English fluently. According to his admissions, he had been in Hamburg as lately as March 1914 and was in Switzerland just before war broke out. In May he was sent to Amsterdam and Rotterdam, probably to receive instructions in the School of Espionage. He arrived at Tilbury from Holland on 30 May and after staying for five days in London, where he asked quotations for horses and cattle, he went north. So far he had transacted no business.

As a spy he was one of the most inept that could have been chosen. Even on the journey north from King's Cross he asked so many questions of casual acquaintances that they became suspicious and took upon themselves to warn him not to go anywhere near the coast. In fact, they were so hostile that he left the compartment at Lincoln and spent the night there. Nor was his reception in Edinburgh any more auspicious. When he came to register with the police he was put through a searching inquiry. He was very careful to tell everyone at Loch Lomond that he had come for the fishing, but it chanced at that moment that certain torpedo experiments were being carried out in the loch and the presence of foreigners at once gave rise to suspicion. The sending of the two postcards was quite in accordance with ordinary German espionage practice. In order to divert suspicion the spies were instructed to send harmless postcards in English addressed to different places. Moreover, a bottle of a certain chemical secret ink was found in his luggage. He was tried on 20 August, found guilty and executed at the Tower on 17 September. He went to his death with admirable courage and declined to have his eyes bandaged when he faced the firing-party. Some time after his execution a Dr Emilio Roggin was removed from a steamer bound from Holland to South America. He turned out to be the brother of the dead spy and was greatly distressed at the news of what had befallen him. It transpired that he was in Germany on the outbreak of war and had been compelled by the German government to serve as a medical officer with the troops in the field. It had taken nearly two years for him to obtain his release and he was now on his way back to Uruguay.

Roggin was at large in England only for eleven days and therefore he was unable to send any information of value to his employers. Nevertheless, he was a hired spy and it was at that time most necessary to make the business of espionage so dangerous that recruits would be difficult to get.

About the same time a well-educated and well-connected Swede of between fifty and sixty years of age named Ernst Waldemar Melin arrived in this country. He had been a rolling-stone all his life. At one time he had managed a Steamship Company at Gothenburg, in Sweden and then on the breakdown of his health he began to travel all over the world. He had found casual employment in London, Paris and Copenhagen and at the beginning of the war he found himself in Hamburg without any means of subsistence. He applied, without success, to his relations and then, hearing that there was plenty of remunerative work to be had in Antwerp, he went to Belgium with the genuine desire to obtain honest employment. There at a café he came into touch with one of the espionage recruiting agents, who were always on the look-out for English-speaking neutrals. At first, according to his own account, he resisted the temptation, but at last, being utterly penniless, he succumbed and was sent to the Espionage Schools in Wesel and Antwerp. At Rotterdam he received his passport and the addresses to which he was to send his communications. He put up in a boarding-house in Hampstead as a Dutchman whose business had been ruined by the German submarine campaign and who was anxious to obtain employment a shipping office. He made himself agreeable to his fellow lodgers, who fully accepted his story.

He was under police suspicion from the first, but there could be no confirmation until he began to write. His first communications were written on the margin of newspapers, a method which the Germans had then begun to adopt. He took his arrest quite philosophically. Fortune had dealt him so many adverse strokes that she could not take him unaware. A search of his room brought to light the usual stock-in-trade at that time – the materials for secret writing and a number of foreign dictionaries used as codes, as well as a Baedeker. He made a clean breast of his business, protesting that he had no real intention of supplying the Germans with useful information. All he meant to do was to send some quite valueless messages that would procure for him a regular supply of funds. He was tried by court-martial on 20 and 21 August. His counsel urged that he had sent nothing to the enemy which could not have been obtained from newspapers, but he could not, of course, put forward the plea that he was not a spy. Melin took this last stroke of fortune like a gentleman. He gave no trouble and when the time came he shook hands with the guard, thanking them for their many kindnesses and died without any attempt at heroics.

One German agent was discovered through the purest accident. It was apparently the practice at that time for the Germans to make use of ex-criminals on condition that they undertook espionage in an enemy country. It chanced that some postal official in Denmark had mis-sorted a letter addressed from Copenhagen to Berlin and slipped it by mistake into the bag intended for London and this letter was written in German by a man who said he was about to start for England under the disguise of a traveller in patent gas-lighters, in order to collect military and naval information. The letter was already some weeks old and there was no clue beyond the fact that some person might be in the country attempting to sell gas-lighters. A search of the landing records was at once instituted and it was found that at

Newcastle at that very moment a young man named Rosenthal was on board a steamer about to sail for Copenhagen, after making a tour with his gas-lighters in Scotland. In another hour he would have been outside the three-mile limit and out of reach of the law. He proved to be a young man of excitable temperament and a Jew. He was very glib in his denials: he had never lived in Copenhagen, he was not a German, he knew nothing about the hotel from which the letter had been written. It was growing dusk and so far the letter had not been read to him, but he had given me a specimen of his handwriting, which corresponded exactly with that of the letter. Then I produced it and read it to him. While I was reading there was a sharp movement from the chair and a click of the heels. I looked up and there was Rosenthal standing to attention like a soldier. 'I confess everything. I am a German soldier.' But the remarkable part of this story was that he was never a soldier at all. On a sudden impulse he had tried to wrap his mean existence in a cloak of patriotic respectability. Subsequent inquiry showed that his full name was Robert Rosenthal, a German born in Magdeburg in 1892. As a boy he had been apprenticed to a baker in Cassel. He disliked the work, returned to Magdeburg and at a quite early age was sentenced to three months' imprisonment for forgery. After his discharge he became a rolling-stone and went to sea, but he was in Hamburg on the outbreak of war and was engaged for a time by the American Relief Commission. It is not clear whether he was actually liberated from prison for the purpose of espionage, but espionage was the kind of work for which undoubtedly he was most suited. It was not surprising that such a man should try to save his life by offering to disclose the methods of his employers.

When he found that acquittal was hopeless he tried to carry off the pretence of patriotism at his trial, but after his conviction he made two unsuccessful attempts to commit suicide. Unlike the other spies, he was sentenced to be hanged and was executed on 5 July 1915. He had some ability, for he wrote English very well and was profuse in written accounts of his adventures.

The next spy to be arrested in England was a Peruvian whose father was a Scandinavian. Ludovico Hurwitz-y-Zender was a genuine commercial traveller, though far better educated than most men of his calling. In August 1914 he went to the United States with the intention of coming to Europe on business, for he was already the representative of several European firms in Peru. Probably it was not until his arrival in Norway that he got into touch with the German Secret Service agents, who were then offering high pay for persons with the proper qualifications who would work for them in England. It happened that the Cable Censor began to notice messages addressed to Christiania ordering large quantities of sardines. Now, it was the wrong season for sardine-canning and inquiries were at once made in Norway about the bona fides of the merchant to whom the messages were addressed. He turned out to be a person with no regular business, who had frequently been seen in conversation with the German Consul. The messages were then closely examined for some indication of a code. They had been dispatched by Zender. On 2 July, Zender was arrested at Newcastle, where he had made no secret of his presence, he professed great surprise that there was any suspicion against him and freely admitted that he had been at Newcastle, Glasgow and Edinburgh. In none of these places did he appear to have transacted any real business and on account of the season the experts in sardines laughed to scorn his suggestion that his order for canned fish was genuine. When all arrangements had been made for his trial by court-martial Zender demanded that certain witnesses should be brought from South America for his defence. The proceedings were therefore postponed for eight months and it was not until 20 March 1916 that it was possible to bring him to trial. The witnesses that had been brought at great trouble and expense could really say nothing in his favour and in due course he was found guilty and executed in the Tower on 11 April, nine months after the date of his arrest. Zender was the last German spy to be executed in this country during the war. Others were tried and convicted, but for various reasons the death sentences were commuted to penal servitude for life.

It became evident throughout the war that the only form of espionage that is really worth undertaking is the gathering of intelligence just behind the enemy lines and on the lines of communication. To be of any real value in an enemy country a spy must be highly placed. The enemy must, in fact, buy someone who is in naval and military secrets, for even the ordinary citizen of the country is very rarely in a position to give useful information. As the war dragged on the Germans became increasingly concerned with the question of morale. They had based their air-raids and their submarine campaign upon false reading of the British character. They thought that they were breaking down the war spirit and that it was becoming evident that the British would be tired of the war before they were.

Perhaps the most astonishing figure that bubbled up to the surface during the war was that of Ignatius Timothy Trebitsch Lincoln. That a Hungarian Jew should succeed in being by turns a journalist, a Church of England clergyman and a Member of Parliament in England shows an astonishing combination of qualities. His original name appears to have been Trebitsch. He was born at Paks, on the Danube, about 1875. His father, a prosperous Jewish merchant, had started a shipbuilding business and Ignatius was intended to enter the Jewish Church. He made a study of languages and when he was little more than twenty he visited London. On his return to Hungary there were quarrels between father and son and in 1899 Ignatius went to Hamburg and was received into the Lutheran Church. Later he crossed to Canada to assist in a Presbyterian mission to the Jews and when that mission was transferred to the Church of England Trebitsch changed his denomination. He had a gift of oratory and made some impression in Canada. When he came back to Europe he applied for an English curacy, was ordained and appointed to the parish of Appledore in Kent. It cannot be said that he was a successful curate. Probably fiery oratory in a strong foreign accent would not have appealed to a Kentish congregation under any circumstances. He left his curacy and went to London, where for some two years he supported himself as a journalist.

About 1906 he came into touch with Mr Seebohm Rowntree, who was so much impressed with his abilities that he engaged him as his private secretary. Mr Rowntree was at that time in close touch with the leading Liberals and this brought Lincoln, as he then was, into constant communication with the organisers of the party, who at last put him up to contest the unionist constituency of Darlington in the Liberal interest. Who can fail to admire the audacity with which this election was successfully fought?

The House of Commons is no more impressed with fiery oratory in a foreign accent than a Kentish congregation and Mr Lincoln was glad to absent himself from the House in order to undertake an inquiry into economic conditions on the Continent, which would bring him into close communication with notable personages, for high politics had fired his imagination and he began to regard himself as destined to become one of the future great figures in European history.

I do not think that when the war broke out Lincoln had any idea of giving information to the enemy. He had lost his seat in the House of Commons and he was in financial straits, but his first inclination was undoubtedly to offer his services to England. The first step was to apply for a position in the Censorship for Hungarian and Romanian correspondence and for the short time of his employment he is believed to have done his work conscientiously, but he was not popular with his colleagues and their treatment of his friendly overtures must have galled him. The iron entered into his soul and from that time he was definitely anti-British in his sympathies.

His first act of disloyalty was to attempt to obtain admission into our own Intelligence organisation. He professed to be able to tempt the German Fleet out into the North Sea, where it could be destroyed and for that purpose he proposed to cross to Holland and offer his services to the German Consul. Though his application was rejected, he did succeed in obtaining a passport and on 18 December 1914 he arrived in Rotterdam. The German Consul, Gneist, was a very active espionage agent and Lincoln appears to have made some impression upon him at first, for he did entrust to him some valueless information to carry back with him to England. With this he again pestered the authorities to take him into the Intelligence Service, but he was so coldly received that he took alarm and left for New York on 9 February. Here he made a living of some kind by journalism, in ignorance of the fact that the authorities in England were investigating a certain signature to a draft for £700. It transpired that Lincoln had forged Mr Seebohm Rowntree's name for that amount. Chief Inspector Ward, who was afterwards killed by a Zeppelin bomb, was sent over to the United States in connection with the extradition proceedings and on 4 August 1916, Lincoln was arrested. After the usual delays in such cases he was brought to England, was tried at the Old Bailey and received a sentence of three years' penal servitude. When his sentence expired in the summer of 1919 it was intended to send him back to his own country, but at that time Bela Kun was in power and the plan had to be deferred. When the communist government fell the deportation was carried out and in September 1919 Lincoln found himself again in Buda Pesth. The atmosphere of that city, just recovering from the communist orgy of misrule, did not suit him. He went to Berlin and renewed his acquaintance there with Count Bernstorff, the former German ambassador at the United States. It is said in Germany that the extreme right will swallow anything. Their political sagacity has never been conspicuous. Kapp was at the moment secretly preparing for his putsch and it surprised no one when it was reported that Ignatius Timothy Trebitsch Lincoln had solemnly been appointed Propaganda Agent to the short-lived Kapp government. How many days the appointment lasted is not quite certain, but apparently even Colonel Bauer found him more than he could manage. The troubled waters of Central Europe are the only fishing ground in which a man such as Lincoln could hope to make a living. We may even hear of him again.

CHAPTER 13

THE LAST EXECUTIONS

IRVING GUY RIES was a German-American who had been recruited by the Germans in New York. He landed at Liverpool in the guise of a corn merchant, though in private life he was actually a film operator. After a few days spent at a hotel in the Strand he, too, visited Newcastle, Glasgow and Edinburgh and went through the routine of calling upon a number of produce merchants as an excuse for his journey, but, like the other spies, he did no genuine business with them. He returned to his hotel in London on 28 July after a fortnight spent in the north. He was more careful than most of the other spies, for he preserved copies of every business letter that he wrote. Unfortunately for him, his employers had not kept him properly supplied with money and by ill chance the Censor intercepted a letter addressed to him from Holland which contained the exact amount of the remittance usually made to spies. Ries carried an American passport and the first step taken was to ask the American authorities to withdraw from him his passport in order that it might be examined by experts. It proved to be forged and on 19 August late at night the police went to Ries's hotel and arrested him just as he was going to bed.

He was a grave and measured person who answered all my questions very deliberately and thoughtfully. On one point he refused altogether to be drawn. He would not tell his true name, but he explained that this was only because if the name ever came to be published it would give pain to his relations. About his movements he was frank enough. He explained that he would have already left for Copenhagen if the Americans had not required him to surrender his passport. Among his effects was found a letter from Rotterdam, directing him to meet a certain person in Copenhagen and report to him the result of his investigations in England. He was asked to account for this and he immediately dropped all the pretence that he was in this country on genuine business. 'I am in your power,' he said. 'Do what you like with me.' There was no doubt whatever that he was a spy, but his case differed from the others in the fact that it could not be shown that he had ever sent information to the enemy. In fact, it seemed clear that the Germans were adopting new tactics and that they intended in future to send spies on flying visits to England and get them to come and report the result of their observations verbally. He was tried on 4 October, was found guilty and sentenced to death. He took his condemnation with perfect philosophy. He spent all his time in reading and he gave his guards the impression that he was a man who had divested himself of all earthly cares and felt himself to lie under the hand of Fate. If he expected that the American government would press for a reprieve and would be successful he never showed it.

On 26 October he was removed to the Tower and as soon as he knew that a date was fixed for his execution he called for writing materials and made a full confession, giving at the same time his true name. This, of course, cannot be published in view of the considerations that had made him conceal it when he was arrested. He was permitted to shake hands with the firing-party and he said, 'You are only doing your duty, as I have done mine.'

I have said that throughout the war there was no case of espionage by any Englishman, but there was one curious exception. In November 1917, it came to our knowledge that a young bluejacket who had deserted his ship in Spain had gone straight to the German authorities in Madrid and given them such naval information as a bluejacket might be in possession of. He had then given himself up as a deserter and had been discharged from the service. He had since obtained work in a munitions factory in the north of England near his home. He was arrested at Barrow and sent to London and so uneasy was the Labour situation at the time that a strike was immediately threatened until the nature of the charge was explained to the responsible leaders.

The young man did not attempt to deny the charge. He was the youngest of a family who were all serving in the war in some form. His explanation was that he went to the Germans in Spain in order to find out their military secrets but, though there could be no doubt about the facts, there was doubt about his mental condition and as his family made themselves responsible for his future good behaviour he was discharged to their care.

Courtenay Henslop de Rysbach was a British subject, but his father was an Austrian naturalised in this country. De Rysbach was a music-hall artist, who, on the outbreak of war, had an engagement in Germany. He was a comedian, one of those who can sing and juggle and play tricks on bicycles. Like the other foreigners, he was swept into Ruhleben and when the Germans separated those who favoured

Germany from the others and accorded them better treatment he began to listen to suggestions that he should undertake work for the enemy. He was removed to Berlin to undergo a course of training. From Berlin he went to Zurich and to Paris in the guise of a British subject who had been released from internment on account of his health. He landed at Folkestone on 27 June and at once found himself free to move about the country without restriction.

One day the Postal Censor detained two songs addressed to a man in Zurich. One was called 'The Ladder of Love' and the other, 'On the way to Dublin Town'. The songs were signed 'Jack Cummings, Palace Theatre, London'. No such person existed and for some time there was nothing to indicate the sender. An examination of the songs with a suitable developer brought up between the bars of music an account of what the writer had seen in this country. De Rysbach was then appearing at a local music-hall in Glasgow with a female trick cyclist. As soon as his identity with Jack Cummings was established he was brought to London and put through a detailed examination. It transpired that after his arrival in this country he had attempted to obtain a post in the Censorship, though employment in that department can scarcely have been more remunerative than his earnings in the music-halls. He told us that with a view of gaining his liberty he had promised to serve the Germans, though he never intended to fulfil his promise. He admitted that he had been supplied with a secret ink made up in the form of an ointment, but declared that he had thrown it away while crossing Lake Constance and had kept only one tube as a souvenir. Being a British subject he was tried at the Old Bailey before a judge and jury. The jurymen were so far impressed with his story that they disagreed. Probably he expected then that he would be released, but he soon found that he was to undergo a new trial. In October 1915 he was found guilty and sentenced to penal servitude for life, though his guilt was really greater than that of several of the spies who had been executed. His name was not made public at the time; only the fact that a British subject had been found guilty of espionage was disclosed and the newspapers began to wonder why a British spy had been so leniently treated. Soon after his sentence de Rysbach offered to give much fuller information about the German espionage methods on condition that he was released. His offer was not accepted.

De Rysbach was not the only Ruhleben prisoner of whom the Germans made use. Among the British subjects interned were, of course, certain Germans who had been naturalised in this country. Among these was a German Jew – we will call him Preiznitser – whose history is instructive. He came over to England as a boy and in furtherance of his ambition he obtained naturalisation. He married an Englishwoman and rose to be manager of his company. In the course of business he was in Germany on the outbreak of war. It is doubtful whether he had any real national allegiance at all, but certain unguarded utterances had aroused the suspicions of his fellow prisoners, who made a clandestine examination of his personal effects. Among these were discovered copies of articles apparently furnished to German newspapers, abusing the allies and particularly the British. There was one paper, evidently the copy of a letter, in which he suggested that he should act as a guide to Zeppelins attacking England, on account of his intimate knowledge of the English roads through motoring in the course of business.

A few days before this Preiznitser had disappeared from the prison and it soon became known among the prisoners that the Germans had released him. Some of the British then made it their business to have the copies of Preiznitser's incriminating letters conveyed to me. After some weeks, for some unexplained reason, the Germans put

Preiznitser back in Ruhleben and it may well be understood that his reception was neither flattering nor cordial. In fact, his life became such a hell that he determined to escape. That was his story. How far it was true, how far the Germans connived at his escaping it was impossible to determine, but he did arrive in England and he did present himself at my office, without knowing that I had in my possession copies of his letters written from Ruhleben. It was there that he told the marvellous story of his escape.

All went well until I produced his letters and read them to him. He was abashed for a moment, but only for a moment. His explanation was that his object in offering to guide Zeppelins to England was to be sent over here in order to offer his services to the Air Ministry as a guide for aeroplanes bombing Germany. I think that during the war I never met a more loathsome type of international. He was ready to serve any and every master if only it should be to the advantage of Lionel Max Preiznitser. And we could do nothing more drastic than intern him until the end of the war.

The spy who made the worst impression was Albert Meyer, a Jew, with a very mean history. He was one of those young scoundrels who live upon women, defraud their landladies and cheat their employers. A letter was stopped in the Censorship which proved on examination to be full of secret writing. The name and address of the sender were false. There was nothing to do but to sit down and wait. During the next few weeks many more of these letters were stopped in the same handwriting, but with different names and addresses. All that could be gathered from them was that the writer was of foreign nationality and that he was living somewhere in London. After a long and patient search a little Jew of uncertain nationality named Albert Meyer was arrested in a lodging-house. He had been moving from one lodging-house to another, promising the landladies that he would pay them as soon as his remittances arrived from 'his parents abroad'. He was living the kind of life which spies affect – dining one day in an expensive restaurant and the next, when the money was exhausted, begging a meal from an acquaintance. He could not even keep faith with his employers, for his communications contained a mass of fictitious information. When he was required to furnish a specimen of his handwriting and the similarity with the writing in the letters was pointed out to him, he explained it by saying that it had been the malicious work of a so-called friend and the invisible ink found in his possession had been also planted on him by this 'friend'. He was tried by court-martial on 5 November and sentenced to death. His end was characteristic. He had behaved quietly during the weeks that followed his sentence, but as soon as he knew his fate and was taken from his cell to the place of execution he struck up the tune of 'Tipperary'. On reaching the miniature rifle-range he burst into a torrent of blasphemy and he had to be placed forcibly in the chair and strapped in. He tore the bandage from his eyes and was still struggling when he died.

The most curious and ineffective of the German spies during the war was Alfred Hagn, a young Norwegian whom we arrested on 24 May 1917. He was one of those young people who write novels, paint Futurist pictures, compose startling poetry and prose for the magazines and fail to arrive anywhere. He had gone to America in the hope of selling his pictures and had returned penniless in 1916. We were afterwards told that his parents, who were in quite humble circumstances, were really to blame for his misfortunes. They had educated him above his station and filled him with the belief that he was destined to become a great artist.

In the autumn of 1916, while he was trying to dispose of some of his pictures in Norway, he met a German painter named Lavendel and a member of the German Intelligence who called himself Harthern. To those men he related to what straits he was reduced and they suggested to him in a joking manner that he should go to England as an agent. He rejected this suggestion at the time, but later, on the assurance of Harthern that, as a correspondent of a Norwegian newspaper, he was not at all likely to be suspected, he consented. He approached the editor of a daily paper, offering to act as special correspondent and the low price which he was prepared to accept for his articles, which were to be contributed free of any claim for expenses, clinched the matter. He arrived in England on 10 October and for some weeks gave no ground for suspicion. He wrote a few articles for his Norwegian newspaper and then returned to Norway. Here the German agents again got hold of him. His money had run short and there was nothing for it but to undertake another trip. His second arrival was on 13 April 1917. He went to a boarding-house in Tavistock Square. Here he appears to have excited suspicion by his taciturnity. An Italian professor who was staying in the same house came to the conclusion that a man who had evidently so much on his mind must be a German spy. While at this boarding-house he received a notice calling him to join the Colours, which had been sent under the impression that he was a British subject. He called at the recruiting office to explain that he was not liable.

It was to the Italian professor that the credit for unmasking Hagn's real employment was due. He was so convinced by his conduct in the hotel that he called at the nearest police station to denounce him as a German spy. There were many hundreds of such denunciations, but they were all passed to the proper department. A careful examination was made of the documents produced by Hagn when he received permission to land in this country. Though there was nothing incriminating in these there was some reason for suspecting that he might be using a new secret ink. His room was visited and on the table was noticed a bottle labelled 'Throat Gargle'. A little of the liquid was abstracted for analysis and it proved to be an ink with which invisible writing might be produced. On 24 May, therefore, Hagn was taken into custody. He took his arrest quite calmly. In fact, he behaved as if he had been expecting it. When a search was made of his effects the police discovered pieces of cotton-wool bearing traces of ammonia, a drug which had to be used with this ink. In examination it transpired that he had written only two or three articles, for which he received £2 a piece and that his expenses in England had come to much more than this. He could not account for the source of his livelihood, but in the end he broke down and admitted everything. He told us that his mission was to obtain particulars of the alleged misuse of hospital ships: probably he had not sent the Germans anything of importance. It transpired that among other things he had made application for permission to visit the Western Front on behalf of his newspaper.

He was brought to trial on 27 August 1917, when his counsel told the whole of his unhappy story. He had been a spoilt child, whose every whim had been indulged by his parents. All went well while his father lived, but at his death the mother was left nearly destitute. She brought her son back to Norway in the hope that he would be able to support her, but what can a Futurist artist, whose pictures no one will buy, do to support himself, much less a dependent? And, to crown his troubles, Hagn was suffering from unrequited love. His death sentence was afterwards commuted to imprisonment for life. He gave no trouble in Maidstone Prison for two years and then he went on hunger strike – not for the usual reason of forcing the hands of the authorities, but because he had become convinced that such a wretch as he had no longer the right to cumber the earth. It was a form of delusional insanity. Counsel was taken with the Norwegian government and on 13 September 1919 he was sent back to Norway on an undertaking that he would never come to England again.

After Hagn's conviction there was a lull. A good many suspects were interned or deported during 1917, but it was not until September that another real spy landed in England. Jose de Patrocinio, a Brazilian half-caste, the son of a well-known journalist in Brazil who had been largely concerned in the liberation of the slaves, arrived at Gravesend from Flushing. He cut so unsatisfactory a figure while he was being questioned that the port authorities felt sure that he was a spy. He was taxed with it and almost immediately he made a confession.

According to his story, he had gone to Paris in 1913 as a correspondent for a newspaper and while there he had been offered an appointment as attaché to the Brazilian Consulate. In 1916, however, his appointment came to an end and he found himself in Amsterdam short of funds and with a wife to support. He was actually considering how he could get money enough for returning to Brazil when a German agent came into touch with him. To this man he related all the squalid little details of his struggle to accumulate sufficient money for his passage. The next day a man named Loebel, afterwards known as a recruiter of spies, began to talk about his approaching visit to Brazil. 'How are you going?' he asked. 'There are no Dutch boats.' Patrocinio told him that he would go first to the United States and thence to South America. Loebel said that in his opinion it was a stupid plan. He might make a great deal of money if he stayed in Europe. In the end Patrocinio promised to be in the same café at a fixed hour the next day in order to be introduced to a person who would put him in the way of making this money.

The newcomer turned out to be a sallow, swarthy person with ingratiating manners, who wore spectacles and perpetually rubbed his hands. He gave his name as Levy and declared himself to be a Brazilian. Patrocinio thereupon addressed him in Portuguese and was immediately aware that whatever Levy's nationality might be he was not a Brazilian. Levy went on to say that he had been born at Rio Grande do Sul, but on hearing that his Portuguese accent was not all that it should be, he said, quite unabashed, 'Oh, but I am a naturalised Brazilian.'

Then Patrocinio pressed his questions and said at last, 'You see, you have never been to Brazil at all.'

Mr Levy was not in the least abashed. He laughed and said, 'You are very clever. You are just the kind of man I want.' He then told him he was a Swiss, but wanted a Brazilian passport with which to go to England and would pay a great deal of money for such a passport. In the subsequent conversation about the use of fraudulent passports, Levy whispered to him, 'I can put you in the way of getting £1,000,' and then, a little later, 'How would you like to look after my affairs in England and France?'

'You see, I know nothing about your business.'

'You are an intelligent man. If you want to earn £1,000 try to find out where the next offensive in France will take place.'

According to Patrocinio, he decided at that moment to track down this ingratiating and shameless person as a service for the Allies and for Brazil. That was an oft-told tale. According to his story, he then asked Levy how he could communicate such information even if he found it out.

'I will tell you everything. I am specially employed by the police in Berlin. If you are faithful to us we can protect you both in France and in England and if you are willing to obtain this information we will give you a secret ink in which you can write your messages in perfect safety and we can give you addresses which no one will suspect.'

Patrocinio asked for the ink.

'Oh, I don't carry that about with me. Come and see me again at Loebel's house and we will have another talk.'

Late in the evening he met the two men again, as arranged and Levy said, 'You must not go unwillingly. There is plenty of time to draw back if you are afraid.' Patrocinio resented the suggestion of fear, but said that he did not altogether like being branded as a spy. 'But £1,000!' whispered the tempter and Patrocinio fell. As a parting injunction, Levy said, 'Remember if you betray us I can have you assassinated either in London or in Paris.' There were claws beneath his velvet gloves!

The instructions Patrocinio received were that he was to obtain news of the movements of troops and forward it written in secret ink between the lines of an ordinary letter to six addresses, of which some were in Switzerland and some in Denmark. At the end of six weeks he was to go to Switzerland and write a letter to Frankfurt-on-Main announcing his arrival. He would be paid according to the value of his information and if he served faithfully he would receive further employment. Levy then took Patrocinio into another room and gave him instructions in the use of this new secret ink, which was contained in a soft linen collar and two or three handkerchiefs. These had to be soaked in water and the water then became the ink. He gave a demonstration by writing a message, but when Patrocinio asked how it was to be developed the claws again peeped from the velvet gloves. Patrocinio went back to his wife thoroughly frightened and it was probably due to her intervention that the confession was made. It appears that as the boat conveying Patrocinio and his wife to England left the quay at Flushing one of the passengers saw the little Brazilian lean over the side and throw some collars into the sea. This seemed to him so remarkable a proceeding that he kept the little man under observation. And, to make Patrocinio's fears even more acute, a lady, addressing his wife in his hearing, asked whether she knew a Mr Rene Levy, who was staying in the hotel and said he was a Brazilian. A few minutes later the fellow passenger who had noticed the incident of the collars came up to him and asked him whether he had had any dealings with Germans while he was in Holland.

By this time Patrocinio's nerves were so shaky that he blurted out to this stranger a great deal of what he afterwards confessed to us. On the whole, it seems doubtful whether Patrocinio ever intended to act as a spy, though he had certainly promised the Germans that he would become one. If he had really intended to unearth the conspiracy and bring the information to England he would have lost no time in making a full report, but being a timid person he very foolishly told falsehood after falsehood until his story had become so involved that the whole of it was suspected.

He was detained while a communication was made to the Brazilian government. It then appeared that his father was regarded as a sort of national hero and was known as the liberator of the slaves and that if anything happened to his son there would be an outburst of popular feeling in Brazil. For this reason Patrocinio was sent back to Brazil with the usual warning.

In February 1916 we had information that a young man of good family named Adolfo Guerrero was on his way to England in the employment of the Germans. The port authorities allowed him to land in order to keep him under close observation. He told them that he was a Spanish journalist representing a Madrid newspaper, *Libral*, and they made the astonishing discovery that he could not speak a word of English. How the Germans could have brought themselves to engage such a person passed their comprehension. Guerrero had brought with him as far as Paris a young woman, a professional dancer, who called herself Raymonde Amondarain, with the 'sub-titles' of 'Aurora de Bilbao' and 'La Sultana'. Guerrero first set to work to pull the strings to obtain permission for this young woman to come to London and he found a Spanish merchant in Fenchurch Street who was ready to write a letter telling her that he had a clerical position in his office open to her if she would come. It did not seem to strike either of them that a young dancer with an extensive wardrobe was scarcely the kind of person who would settle down to clerical work in a city office, but it was good enough for the French Passport Office; and when Amondarain announced at the port that she had come to join her future husband, Señor Guerrero, she was detained, for it was found that she had given false answers to the questions put to her for passport purposes. On 18 February 1916 Guerrero was arrested and brought down for examination. From his point of view, it was tragic that the lady was lodged, all unknown to him, a few streets off. For a time he adhered to his ridiculous story that he was to be a correspondent for the *Libral* on payment of £2 an article. In sixteen days he had written two such articles and he was proposing to keep himself and Amondarain on the earnings of his pen.

It was now necessary to ascertain who Guerrero really was. Officers were sent out to Spain and they found that part of the story was true. He did belong to a noble family, but he had fallen into wild habits and had become an easy victim to the German agents then living in Spain. The editor of the *Libral* had never heard of him. It was not until 13 July that he appeared at the Old Bailey, but before this it had been decided not to include Amondarain in the charge, because her strenuous advocacy of her intended husband and the inquiries we had made about her antecedents seemed to make it clear that she was not implicated in espionage. She was, however, kept in custody until the issue of Guerrero's trial and then sent back to Spain. He was found guilty and sentenced to death.

A few days after his trial he wrote to say that if his life was spared he would give information that would break up the whole of the German espionage system, but his confession proved to be a tissue of fiction. He said that his name in the German Secret Service was Victor Gunantas, that he was known as No. 154, which meant that he was the 154th spy who had come from Spain to England. He was to visit mercantile ports and report merchantmen who were about to sail to ensure their becoming a prey to the submarines; he was to receive £50 a week and a commission on all ships sunk as the result of his information. No man ever deserved the extreme penalty more richly, but influences had been at work in Spain and, in deference to the representations of the Spanish government, his life was spared. I am not sure that there have not been moments during Guerrero's imprisonment when he wished that his friends had not been so insistent in his behalf.

It was a curious fact that among the papers found upon him was a letter telling him to call on a certain number in Stockwell Road, Brixton, the address of the spy, de Rysbach, who had been arrested in 1915.

Early in 1916 we learned that, besides the perennial question of movement of troops, the Germans were anxious to locate our munitions factories. But they were even more anxious to know about our national morale, probably because their own was beginning to give them cause for anxiety. We learned that a certain Dutch Jew who passed under the name of Leopold Vieyra was being sent to England specially to report upon these points and that the Germans had given him a sum of money calculated at the rate of 50s. a day for the expenses of his trip. He was allowed to land and very careful observation was kept upon him. It was found that he was communicating with a person in Holland whom he addressed as Blom, that he had once dealt in films under the name of Leo Pickard and that he had been getting his living in buying and selling films, both in England and in Holland. In July 1916 he mentioned in a letter to Blom that he was about to return to Holland and in one of Blom's letters occurred the passage, 'If you cannot do anything in London try the provinces.' It was arranged that a call should be made at Blom's address and it was found that no one lived there except a Mrs Dikker, who admitted that her maiden name was Sophia Blom. Further inquiries showed that this address was an ordinary post-box for letters addressed to the German Secret Service. In August Vieyra was arrested, his house was searched and in it was found the usual outfit for secret writing. His explanation of his connection with Blom broke down under interrogation. He was tried by court-martial on 11 November, found guilty and sentenced to death, but the sentence was afterwards commuted to one of penal servitude for life.

The most absurd person employed by the Germans was Joseph Marks. I was watching the work of the port officers at Tilbury one summer afternoon when one of my inspectors whispered to me that in the next room was a person over whom they would be glad to have my help. He said that his very first question had reduced the man to a pitiable condition of fright and that when he was told that within a few minutes he would have an opportunity of making his explanations to me in person he collapsed, murmuring, 'Then Basil Thomson knew I was coming or he wouldn't be here.'

Adopting a manner suitable to the occasion, I sat down at a table and sent for Marks and there stumbled into the room a positive mountain of flesh, over 6 feet in height and proportionately broad and deep: he must have weighed at least sixteen stone. At the moment the whole mass was trembling like a jelly. The passport he produced was Dutch, but almost at my first question he broke down and said:

If you will have patience with me I will tell you the whole story. When I saw one of your men on board the steamer watching me I knew I was in a trap and if you hadn't been here to meet me I should have gone straight to your office tomorrow morning.

(His guilty conscience had converted an ordinary fellow passenger into a police agent.)

According to his story, he belonged to an important commercial family in Aix-la-Chapelle, where he had three times been accused by the Germans of being an agent for the French. They told him that he could clear himself from suspicion only by proceeding to England to obtain naval information for them. He preferred to take his chance of escaping discovery in England to being shot as a French spy by his own people. He attended a spy school, where they furnished him with an album of postage stamps – a method of conveying information that was new to us. He was to send to Switzerland stamps indicating particular classes of warships. Thus, ten Uruguay stamps taken in conjunction with an Edinburgh postmark would mean that ten battleships were lying in the Firth of Forth and so on. Whether he ever intended to carry out his instructions is uncertain: usually so well-fed a person has no stomach for adventure, but he was put on his trial for having come to this country after being in communication with an enemy agent and was sentenced to five years' penal servitude. In a convict prison he was safe for the duration of the war and when he was repatriated in October 1919 he was profuse in his gratitude. Probably no one has ever gone to prison with a lighter heart. I imagine that any philatelist who may in future produce his album for the inspection of Mr Joseph Marks will be startled by the effect he will produce.

The bottom rung of the ladder of infamy was touched by a young

Fleming whom I examined in 1917. He had been employed by the Belgians to pilot young Belgians over the Dutch frontier. He proposed to a Frenchman that they should sell the secret to the Germans and divide the money. He said that eight men were to cross that night: for a few gulden he would have sacrificed the lives of eight of his fellow countrymen who had trusted him. With great presence of mind, the Frenchman gave him to understand that he himself was a German agent and that he would arrange the whole business and further, that if he would make a trip with him to England at once he would earn a much larger sum. So great was the Fleming's cupidity that he embarked and was received on landing by Special Branch policemen.

CHAPTER 14

SOME AMERICANS

I T WAS NOT to be expected that the Germans would do no recruiting among Americans as long as the United States remained neutral. American journalists were travelling to all the belligerent countries and were allowed to see much that could not properly be shown to private citizens. I believe that all the reputable American newspapers were very careful in the selection of their foreign correspondents during the war and it is, perhaps, for that reason that there was no cause for suspicion until late in 1916. About that time two so-called American journalists, B— and R— arrived in Europe. The former had spent several weeks in England before he applied, on 20 September 1916, for permission to travel to Rotterdam as European representative of the Central Press of New York. Before leaving he told the people in his hotel that he was going to a certain hotel in Rotterdam which was known to us as being the resort of German spies and he wrote a letter to a person in Amsterdam named D—, against whom there was already suspicion, about the production of a cinema play. It was noticed that the letter contained a number of underlined words. In the meantime he had left for Holland. All that could be done was to keep observation upon him in that country and it soon became known that his only associates were two Americans, one of whom, R—, was marked down for arrest if ever he came to this country. B— did appear to have made a few inquiries from film dealers, but that was all. On 3 November he landed at Gravesend and, probably to disarm the suspicions of the port authorities, he volunteered a statement that while in Amsterdam a Dutchman had tried to pump him for information, but he had indignantly refused to have anything to do with him. His luggage was searched, but not in a way that would allow him to think that he was under suspicion. He stayed in London for a few hours and then left for Worcestershire. He travelled about the country for a month, sending occasional articles to New York; then he left for Ireland and visited Dublin, Cork, Killarney and Belfast. At that time the Germans were specially anxious to receive news from Ireland subsequent to the Rebellion, because they were being pressed to furnish a fresh supply of munitions together with German troops.

Meanwhile, careful inquiries had been made in Holland regarding the man D—, to whom B— had written when he was last in England, and it was found that he was a German and that he consorted with persons who were known to be in the Secret Service of the enemy. On this a letter was written to B— asking him to call at Scotland Yard and he crossed from Dublin on the night of 8 December. He could give no satisfactory explanation as to why he had underlined certain words in his letter to D— and he professed the greatest astonishment when he heard that D— himself was suspected of being a German spy.

A search of B—'s effects produced the usual ball-pointed pen, unglazed notepaper and a bottle of mixture which could be used as invisible ink. Moreover, he was in possession of a draft for £200 issued to him on 19 October. It was found that he had attempted to obliterate the address of D— in his notebook and he had the name and address of a certain person in Rotterdam, who had been known to us for months as an enemy agent.

Now it chanced that our authorities in New York were in full possession of the details of the new German conspiracy to flood this country with journalists. The spies were recruited by a man who passed under the name of Sanders, who was believed to be closely in touch with the disaffected Irishmen in America. For this reason the spies were to take an opportunity of visiting Ireland and, after gathering all the information that they could they were to go to Holland, impart it to the German agents there and receive the wages of their hire. They had instructions also to get into touch with wounded officers lately returned from the Front and obtain their views on the morale of the troops.

Now B— had done all these things: he had visited Ireland, he had made friends with a wounded officer and had even suggested to him that they should make a trip to Scotland together; he had gone to Holland and had upon him a draft for £200, the equivalent of the $1,000 which was always given for preliminary expenses. This man had heard that B— had been provided with a wonderful new invisible ink disguised as a medical mixture, which could be used only on un-glazed paper with a ball-pointed pen. There was also a statement that an American journalist whose name began with 'R' was already doing good work for the Germans in London.

While B— was under detention he received a letter from R— in Holland: 'Wish old "C" had been here to help me read the letter.' Why should R— require any help in reading a letter unless it was written cryptographically? So far, the case was one of suspicion, but on 3 February 1917 B— wrote from Brixton Prison, asking that he might be visited by someone in authority to whom he was prepared to make an important statement. A senior officer was sent to Brixton and to him B— made a full confession. He had formerly been the New York publicity agent for a well-known firm of film producers. One day he received a telephone message from a man with a foreign accent, asking whether he would care to go to Europe. He said that it was for very special work, for which he would be well paid. The voice directed him to call at an office in New York, where he would meet a man named Davis. Davis was a pseudonym for Charles Winnenberg, who told him frankly that the special work was to obtain information which would be useful to the German government. The Germans wanted particulars about our anti-aircraft defences, the movements and the morale of our troops and the actual position of British squadrons in Scottish waters, together with anything he might be able to glean about our new battleships. Not unnaturally, B— referred to the danger of such a service, but Winnenberg treated this with great scorn, saying, 'They have only caught two or three and they were all fools. There will be no suspicion against you. We will pay you £25 a week and give you liberal expenses.'

Then, according to B—, Winnenberg became confidential and said that he intended to go himself to London, whence one of his agents, known as Robert W— had already sent him useful reports. He gave him particulars of the people in Holland with whom he was to communicate and added that there were three or four Americans in that country who would relay his messages if necessary. When B— pointed out that the Censor would probably intercept his messages, Winnenberg said, 'As soon as you have got your passport I will give you the secret of fooling the Censor.'

On this B— called on the Central Press and told them that as he was going to Europe on business he would be prepared to collect war pictures for them on commission and in this they acquiesced. Thus he had a business cover for his journey and no difficulty was made about his passport. He then called on Winnenberg again, who was much pleased with the energy he had displayed. 'Have you got a pair of black woollen socks?' he asked. B— had not. 'Well, go and buy a pair at once.' When this was done Winnenberg produced a collapsible tube, from which he squeezed a thick brown liquid. This he smeared all round the top of the socks. 'There,' he said,

> *That is a secret ink which the English will never discover. All you have to do is to soak these socks in water and use the fluid as an ink. You must use a ball-pointed pen and a rough paper, on which the ink will not run. You must mark all your reports 'M', which will stand for 'Marina, Antwerp'. That is the only place which knows the secret of developing the ink.*

B— was given a thousand-dollar bill for preliminary expenses and was told that if he got good information he would be treated very liberally. He explained his visit to Worcestershire by saying that the wounded officer whose acquaintance he had made had asked him down there and he tried to excuse himself with the usual plea that he had not intended to give the Germans anything of value, but merely to draw money from them. As a matter of fact, when he went to Holland he was nearly at the end of his resources and probably it was in the hope of obtaining a draft for £200 that he went.

It became clear from subsequent investigations that B— was trying to spread his net wide. His wounded officer friend was nominally to be made a representative of a big shipping firm in America, but actually of another German agent who was to use him without his knowledge. B— was also suggesting to a girl acquaintance that she should obtain a post in the Censorship.

B— was tried by court-martial on 17 March 1917.

His counsel stated that he could trace his descent back to 1644, that his ancestor had fled to America after the battle of Marston Moor and that his mother's ancestors had fled from France at the time of the Edict of Nantes. He was said to be a Bachelor of Arts in the United States, but the only defence put forward was that he had yielded to a sudden temptation to make money. He was sentenced to death by hanging.

Fortunately for B— the United States was about to enter the war and his value as a witness against the numerous persons who were being arrested was realised. It was decided to send him over to New York under arrest. On his arrival he was charged with a breach of neutrality laws and sentenced to imprisonment for a year and a day, for the sentence pronounced by the British court-martial could not, of course, run in America. While imprisoned in the United States he gave evidence against the German master spies and he seems to have greatly recovered his spirits, if we may judge from a letter that he wrote to a friend in England, asking him to try and forward the balance of the money which he had received from his German paymasters.

Winnenberg, alias Davis and Sanders, were arrested and convicted. The former made a full confession, which contained, no doubt, a good deal of romance, for he tried to inculpate many other foreign representatives besides Germans. According to his story R— entered England as an American journalist sent to write articles on the food situation in Europe for publication in American newspapers. He lost little time in communicating with a certain Cookery School organisation which was employed by the government for instructional purposes. R— made frequent trips to and from Holland and then, having run what he thought was more than his share of risk, he persuaded the Germans to allow him to remain in Holland as one of their chief agents to deal with any American journalists who might come after him. Arrangements were made to arrest him as soon as he set foot again in this country, but that moment never came. Even when he communicated articles to the British press on the international food question he was careful to arrange that payment should be sent to him in Holland. After the articles had been published it was brought to the notice of the editor that the writer was under strong suspicion. Payment was withheld. R— then wrote asking for a cheque and received the reply that if he would come to England the money should be paid, but he never came and it is not known what became of him.

Two other American journalists who were believed to be agents of Winnenberg were stopped, but since the evidence was insufficient for bringing them to trial they were sent back to America with a strong caution against returning to England. It must be understood that the vast body of American correspondents was quite above suspicion. These spies were needy freelances who were on the outskirts of the profession.

CHAPTER 15

WOMEN SPIES

I T IS NO disparagement of the sex to say that women do not make good spies. Generally they are lacking in technical knowledge and therefore are apt to send misleading reports through misunderstanding what they hear. Their apologists have urged that one of their most amiable qualities, compunction, often steps in at the moment when they are in a position to be most useful: just when they have won the intimacy of a man who can really tell them something important they cannot bring themselves to betray his confidence.

Throughout the war, though women spies were convicted, no woman was executed in England. In France there were one or two executions apart from any that may have taken place near the Front, where espionage was highly dangerous. The case of Margaret Gertrud Zeller, better known as Mata Hari ('Eye of the Morning'), has overshadowed all the other cases. Her father was a Dutchman who, while in the Dutch East Indies, married a Javanese woman. He brought her home to Holland, and there the daughter became known as an exponent of a form of voluptuous oriental dancing that was new to Europe at that time. She was tall and sinuous, with glowing black eyes and a dusky complexion, vivacious in manner, intelligent and quick in repartee. She was, besides, a linguist. When she was about twenty she married a Dutch naval officer of Scottish extraction named Macleod, who divorced her.

She was well known in Paris and until the outbreak of war she was believed to be earning considerable sums of money by her professional engagements. She had a reputation in Holland, where people were proud of her success and, so cynics said, of her graceful carriage, which was rare in that country.

In July 1915 she was fulfilling a dancing engagement in Madrid, when information reached England that she was consorting with members of the German Secret Service and might be expected before long to be on her way back to Germany via Holland. This actually happened early in 1916. The ship put into Falmouth and she was brought ashore, together with her very large professional wardrobe and escorted to London. I expected to see a lady who would bring the whole battery of her charms to bear upon the officers who were to question her. There walked into the room a severely practical person who was prepared to answer any question with a kind of reserved courtesy, who felt so sure of herself and of her innocence that all that remained in her was a desire to help her interrogators. The only thing graceful about her was her walk and the carriage of her head. She made no gestures and, to say truth, time had a little dimmed the charms of which we had heard so much, for at this time the lady must have been at least forty.

I have said she was openness itself. She was ready with an answer to every question and of all the people that I examined during the course of the war she was the 'quickest in the uptake'. If I quoted to her the name of some person in Spain with whom it was compromising to be seen in conversation she was astounded. He a suspect? Surely we must be mistaken.

'I see how it is,' she said at last. 'You suspect me. Can I speak to you alone?' The room was cleared of all but one officer and myself. She looked at him interrogatively.

'I said "alone".'

'Yes,' I replied. 'This gentleman and I may be regarded as one person.'

'Very well,' she said. 'Then I am going to make a confession to you. I am a spy, but not, as you think, for the Germans, but for one of your allies – the French.'

I do not know to this moment whether she thought we would believe her, but she plunged then into a sea of reminiscence, telling us of the adventures she had undergone in pursuit of the objects of her employers. I wondered how many of them were true.

We had altogether two long interviews with Mata Hari and I am sure that she thought she had had the best of it. We were convinced now that she was acting for the Germans and that she was then on her way to Germany with information which she had committed to memory. On the other hand, she had no intention of landing on British soil or of committing any act of espionage in British jurisdiction and with nothing to support our view we could not very well detain her in England; so at the end of the second interview I said to her, '*Madame*,' (she spoke no English) 'we are going to send you back to Spain and if you will take the advice of someone nearly twice your age, give up what you have been doing.' She said, 'Sir, I thank you from my heart. I shall not forget your advice. What I have been doing I will do no more. You may trust me implicitly,' and within a month of her return to Spain she was at it again.

This time she was captured on the French side of the frontier and, as I heard at the time, with compromising documents upon her. I should have thought that so astute a lady would have avoided documents at all hazards. They carried her to Paris, put her on her trial and on 25 July 1916 condemned her to death, but there was, as there is usually in such cases, an interminable delay and it was not until 15 October that she was taken from Saint Lazare Prison to Vincennes for execution. A French officer who was present described to me what happened. She was awakened at five o'clock in the morning and she dressed herself in a dark dress trimmed with fur, with a large felt hat and lavender kid gloves. With an escort of two soldiers, her counsel and a padre, she was driven to Vincennes. When she came into sight of the troops she gently put aside the ministrations of the padre and waved a salute to the soldiers. She refused to be blindfolded and she was in the act of smiling and greeting the firing-party when the volley sent her pagan spirit on its journey.

Another lady who was taken off a ship in transit from Rotterdam to Barcelona was the cause of diplomatic remonstrances. She was a German named Lisa Blume and she was accompanied by an aged German duenna who had been a governess in her earlier years. Attention was first called to Fräulein Blume by the enormous quantity of baggage she was carrying. She had no fewer than seventeen trunks filled, for the most part, with expensive clothes, which hardly seemed to fit in with her story that she was housekeeper to a member of the German embassy in Madrid. She was most indignant at her treatment and she refused to answer any questions at all. Her duenna, however, was more communicative. Fräulein Blume, she said, was the daughter of a railway official in Germany and though undoubtedly housekeeper, she was also in confidential relations with the Counsellor of the embassy. When we came to search her baggage we discovered a ration of nine iron crosses, which she appeared to be conveying to the personnel of the German embassy. There was reason to believe, moreover, that she was the bearer of messages probably committed to memory, from the German government to their representatives. Under these circumstances we interned her and retained the decorations, but the duenna was allowed to proceed upon her journey. We thought it likely that the incident would not be allowed to pass without comment and in due course representations were received from two neutral Powers who, when the true relations of Fräulein Blume with her employer were explained, appear to have dropped the question rather hurriedly.

Towards the end of 1915 some very remarkable telegrams were handed in at Malta. They were a meaningless jumble of words and evidently a code and it was decided that the sender was a woman who called herself Madame Marie Edvige de Popowitch, a Serb, who had come to Malta for the state of her health. She looked astonishingly well for an invalid. Her flow of eloquence was reported to be extraordinary. Among her effects was found a Dutch dictionary in which certain words were underscored and some of these words occurred in the telegrams. On probing the possibility of this dictionary providing a code, it was found that the messages that were to have been dispatched to a certain port in the Mediterranean detailed the sailing of steamers from Malta. It was decided to send her to England to be dealt with and she was put on board HMS *Terrible*, together with two canaries, from which she refused to be separated. The voyage was stormy in more than one sense and the captain did his best to placate his prisoner, but it was whispered that on one occasion when he went to listen to her complaints about her rations she flung a beef-steak full in his face.

It was with this reputation that she came before us. On that occasion three officers were present besides myself. The lady entered my room calm but determined. She was one of the shortest women I have ever seen and certainly the broadest. Sitting in the low armchair, her head scarcely reached to the top of the table, but it would have been a mistake, I saw at once, to treat her as negligible in any other respect. She spoke French. In the earlier stages of our interview I was '*ce monsieur*', at a later stage I was '*ce maudit* policeman'. It was my rather searching inquiry into her reasons for possessing an ancient Dutch dictionary that provoked the change. The difficulty was that when any question was put to her she never stopped talking even to take breath. Her voice rose and rose until the very walls reverberated with it. I do not know what a welkin is, but I am quite sure that if we had had one over our heads that morning it would have been rung. Her excitement rose with her voice and, finding herself at the usual disadvantage in sitting in a low chair, she got up from it and came nearer and nearer until her gesticulations began narrowly to miss our faces. There was a point at which one of the officers with me began unostentatiously to remove the paper-knives, pens, rulers and other lethal weapons that lay at my right hand and to push them out of her reach, but she became at last so violent and her hands were so nearly at the level of our faces that we rose too and as she advanced upon us, still talking, we gave way, until she was at the table and we were half way to the door. As nothing would stem the torrent of her eloquence it was suggested in a whisper that we should all bow gravely to her and leave the room, sending in the proper people to get her into a taxi. I do not suppose that those silent and dignified vaulted corridors have ever re-echoed such language as the lady used on her way to the taxi. I was told afterwards that the storm would have been far more severe if it had not occurred to the wily inspector who had to deal with her to talk to her soothingly about her canaries.

Madame Popowitch was medically examined as to the state of her mind and we were advised that it would not be wise to try her on the capital charge. It was therefore decided to keep her in internment until the end of the war. She was removed to Aylesbury, where she bombarded the authorities with a myriad complaints. Nobody seemed to have pleased her except the captain of HMS *Terrible*, who, she said, never failed to inquire after the health of her canaries. All this time these canaries were being looked after by the police, but at the suggestion of the prison authorities they were sent to Aylesbury, where it was reported they had a calming effect upon their mistress. In the end Madame Popowitch was certified insane and removed to an asylum.

Eva de Bournonville was probably the most incompetent woman spy ever recruited by the Germans. She was a Swede, of French extraction, well educated and a linguist. Life had not prospered with her. She had been a governess in the Baltic Provinces, an actress (I should think a very bad one) and a secretary and typist employed occasionally at foreign legations. In the autumn of 1915 she was out of work, when she was approached by one of the spy-recruiting agents in Scandinavia. It chanced that she had an acquaintance in Scotland whom she had met in Sweden. To this lady she wrote that she was coming to England for the sake of her health and proposed to pay her a visit. Provided with a Swedish passport, she had no difficulty in entering the country: she was, moreover, a lady by birth and her manners were perfect.

On her arrival in London she put up at a cheap hotel in Bloomsbury and wrote to her friend in Dunbartonshire, saying that after a good rest she proposed to apply for a post in the Censorship, for which her friend might give her a recommendation. The Scottish lady sent her the address of some acquaintances in Hackney and advised her to call upon them. She did so and, finding that they were not at home, she left a card on which she had given the Danish Legation at Pont Street as her address, for it appears that she had made arrangements to have remittances sent to her through the Danish Legation. On this she received an invitation to Hackney where, however, she soon began to excite uneasiness in the minds of her new acquaintances. With all her education she was remarkably stupid at the business of espionage. She called again and again and went out walking with the family. There were a good many Zeppelin raids in those days and she was continually plying her host with questions about the anti-aircraft defences. Could she be taken to see the nearest gun? How many guns were there in London? How far could they shoot up in the air? And once, when she accompanied the family to Finsbury Park, she said, 'Oh, this is Finsbury Park. Where are the Zeppelin guns placed here?'

At last she asked her host to recommend her to the Postal Censorship and here he put down his foot and said, 'You see, if anything went wrong we should get into serious trouble.'

On this she dropped the family in Hackney, who remembered afterwards that she had said on one occasion, 'The Germans know everything that passes here. You cannot hide anything from them.'

She failed in her application to join the Censorship, chiefly on account of the lack of satisfactory English references. She told the lady who interviewed her how her father had been a general in the Danish Army and her grandfather a music-teacher to Queen Alexandra, while an aunt was still acting in that capacity to the Danish royal family.

She left Bloomsbury for lodgings in South Kensington and later for a certain ladies' club. Then she returned to Bloomsbury and put up at a private hotel in Upper Bedford Place, where army officers were wont to spend their leave. She was unremitting in her questions to subalterns.

For some time afterwards, letters proved to be in her handwriting, containing information that would not have been of much use to the enemy had he received it, had been intercepted, but beyond the handwriting there was nothing that would give the identity of the writer. At last certain observations in one of the letters pointed to a particular hotel in Upper Bedford Place, but in that hotel there were more than thirty guests and it was impossible to determine which of them was the spy. A certain officer who was employed on the case determined to test the matter in the simplest possible way. He selected one or two of the most likely of the guests and whispered to them incredible stories about secret engines of war that were in preparation. The most incredible of all was told to Eva de Bournonville and on the following day a letter was intercepted containing this very information which, if it had reached the German spy agent, ought to have caused his remaining hairs to rise in their places. De Bournonville was arrested on 15 November 1915. She expressed great surprise and made no admissions. In my room on the following day she made a brave show of innocence until I produced her letter and showed it to her, with the messages in secret ink between the lines developed. She opened her eyes very wide and said, 'Yes, it is my handwriting, but how did you get it?' I told her that I had got a good deal more. She then asked to be allowed to see me alone and the room was cleared of all but a military officer.

'You may think it curious,' she said,

> but I always wanted to work for you and not for the Germans. I am very fond of the English and the Belgians and I do not like the Germans at all. Never have I forgotten their behaviour to Denmark in 1864. My idea was to

make the Germans believe I was working for them until I was fully in their
confidence and then offer my services to you. I only did this for adventure.

It then appeared that the German military attaché in Sweden, acting with an agent of the Secret Service, had induced this wretched woman to imperil her life for £30 a month. A cheque for that amount was actually found in her possession on her arrest and she claimed to be allowed to keep it. She was tried before Mr Justice Darling at the Old Bailey on 12 January 1916 and was sentenced to death by hanging. Following our universal practice of not executing women, the King commuted the sentence to one of penal servitude for life. She was sent to Aylesbury to serve her sentence and was repatriated in February 1922. It transpired in the course of this case that the Germans were instructing their spies to address their letters to non-existent Belgian prisoners of war.

Towards the end of 1917 the Germans had ceased to employ agents in England for obtaining naval and military information. What they were then concerned about was the public morale, I suppose because their own was giving premonitory symptoms of crumbling. We first became aware of this through the letters written by a Mrs Smith to her relations in Germany. Mrs Smith proved to be a working housekeeper.

Originally she had been a German nurse in Switzerland, where she had married one of her patients, an English doctor, not long before his death. Having thus acquired British nationality, she came to England, where she found herself obliged to eke out the slender provision her husband had made for her by taking work as a housekeeper. Her letters, written in German, contained gems like the following:

Tell Uncle Franz that Fritz is perturbed at seeing so many of the trout in his
fish-pond eaten by the pike. If more pike get into the pond there will soon be
none of his trout left. It makes him very angry and frightened.

And in another letter she writes:

> *On Sunday I went out to see the place where the big birds roost. It was full of birds and some of them are very big indeed. It is said that they will soon take longer flights. I do not think that the great eagles that fly over us are frightening these birds; they only make them angry.*

Mrs Smith made a brave attempt to explain these letters away. She had, she said, an uncle named Franz who bred trout in a fish-pond and who had written to her about the depredations of pike. And about the great birds she ventured the suggestion that they were herons; but when we put before her our own interpretation of this simple code she became silent and resigned and she retired into internment at Aylesbury with a philosophic heart.

CHAPTER 16

CURIOUS VISITORS

O N 6 JANUARY 1916 a Dutch liner called in territorial waters at Falmouth and was boarded by naval officers. On the steamer were Colonel von Papen and Captain Boy-Ed, the German military and naval attachés from Washington. The boarding officer was quite polite, but he declared his intention of looking through their papers. On this von Papen protested vigorously that his papers were covered by the 'safe-conduct' that had been given by the British government. It was pointed out to him that the 'safe-conduct' applied to his personal liberty but not to his baggage or papers and without further ado the officer took possession of these and, among them, of all his used cheques, chequebooks and paying-in slips, which proved to be a mine of information. There were payments to a man who was known in the United States as a wrecker of bridges and to others who were known to have been guilty of sabotage. There were payments to Kuppferle, who committed suicide in Brixton Prison and to von der Goltz, as well as to other suspects.

It is said to be the fashion in Germany to lay much of the blame for defeat upon the ineptitude of the German diplomatic agents abroad and certainly Colonel von Papen, either by bad luck or bad management, had helped us not a little, for not long before this date Bernstorff had made a solemn declaration that no member of the embassy had had anything to do with sabotage or with espionage.

Bernstorff was not the first to use the diplomatic machinery for espionage. The foreign ambassadors at the Tudor and Stuart courts made considerable use of secret agents. In 1745 Monsieur Tiquet, the French diplomatic agent at Brussels, obtained from Grieling, a Brussels shopkeeper, plans of the fortresses of Nieuport and Dunkirk, in which, following German methods in our own day, he had worked as a labourer.

In the war of the Austrian Succession Count de Tilly, the French minister at Mannheim, got from an Italian named Pasetti, who was actually serving as an officer in the Austrian Army, information that determined the choice between the Rhenish and Flemish theatres of war. Belgium and Holland were then, as they have been in our own time, hotbeds of espionage against England, but one may read between the lines that even during the Seven Years' War the British Intelligence Service was more than a match for the French and that Louis XV spent very large sums to little purpose. In those days the *agent double* seems to have been as common as he is now.

Louis had scruples that would have seemed curious to the German General Staff in the late war. He would not listen to a scheme for causing a run upon the Bank of England by means of forged notes, or to employing Ivan Golofskin, the friend of the secretary to the Duke of Cumberland, who was exceptionally placed for obtaining information, but he was not above using duplicates of the Russian ambassador's dispatches addressed to his own government, or to arranging with the Czarina Elizabeth to pay her new ambassador £100,000 a year to send to the French government information about military plans of the British and especially the plans of the projected invasion of the low countries.

Spies in those days were treated with remarkable leniency. Robinson, a French spy arrested in London, was imprisoned for six months in the Tower in 1757 and was then released. Dr Hensey was arrested in London in June 1758 and sentenced to be hanged, but it is not certain that the sentence was carried out. This unusual severity was sufficient to frighten the other agents of the business.

It must not be supposed that no German spies in England went undetected. We learned of the operations of two or three after they had left the country and they were wise enough to attempt no second visit, but if one may judge from the character of the information supplied by those who were arrested the intelligence they gave to the Germans cannot have been of great value. Probably the spy who brought them the most useful information was a certain American journalist.

As the activities of German agents in America were gradually unfolded the American government began to take more drastic action. They opened the safe of von Igel and found there documents of extraordinary interest. To me the most interesting was a letter from the German Consul General at Shanghai to the Foreign Office in Berlin, in which he deplored his ill-fortune and gave an accurate account of the German Secret Service activities in the Far East, for there was nothing in the document that we did not know before; it might have served for a précis of German activities written in any British Intelligence Office.

The Germans made great use of sabotage in America. Unquestionably, they would have done the same in England if they could, but it would not be safe to say that none of the accidents that took place during the war was caused by sabotage. The difficulty was to know how much was due to criminal carelessness, how much to fanatical pacifism among our own people and how much to German agents or to Sinn Fein. I remember one case where matches were picked up in the mixing machine of a high-explosive factory. If even one of them had gone down into the mixer many hundreds of people would have lost their lives. The man who found the matches brought them to the foreman and received the thanks of the manager, but the police inspector who was sent down to investigate was a sceptical kind of person and insisted upon the finder of the matches re-constituting the crime by placing matches in the exact position in which he found them. The extreme uneasiness of the workman confirmed the inspector's suspicions and after a prolonged interview the man confessed that he had put the matches there himself and had taken them to the foreman in order to win credit and promotion from his employers.

From time to time bolts and hammer-heads were found in the crank cases of aeroplane engines, where they had evidently been placed by design. It is hard to believe that the man who put them there intended deliberately to send an airman to his death; perhaps all he aimed at was to wreck the machine during its bench test. The criminal in this case may have been a discontented workman or a fanatical pacifist of the 'stop-the-war committee' type.

It must certainly have been a man of this type who dropped a hammer-head into the gearing of a new tunnelling machine which was designed to bore tunnels 5 feet in diameter far underground. Fortunately, the obstruction was found before it had time to do any damage.

The propaganda carried on by the opponents to conscription during 1916 and 1917, particularly among the engineers and electricians, was certainly disturbing. Some of the electricians in one of our filling factories had been heard to enunciate violent revolutionary sentiments and their technical knowledge was such that they could at any time have contrived an accident which, while destroying the factory, might have caused no loss of life if it were so timed as to take place when the hands were at home.

In October 1917 there was a fire and explosion at a large factory in Lancashire which caused the death of ten people and enormous devastation. Sabotage was suspected, particularly as the factory was situated in a part of the country where Sinn Fein influences were strong, but nothing was ever proved.

At five minutes to seven on the evening of 19 January 1917, I was at a house in Kensington when the Silvertown explosion shook the house to the foundations. Our first thought was that a bomb had fallen quite near; our second that a gasometer had exploded. People in the street suggested an explosion at Woolwich Arsenal. The telephone cables had been cut by the explosion and it was some time before we knew what had happened. I visited Silvertown, the scene of the explosion, on the following afternoon. The devastation was extraordinary. For quite a mile before we reached the spot we drove through streets of broken windows and here the explosive had shown its usual caprice, for many panes of glass much nearer to the scene were intact. The firemen located the buried mains and coupled up their hose with wonderful rapidity and they soon had the fire under control. Meanwhile, the guards had carried out the very dangerous duty of searching for bodies. Forty-five persons were known to have been in the works at the time of the explosion, but practically no traces of them were to be found.

The fire had broken out in an upper storey, where a man and a woman were employed in feeding trinitrotoluene (TNT) into a hopper. Two women on the ground floor called up to ask whether they had sufficient explosive for the next twenty minutes and on hearing that they had they left the building for about a minute. As they came out the whole floor burst into roaring flame.

Now, it is known that a piece of a certain chemical substance no larger than a Brazil nut introduced into TNT will lie in it innocuous for months, but that on the application of heat it ignites the whole mass. The TNT was falling from the hopper into a temperature of 130 Centigrade: a small piece of the chemical would not have been noticed by the people feeding the hopper. This particular batch of explosive had been brought by train from the north of England and at any stage of its journey it would have been possible to introduce the chemical into one of the bags. But while the facts were consistent with sabotage there was no proof and the case of Silvertown must remain among the mysteries of the war. If it was sabotage surely eternal justice demands that some special place of chastisement be reserved hereafter for the fiend who caused it.

If the explosion at Arklow during the previous September, in which a number of people lost their lives, was not due to sabotage, the coincidence was remarkable, for threatening letters had been received by the management, but in that case it is probable that the Germans were not concerned.

There were many dramatic and a few amusing incidents during the examinations of suspected persons. The Germans had been using as spies people belonging to travelling circuses and shows, as being less likely to invite suspicion than the pseudo-commercial travellers, of whom we had taken a heavy toll. Consequently, a sharp look-out had been kept for messages from such people. One day a telegram to a world-famous American showman announced that the sender was ready to book his passage to New York. He was invited to call, the stage was set, the chair was ready – and there walked into the room a blue man! His face was a sort of light indigo set off with a bristling red moustache. He was a really terrifying spectacle. If we were surprised we did not show it. All we dreaded was what would happen to the stenographer when she would steal a glance at the object sitting beside her. Then the moment came. She leaped a foot from her chair with a little sob. He turned out to be an ex-cavalry sergeant who had turned blue after his discharge and now got his living honourably as a blue man. The stenographer was accustomed to men of colour, but never to that particular shade.

Among the curious persons who drifted into my room was a Dutch socialist Member of Parliament who had been admitted to the country on 19 May 1916, on condition that he gave an account of his intentions at Scotland Yard. As it turned out, he had been sent over to study food legislation in England, for the Dutch were in the uncomfortable position of having to contend with high food prices without a corresponding rise in wages and the government was attempting to regulate the maximum retail prices for all commodities, without much chance of success. He was astonished to hear that the only controlled commodities in England were sugar and coal. He was very indignant with the Amsterdam *Telegraaf*, in which Mr Raemakers's cartoons were being published. He said that the paper was trying to force Holland into war. 'We are a tiny country crushed between two giants.' He was very contemptuous of the official socialists in Germany, who he said did not represent their Party. They were elected over and over again as a matter of routine and when the government squared them, as it always did, the Party itself remained unaffected. In his opinion Liebknecht had a very large following even in the army itself. He said that the food riots reported from Germany were more serious than was generally supposed.

A few days later a Dutch socialist journalist came in. He was cheerful but very dirty and when I hinted that people were suspicious of him he said that it proceeded from envy and lack of principle. As for him, he lived by principle: he was an anti-smoker, an anti-drinker, a vegetarian and he wore no socks – all from principle. At this point he pulled up the leg of his trousers to prove his case, much to the scandal of the lady stenographer who was present. If I felt inclined to ask whether he went unwashed from principle I restrained myself.

It was about the same time that a mysterious person calling himself Colonel Dr Krumm-Heller was taken off a Danish steamer at Kirkwall. He must have expected that this would happen because he had been sending anticipatory protests by wireless all the way over. He claimed to be the Mexican military attaché in Berlin and to be well known in Mexico for his scientific, literary and philosophical works. His mission, he said, was to study schools in Scandinavia and not to become military attaché until he entered Germany: his real mission, we felt sure, was propaganda. When I told him that he might have to go back to Mexico he began to cry and said that Carranza would most certainly dismiss him. It became known to me a little later that he was carrying a letter from Bernstorff to the German government, but that when he found that he was to leave the steamer he had passed it to a Russian for delivery. The next day Colonel Dr Krumm-Heller offered to make a bargain with me. If I would not send him back he would reveal a new German plan and would thus save the Allies thousands of lives. But when it came to the point he had nothing at all to tell and back he went. In due course a demand was made upon the government for £10,000, at which he assessed his 'moral and intellectual' damages.

All this time England was seething with excitement about the battle of Jutland. The editor of a certain daily newspaper called on an officer of the Admiralty and said, 'We are not satisfied with Admirals Jellicoe and Beatty.'

'Who is "we"?' asked the officer.

'The public.'

'Oh,' said the naval officer,

then you are one of those people who, if you had lived a hundred years ago, would have said, 'Who's that one-eyed, one-armed beggar in charge of our Fleet? Have him out.' Now, look here, supposing you and I had a row in this room and you knocked my teeth out and I kicked you out of that door and you stood cursing in the passage, not daring to come in, would you say you had won a victory?

The same officer, when questioned by a pressman as to why the German fleet had come out, replied, 'They came out to get a mutton-chop for the Kaiser. I believe there were some other reasons, but these I am not at liberty to tell you.'

We were busy talking about the end of the war as early as October 1916, so busy that some satirist circulated the following rhyme:

Accurate evidence have I none,
But my aunt's charwoman's sister's son
Heard a policeman on his beat
Say to a nursemaid down our street
That he knew a man who had a friend
Who said he knew when the war would end.

One of the most romantic incidents in the war experience of Scotland Yard was the arrival in England of an educated Jew who had, against his own will, been closely associated with Djemal Pasha, the

Commander of the 9th Army in Palestine. According to his account, there had been attempts on the lives of both Djemal Pasha and Enver. In one attempt Djemal had received a bullet in the cheek. He gave a very curious account of the relations between Enver and Djemal. According to rumour, though they kiss one another on both cheeks and travel in the same car, each man has his hand upon his revolver as they sit side by side. The popular rumour at the time was that Enver had 600 men specially told off to protect his life and in 1916, when a plot against him was reported, he executed forty-two people merely on suspicion without any trial.

This man was a native of Haifa, in Palestine and was therefore a Turkish subject, though his parents had come from Romania. As a young man he had taken to scientific research work in agriculture and had gone through a course in Berlin. He was director of the Jewish Agricultural College. Djemal used to apply to him for advice on agricultural and economic matters. He said that all the Jews and Christians had been put into a labour battalion, where they were employed in road-making, on very slender rations. In some places they were under German direction, but in others under Turkish officers. In 1915 there had been a locust plague and in 1916 they had the worst harvest that had been known for thirty-five years and the population of Palestine was in dire straits. He believed it to be the policy of the Turkish government to allow them to starve, for Djemal Pasha did not approve of open massacres, but preferred starvation as a means of purging the population of what he regarded as its undesirable elements. He said there was great friction between the German officers and the Turkish and it was common talk in the German mess that they were more likely to fall from a bullet in the back than in the front. Very few of the Turkish officers seemed to believe in success. They talked of this campaign as their last fight and that they wanted to fall in it like men.

He had for some time been trying to get out of the country. He must have played his cards well, for in the end he obtained leave from Djemal Pasha to go to Berlin en route for Denmark for scientific agricultural study and from Copenhagen he succeeded in obtaining leave to come to England.

I heard afterwards that this man had been out to Egypt and Palestine, where he had put his local geological knowledge to good use. A year later he came to see me and he was convinced that from El Arish northward there is a water zone where water can be tapped at semi-artesian depths. This he had discovered when he was Agricultural Adviser to the Zionists. Borings in this area produced water, which rose to within 30 feet of the surface. He was a great reader and he told me that his attention had been first called to the water question through reading Josephus, who describes Caesarea as being surrounded by gardens for an eight hours' walk in every direction, whereas now it is a sandy desert right up to the walls through the encroachment of the sand. He said that he had tried very hard to persuade our engineers to try the experiment, but when at last they did there was an abundant supply of water and it was no longer necessary to bring tanks by rail from Egypt. He was convinced that experimental borings in the Sinai desert would produce water in the same way and thus the Mosaic miracle of striking the rock with a staff may be performed again in the twentieth century.

After the Armistice I saw this man again in a new capacity. He was a member of a deputation of Zionists to the Peace Conference. He had a tragic end. He took an aeroplane to fly to London on some urgent business; the machine came to grief and he and his companions plunged into the Channel and were lost.

CHAPTER 17

THE END OF RASPUTIN

S EVERAL ACCOUNTS HAVE been published of the assassination of Rasputin, differing in detail. This event had so much to do with the collapse of Russia that I took pains to collect evidence as to what actually happened.

As everyone knows, during the autumn of 1916 Rasputin had succeeded in gaining complete ascendency over the Czar and Czarina. He was a person who could have existed only among the Russians. He gloried in being a peasant of the grossest and most common clay, but, just as a filthy fakir in India can acquire a reputation for holiness by his self-imposed penances, so a Russian moujik can do the same if he has personality, cunning and a smattering of ecclesiastical lore. Rasputin had all these and he was, besides, a creature of immense physical strength and physical temperament. His doctrine was that the cure for all human ills was humility and he set out to humble the great ladies of the court. He had some curious magnetic power which he exercised more successfully over women than over men, but even men felt it. His influence over the royal family was such that he was able to persuade the Czar that the only medical attendant to whom he should listen was the Tibetan herbalist, Batmaef, whom Rasputin described as a doctor appointed by God. The story in court circles was that Batmaef administered herbal decoctions to the Czar himself and, by this means, weakened his will-power.

In the late autumn there were rumours that Rasputin's influence had been bought by the Germans to persuade the Czar to make a separate peace and Youssoupov, one of the young nobles, determined to worm himself into Rasputin's confidence in order to ascertain the truth of these rumours. After some weeks he succeeded in winning his confidence and at last, in an interview lasting for two hours, Rasputin revealed the whole plan to him. A separate peace was to be proclaimed by the Czar on 1 January 1917 and it was then the second week in December. There was, therefore, no time to lose.

Rasputin was the most 'protected' person in Russia. He was said to be watched over by two German detectives, a detective appointed by a group of bankers and an imperial detective who was responsible for his personal safety. The little group which was resolved upon his death believed that they were under the direction of a Higher Power because everything fitted in so perfectly and easily with their design. Rasputin seemed positively to cultivate the society of Youssoupov, who called upon him a day or two before Christmas and said that he was about to leave for the Crimea to spend Christmas there and that as Rasputin had never set foot in his house, he had come to invite him to drink tea with him that evening: he would consider it the greatest honour. Rasputin did not demur at all. He said, laughingly, that he would tell the detectives he was going to bed and that they were free for the evening and he invited Youssoupov to call for him in his car at the back door in order to give the slip to any detective who might remain on duty.

In Prince Youssoupov's house there was a dining room in the basement. From this a winding staircase led to the first floor, with a landing halfway giving into the hall. On this landing was a small room. On arriving at the house Rasputin was conducted into this dining room, where bottles of madeira and port were set out. The conspirators had previously obtained from a chemist a drug known in Russian as 'cianistii kalii', which was said to have a very quick action on the heart and to be tasteless when taken in wine. It was in the form of a white powder contained in glass tubes and the quantity introduced into the wine was believed to be sufficient to kill twenty men. During the afternoon the potion had been tried upon one of the dogs in the courtyard and the effect was immediately fatal.

They sat down at the table and Youssoupov plied Rasputin with the wine. There was nothing in this, for Rasputin, like most Russian peasants, had a strong head and was always ready for carousal. He was quite unconscious that there was anything unusual in the taste of what he was drinking, but as time went on and conversation flagged Youssoupov began to realise that the poison would not act upon such a man. He made an excuse for going upstairs to the little room on the landing, where his friends were waiting. The Grand Duke Dmitri lent him his revolver and he went down again, feeling, as he said, that he was not acting of his own volition, but was under the direction of a Higher Power. He found Rasputin leaning on his hands and breathing loudly as if he was not feeling well. At the end of the dining room was a large ikon. Youssoupov went and knelt before it to pray for strength to do what he had to do for the salvation of the country. Then Rasputin got heavily to his feet, came over to the ikon and stood beside him. Youssoupov rose, put the pistol to Rasputin's side and fired. Rasputin uttered a terrible cry and fell backwards on the floor, where he lay motionless. There was a doctor in the little room upstairs and Youssoupov went to call him. All came down with the doctor; some were in favour of firing another shot to make sure, but the doctor, on examining the wound, declared that the bullet had entered the heart and had pierced the liver and that clearly the man was dead. Then they went upstairs to consult about a car in which the body was to be removed. This took some time and then Youssoupov, in whose mind the idea had been working that Satanic power might have kept the man alive in spite of his wound, went down alone into the dining room to make sure. The body was still lying in the same place. He felt the pulse: it was not beating. He opened the monk's robe to feel the heart. At that moment Rasputin, with a terrible cry, sprang up and seized him by the throat. He was throttling him. Then superhuman power came upon Youssoupov, who flung him down on the floor: he lay without motion.

With the horror of this incident upon him Youssoupov ran upstairs. The Grand Duke, the doctor and another officer had gone away for the car and only Poroskewitz, a member of the Duma, was left and he had a pistol with three cartridges left in it. To him Youssoupov poured out his story. They came out on the landing with the intention of descending the staircase and, looking down, they saw the bullet-head of the monk coming up the staircase. He was on all fours like a bear. They shrank back into the room and saw him stagger to his feet on the landing and go through into the hall. They followed. Rasputin fumbled with the door leading to the courtyard, dragged it open and went through into the darkness. The two men ran to the door and saw him against the snow as he was crossing the courtyard. Poroskewitz fired three shots, but he still ran for several paces and then fell close to the gateway which led from the courtyard into the street. Youssoupov had with him a rubber truncheon such as the police use and, finding him still alive, put an end to him with that weapon. It was then seen that one of the revolver bullets had hit him in the back of the skull and still he had lived.

Poroskewitz returned to the house and while Prince Youssoupov was standing irresolute by the body there came a knocking on the gate. The police had been alarmed by the revolver shots and had sent an agent to make inquiries. It was a critical moment because the body was lying only a few feet from the gate. Youssoupov opened the gate and admitted the man, placing himself in front of the body. The policeman wanted to know if anything was wrong. Youssoupov took a high tone with him; said that the Grand Duke had been dining there and had just left in a car; that he was slightly merry and had fired his revolver at a dog in the courtyard and had killed it: that was all. While he was speaking he was edging the police agent towards the gate and at the mention of the Grand Duke the man seemed to be satisfied. It must be remembered, too, that the high rank of the person he was questioning may have had its effect. The report he brought to the police station, however, did not satisfy his superiors. He was sent back to make further inquiries and this time he went to the front door and was admitted without Youssoupov's knowledge while he was engaged in dragging the body across the courtyard. When the Prince re-entered the house he heard voices in the sitting room upstairs. There he found that Poroskewitz, who was a very excitable and nervous man, had blurted out the whole truth and said that they had killed Rasputin. It was a desperate moment. Youssoupov quickly intervened, saying, 'Look, he has gone clean off his head. When the dog was shot he said, "What a pity it was not Rasputin," and now it has become an obsession with him and he thinks that what he wanted has really come to pass.' After a good deal of talking he succeeded in getting the policeman to go.

There was now no time to lose. Several things had to be done.

A dog had to be found and shot and laid exactly in the position of Rasputin's body in order that the blood marks on the snow might be taken for the blood of the dog. Scarcely had this been done when the Grand Duke's car arrived. In Russia grand-ducal cars used to carry a flag on the bonnet which exempted them from being stopped by the police. Together they carried the body into the car, took it to the bridge and dropped it into the frozen Neva, where it was found some three days afterwards.

The next morning there was an interrogation at the police station, but the same story was adhered to and the police could make little headway. It is said that the Czarina was pressing for extreme measures against the assassins, but that the Czar, who was about to return to the Front, refused his consent. People who were about him at the time said that he had never seemed more cheerful than when he heard of Rasputin's death. The assassins were banished to the Caucasus and to Persia.

When will the romance of escapes during the Great War be adequately written? There were stories of Russian peasant prisoners escaping from internment and wandering over the frontier into Switzerland not knowing that they were in a neutral country, living in the woods like wild animals, with hair and nails grown long, unwashed, unkempt, half-naked, subsisting upon food taken from the farms at night and eaten raw. There was one, better authenticated, of a Russian officer who, after five days' wandering, succeeded in crossing the frontier into Holland with his pursuers behind. The Dutch had recently changed their uniform into field-grey, the colour worn by the Germans and, seeing a platoon of grey-coated soldiers in front of him, the wretched fugitive turned back and re-crossed the frontier in full view of the German sentry, who shot him dead.

Who knew at that time that a necessary part of the equipment of an escaping prisoner of war was pepper, because the German dogs would scent him at night in his lair and raise the neighbourhood by their barking? But if he scattered pepper about his resting-place the dogs would sneeze and slink off home in silence.

Though there were escapes of British officers and men and civilians from internment in Germany, I believe that only one German officer succeeded in escaping from Donington Hall and reaching Germany. This was Gunther Plüschow, an aviation officer from Tsingtau, who escaped in his machine when the fortress was captured by the Japanese, made his way to Shanghai and thence to San Francisco and New York. Here he obtained a false Swiss passport as a fitter under the name of Ernst Suse, with which he embarked for Italy. But to his great indignation our interpreter at Gibraltar spoke such fluent German that he was betrayed into unguarded observations. He was arrested and sent to England, where, after many vicissitudes, he proved his identity as an officer and was interned at Donington.

His escape from Donington Hall was managed with great skill. On 4 July 1915, he and an officer named Treffitz reported sick and remained in bed. At roll-call the NCO ticked them off. It was raining hard and they had no difficulty in slipping away to the outer enclosure and hiding in the bushes. At 6 p.m. the doors between the inner and outer enclosures were locked and they remained outside. Other officers were occupying their beds when the roll was taken and at 10.30 'Die Wacht am Rhein' was sung from the windows to inform them that they had not been missed. They climbed the wire entanglements and made for Derby, where they separated, each man finding his way independently to London.

In his book published in Dutch, *Adventures of the Tsingtau Flying Man*, Plüschow gave an account of his proceedings while trying to board the Dutch packet, which did more than justice to his courage and endurance and less than justice to the truth. According to this narrative he spent his nights in Hyde Park, suburban gardens and in a lair under a timber stack at Greenwich. Twice he was plunged into the stinking mud at low water and nearly drowned while setting out in the dark to swim to the mooring buoy. But, in fact, as we discovered too late, he eluded the registration regulations by passing his nights with different women, at whose rooms he was not called upon to register at all, for he was amply provided with money and he knew London well from a former sojourn in 1913. He boarded the buoy to which the *Princess Jidiana* was moored, climbed the cable and hid himself in one of the lifeboats. Probably he stole a landing-card from a sea-sick passenger, or he may, as he says, have walked ashore without one, unchallenged. At any rate, he landed at Rotterdam and was accorded an ovation by the German colony at a public luncheon arranged by the German Consul.

In May 1916, when the last batch of German officers was received at Donington Hall, it was reported that the prisoners were plunged into deep depression by the news from the German front.

CHAPTER 18

RECRUITS FOR THE ENEMY

I SUPPOSE THAT some day or other one of the Assistant Provost Marshals who served in France will be moved to publish some of his experiences. Most of his work was dull and uneventful, but every now and then there flared up one of those sordid little tragedies which human nature, under the stress of war, is apt to give out. One summer day in 1916 the APM at Boulogne received from an Australian escort a grimy envelope on which nothing was written but, 'The APM, Boulogne. Herewith Jim Perry.' (Perry was not the name.) He asked why he should receive Jim Perry and what Jim Perry had done. About this the escort knew nothing at all. All he had to do was to deliver Jim Perry and bring back a receipt for his body. For the rest, the APM had better ask Jim Perry himself. Perry, when produced, turned out to be a well-educated young man born in South Africa, with the marks about him of having undergone a rather strenuous experience, but in this there was nothing unusual as far as the clients of an APM were concerned.

Jim Perry's story deserves to live. As soon as he heard that war had been declared he left South Africa in order to join up in England. He was drafted to the Officers' Training Corps, but finding the corps uncongenial, he deserted and walked off to a certain Australian battalion which was then training in England for the Front. There was a free and easy way about the Australians that pleased a fellow colonial. They welcomed their new recruit and did not think it necessary to report his arrival to the officers. The privates collected some kind of a kit for him from among themselves and as a roll-call never seems to have been taken in this particular battalion, Perry was able to serve with them over two months in England and afterwards to accompany them to France. He was five weeks with them in Abbeville and then they were moved up to the front line. Here he was with them for five weeks more and he might have continued to be an Australian soldier until the Armistice but for a mishap. One day the battalion came out of action with a good many casualties and the younger officers organised a spy hunt. The first step was to do what they had never done before – to call the roll and during this unwonted ceremony it was discovered that they had with them one man more than they ought to have had. Here, obviously, was the spy. Jim Perry was put under arrest and the subalterns held a consultation. The remedy was obvious. Jim Perry should be shot at sight. They were about to carry out the decision of the meeting when one of them said that he remembered reading somewhere that you never shot a man without reporting first to the colonel, so this formality was complied with and the colonel, who saw nothing in the verdict of which he disapproved, remembered to have read somewhere that you never shot a man without first reporting to the brigadier. This was a great disappointment to the subalterns, who were all for action stern and swift.

Now the brigadier happened to know something about military

law and he pointed out that as no court-martial had been convened and no evidence had been called, whatever else was done no shooting could take place. This annoyed the battalion excessively. The decision came just at a time when they were leaving their rest camp and they had no intention of taking with them into action an unmasked spy. Perry could not be shot, but he could be left behind, so they took him into a barn, handcuffed his hands and feet round the post which supported the roof, locked the door and went away. There Perry remained in this extremely uncomfortable position for two whole days and then the South African angel which watched over him ordained that another Australian battalion should march into the village and require the barn, should break down the door and find Jim Perry. He seemed to want food and water very much, so they fed and watered him and made a pet of him and when their turn came to return to the trenches they wanted to take him with them, but here the colonel intervened. To him there seemed to be something irregular about taking a man whom you have found chained to a post into action with your battalion even as a mascot. He reported the occurrence and asked for instructions and these were that Perry should be sent to the base. It was under these circumstances that an escort of the Good Samaritans had brought him to Boulogne with the grimy envelope.

Even an APM has a heart and this one decided to send Perry to England to begin again at the beginning – in other words, to enlist in any regiment that came handy and draw a veil over his past and as Perry had no money he pulled out of his pocket a £1 note. Perry looked at it dubiously and said, 'Money? That's no use to me, sir. I have plenty of money of my own. What I want is my chequebook.' And this turned out to be perfectly true. Perry's father was a wealthy man and the son had a banking account.

Later in the war a large number of German Army reservists in Spain and South America and a certain number of German prisoners of war taken on the Russian Front who had escaped from Siberia began to cross from America in the hope of reaching Holland without being recognised at the English port as enemies. It was a regular business with the German Consulate to furnish them with forged passports. They were Swedes, South Americans and Dutchmen, according to their papers, and they assumed the nationality of the language which they happened to be able to speak. Sometimes we knew when particular persons were coming; at others the naval officers at the ports had to use their own intelligence and very well they did it. There was one rather pathetic case in which I almost wished that they had been less successful. It was reported from Kirkwall that two of the stokers on a Swedish ship were men of above the ordinary education of stokers and that they were on their way down to London. I examined them separately. The first gave in rather quickly. He was the last kind of person who could have hoped to pass muster as a stoker. He had not even succeeded in making his hands rough. He was a Viennese reserve captain of artillery, who had relations in Paris and had been called up straight from the bank in which he was employed. He took his internment as a prisoner of war with perfect philosophy. It was one of the ordinary accidents of war and he would rather be interned in a British camp than under the appalling conditions that prevailed in Siberia, but it did seem hard to have been taken prisoner twice in the same war after walking some thousands of miles across Asia. I sometimes hear from him still. When I first saw the other man I thought that our boarding officer had made a mistake. He was a sooty, smiling, alert little person and he slouched into the room with the regular stoker's lurch. He answered all my questions and picked out on the map the little village in Sweden where he was born. He talked Swedish with apparent fluency and his hands were as dirty as anyone could expect from a stoker. Nevertheless, we sent him to Cannon Row for further inquiry. Cannon Row was his undoing. He had guessed that his companion in adversity must be in a cell not far from his and as the place seemed very quiet he thought it safe to call him up in German through the ventilator. He did not know that a German-speaking police officer was in hearing. His companion replied and the flood-gates of our friend's eloquence were opened. 'They got nothing out of me,' he shouted. 'They really believe that I am a Swedish stoker. How did you get on?' (No reply.) 'The proper way is to bluff them and if you do it well they will swallow anything.'

When he came before me next morning I told him that he had played his part very well indeed; in fact, that if he ever cared to try his luck upon the stage I was sure that he would make a fortune. He grinned a little uneasily, I thought. 'And now,' I said, 'since the game is up you might wash your face and hands, put on a collar and write a letter to your friends in Vienna, asking them to send your military uniform in order that we may treat you in internment as an officer.' His whole manner changed. Instinctively he pulled himself to attention, gave me the name of his regiment and the address of his friends and before he left the room he clicked his heels and walked out of it like a trained soldier. To this day he does not know where my information came from.

From Falmouth they sent me one day a curly headed and rotund young gentleman from Chile. He spoke Spanish like a native and he was bound for Rotterdam to buy cheap cigars for his firm in Valparaiso. Also he spoke English, which he professed to have learned in New York during the course of his business travels. Unfortunately for him, there had been on the steamer an Austrian woman with whom he had spent much of his time and just before he was called to go ashore he had been seen to slip into her hand a folded piece of paper. She retired to the cabin to open and read this note, but one of the boarding officers followed her and recovered it. It was a German letter written in pencil and it said, 'Whatever you do, you must not reveal the fact that I speak German.' This note was on my table when he came in for examination and with me was sitting as Admiralty representative the late Lord Abinger who spoke German fluently. He kept his knowledge in reserve.

The young man was quite charming. He answered all my questions without hesitation; he thought that some generations ago one of his ancestors might have been a German, but he was not well enough versed in the family history to give me full details about this. Many Chileans, he said, had fair curly hair like his and a fresh complexion, because the Chilean sun does not burn the skin as it does in Peru. Yes, he spoke English fluently but not German. It was one of the regrets of his life that he had never learned that language. We gave him writing materials and set the lamp as he liked it and then I said, 'Draw up your chair and this gentleman will set you a piece of dictation.' Then Lord Abinger cleared his throat and dictated the Spanish text of his passport. The handwriting, as I could see, was the same as that of the note. While he was still writing I handed his German note to Lord Abinger who, without break or pause, followed on with the German text. The curly head was not raised. All I could see was a deep flush creeping over the cheek. The hand stopped writing. 'Well,' I said, 'you do not seem to be getting on.'

'The gentleman is dictating in a language I do not know.'

'He is reading from a letter written by yourself.'

There was a long silence, during which the pencil dropped on the floor and at last the young man rose wearily from the armchair and said, 'Well, what are you going to do with me? You have me in your power.' He was quite ready then to answer questions and I believed him when he said that his only object in coming over was to do his duty, because he could not bear to have it thrown in his teeth afterwards that he had taken no part in the Great War. He added, philosophically, that he supposed that they could not reproach him if he was interned in an enemy country and I, looking at his fat hands and his ample proportions, added the comfortable reflection that he would find internment far safer than service in the trenches.

In January 1917, an American boasting the name of Jelks Leroy Thrasher was found on board the Dutch passenger steamer *Zeelandia* when she put into Falmouth on her way to Holland. Mr Thrasher was a young, clean-shaven man who had something about him of military courtesy, which scarcely accorded with the account that he was prepared to give of himself. For this reason he was asked to land and sent to me for an interview. He had quite a marked American accent and yet there was something about it that did not quite carry conviction. After the usual caution he became even more communicative than before and was ready to tell me every detail of his past life from his very earliest years. There was something quite uncanny about his memory. He could describe the colour of people's hair whom he could have known only when he was just out of the perambulator. He was never at a loss for a name and his elaborate description of Quitman, Georgia, where he said he had passed his early life, would have astonished the residents of that little-known centre. There were, of course, a few discrepancies and as the examination proceeded he began to show uneasiness. I said at last, 'Do you know, you are not telling your story very well?' He looked concerned and bowed – from the waist. I said, 'Your accent is not quite American, though it is a very good imitation.' He again bowed, as before, from the waist. What I wanted was a name to put to him and so we adjourned for luncheon to consider what Germans were at the moment loose upon the world on unlawful pursuits. It happened that about this time the German government had had occasion to send a direct messenger to New York in connection with the negotiations for landing arms in Ireland and it was intended, no doubt, that the messenger should afterwards proceed to Holland in the guise of an American. The officer's name was known to be Captain Hans Boehm. There were several other Germans wandering about, but as this man seemed the most likely I thought I would try him first.

After luncheon Mr Thrasher resumed his seat and I again referred unkindly to his American accent, which I pointed out to him was too laboured for an American. At last I said, 'You are not doing this well, Captain Boehm.' He looked surprised, but said nothing. 'No, Captain Boehm, you are not doing it well.' He smiled and again bowed from the waist. I said, 'Take, for example, your bow. No American bows like that.' He laughed and bowed again and, as he made no objection to being called Captain Boehm, I said, 'Perhaps I am not quite fair. You had a very difficult part to play and you played it better than any German officer who has yet sat in that chair.' That pleased him and after a little pressing he told me most of his story. He was the son of an official in Alsace, was well educated and had spent a good deal of his life in America. During 1916 he was commanding a battery of artillery near Wytschaete in Flanders and, on account of his reputation as an American, he had been taken out of the line to be employed upon a special mission. He was now on his way back. He would tell me nothing about the nature of his employment – that we knew from another source – but he did admit that he had met Roger Casement while in Germany. It afterwards appeared that there had been a man of the name of Jelks Leroy Thrasher in Quitman, Georgia, but he was dead. Probably the passport was one of those that had been retained by the German government on the pretence that it had been lost at the Foreign Office when sent thither for a visa. Captain Boehm was treated as a military prisoner and told that as soon as his uniform arrived he would be treated as an interned officer. He wrote to his friends from Brixton on 17 January 1917 saying:

> *I wish to emphasise that the treatment meted out to me right throughout has been very good. From Admiral to seamen, all were very kind to me and the comprehension of the situation was superior. The Admiral said to me, 'We have no interest to make difficulties for an enemy who can do us no more harm.' Please bring these lines to the knowledge of my superiors in the General Staff. If you can do a friendly action to an English prisoner do it.*

A great many neutrals used to come in about this time after their journeys in the enemy countries. One of them had had a talk with von Tirpitz. He had called to give the family news of their son, who was a prisoner of war and while they were at tea von Tirpitz himself came in. He described him as looking like a very untidy old farmer, with socks hanging down over his boots and chalk marks all over his trousers, but his expression exhaled benevolence quite out of keeping with the fire-eating advice he was giving to the German government on the subject of submarines. He complained bitterly of the conduct of the Americans in making munitions for the Allies. My friend pointed out that if the Germans would send ships to fetch munitions, as the Allies did, they could be supplied too and remarked, 'If you had command of the sea, would you not obtain them from us?'

'Of course we would,' said von Tirpitz.

I have said little about that admirably managed department, the Postal Censorship, because much of its work was necessarily confidential, but there was nothing new about its functions. At the time of the Great Fire the General Post Office was situated in Cloak Lane off Dowgate Hill. There was no Postmaster-General; the service was farmed out and the lessee at that time was Katharine, Countess of Chesterfield, acting through her agent, Sir Philip Frowde. Under him was the actual postmaster, one James Hickes, whose claim to fame was that he kept the office open throughout the Great Plague and saved most of the letters on the night of the Great Fire. There was at that time an inventor, Sir Samuel Morland, who, among other inventions, had devised the capstan and the speaking trumpet and we are told that an apparatus for the opening and rapid copying of letters was among the property that perished in the Great Fire of London. What the machine was that kept Charles II three hours 'seeing with admiration and very great satisfaction' the various operations, that copied a letter in little more than one minute before photography was invented, will never be known because Morland omitted to invite Samuel Pepys to a demonstration and allowed his secret to die with him.

All sorts of queer people came to light through the censorship of letters. One would have thought that during the agonies of war there would have been no time for the innocent forms of internationalism, but it is a fact that in nearly every country in the world one could find international chess-players so detached from public affairs that they were actually conducting games by post in 1917. The Censor stopped a postcard in a foreign handwriting addressed to Spain with the usual chess formulae on its back. The card was tested in every possible way for secret writing and it seemed so incredible that any one should be playing chess with a foreign antagonist at such a moment that we concluded that a new form of spy communication by means of chess formulae had been adopted by the enemy. After some search we found the writer. He proved to be a young Spaniard, little more than a boy, who lived in a squalid room near Tottenham Court Road with practically no personal effects except a chessboard. He was genuinely astonished at being hauled before the authorities. During the day-time he was a waiter at a restaurant, but in his spare moments – and there could not have been many of them – he was conducting twenty-four games of chess by post with antagonists in foreign countries whom he had never seen. He had heard that 'there was a war on', but apparently as long as it did not interfere with his games it was no concern of his.

It was clear that the British Navy was doing its work well. A letter found concealed in a parcel addressed to a German prisoner which was intercepted in January 1917 gave us some very useful information. The writer had been recently repatriated from Wakefield via Stratford and he gives the following account of what he imagines he saw:

> We left Stratford in the omnibus on Sunday evening, driving to Charing Cross through London's dark streets, which are fearfully depressing. We saw a few houses destroyed by the Zeppelins, but it was only here (in Germany) that I got some photographs which show that the whole corner from the Haymarket, Piccadilly, the complete block of residences over the Piccadilly Tube Station had been clean swept away.

He went on to give minute instructions, based upon his own experience, how gold and other prohibited articles could be smuggled out of the country without interference from the military and the police – a part of his letter which caused us to stop a number of leaks. In the early days of the war a good deal of gold was successfully smuggled out. One German woman had gone to the expense of having a false bottom made to her handbag, which proved on examination to be floored with sovereigns. Its weight was its undoing.

This verbose correspondent was guarded when he wrote about the state in which he found Germany. 'I will only tell you one thing,' he wrote: 'times are serious; much, much more serious than any one has ever thought. So, for instance, it is in my opinion a direct active meanness if anybody in the camp has had sent to him eatables of any sort, even in the smallest quantities.'

CHAPTER 19

THE DECLINE OF MORALE

I N JUNE 1916 the Germans adopted a new policy. They began to send distinguished neutrals, generally Swedes, who entered the country as ardently pro-British and told us that a recent visit to Berlin had convinced them that the economic situation in Germany was far stronger than in England and that England was faced with the certainty of defeat unless she agreed with her enemy quickly. In one case the Swede proposed that our government should select six businessmen and send them to Holland to meet six Germans and thus convince themselves of the truth of what he said! He was surprised and pained when he heard that his invitation had been refused. I wish I had seen him after the Armistice to remind him of his passionate assurances that the Germans whom he professed to dislike so much were about to triumph.

There were many other indications that the Germans were becoming anxious about their morale. It was common talk among the interned officers in Donington Hall in September 1917 that they could not expect to win the war, but they still hoped to be able to hold out long enough to secure a 'draw'.

The peace feelers of the Austrians led to a very curious incident. In March 1916 two distinguished Spanish gentlemen were ushered into my room. One, who bore an ancient title, was the proprietor of a Madrid newspaper; the other, who spoke English fluently and was married to an American, was vouched for as a person of wealth and position. He explained that he had a scheme for obtaining for the Allies the use of all the Austrian ships interned in Spain and the titled gentleman bowed and smiled as an endorsement, though it was doubtful whether he understood enough English to know what was said. Señor P— had with him all the impedimenta of a wealthy traveller – wife, children, governess, secretary, servants and baggage and he had engaged a suite of rooms. He had interviews with various distinguished people, but there was something rather nebulous about his proposals and he did not produce any written guarantee of his good faith. It happened that on the staff of a certain daily newspaper there was a gentleman who knew Spanish. Upon him Señor P— seized, for he could bring him into touch with the newspaper world and so mobilise public opinion in favour of taking over the Austrian ships. Just before Easter Señor P— informed me that he intended to go to Holland and there meet certain Austrian shipping magnates with whom he hoped to negotiate the transfer. On Good Friday I was rung up by the newspaper man, who asked my advice. Señor P— had begged him to accompany him to Holland. Was there any objection? Knowing that he was to be trusted and that he might keep an eye upon the Spaniard's movements and let me know what it was all about, I helped him with his passport and the two went off together. Two days later I received a telegram from Rotterdam, begging me to meet the pressman in my office on Easter Sunday as he had something important to communicate. The poor man had been travelling all night and was in a state of nervous tension. He told me the following story:

On the way down the river Señor P— had remarked, 'I ought to tell you without delay that all this about the Austrian ships is a blind. What we are really going to do is to negotiate a peace between Austria and the Allies.' With that, he pulled out of his pocket a telegram which read as follows:

> *I appoint Señor P— and Mr H— to be my Plenipotentiaries for making peace.*
> *Lord Robert Cecil*

Mr H— pointed out that this was a forgery; that Lord Robert Cecil would not have sent or signed a telegram in this way, nor would he have thought of appointing either Señor P— or himself as plenipotentiaries. Señor P— burst out laughing. 'Never mind,' he said, 'these little artifices are necessary when great events hang in the balance. I shall show this telegram to the Austrians and they will believe it.'

On arriving at Rotterdam Mr H— found that three Austrian gentlemen had actually arrived and he was taken into a conference in a hotel. Señor P— did most of the talking and was particularly eloquent on the financial question. You could not, he said, have peace without paying for it and peace in this case was worth a million sterling to Austria if it was worth a crown. They haggled for some time over the deal, and Señor P— left the room for a moment to find a document, whereupon the Austrians asked Mr H— what he knew of his Spanish friend. They had made inquiries about him in Berlin and what they had learnt was not very much in his favour. 'But,' they said, 'whether we care to negotiate with him or not, we do welcome the opportunity of meeting face to face the proprietor of a great London daily newspaper.'

'I am not the proprietor,' said Mr H— in amazement. 'I am merely a humble employee.'

They waved this politely aside. Great men often travel incognito. He was, of course, Lord — in disguise. He continued to disclaim the compliment and they said, 'Well, whoever you are, you are in a position to convey to the proper quarter our views regarding a peace between Austria and the Allies.' With that, they handed him the following paper:

M. Emil Karpeles and Mr H—, respectively an Austrian and a British subject, having been brought together at Amsterdam by Mr de P—, starting from the idea of their two countries being in a position to initiate preliminaries for peace and to become for a long period trustees for peace in Europe, undertake to submit to their respective governments the ten clauses named below in order to obtain from them a declaration of their agreeing to them in principle. By giving such declarations the two governments accept these ten clauses as the basis of a preliminary conference to be held as soon as possible within four weeks from today in Holland or Switzerland. The conference is to be composed of the same number of delegates from the two parties and two delegates appointed by His Majesty the King of Spain. This preliminary conference will also arrange conditions and regulations for the exchange of goods between the two countries for the time of an armistice if such be proclaimed.

Clause 1. The re-establishment of the Kingdom of Serbia, with limits as before the Treaty of London, the King to be chosen by Great Britain and Austria-Hungary, the province of Negotin to come to Austria-Hungary.

2. The re-establishment of the Kingdom of Montenegro. Lovcen and the coast to go to Austria-Hungary against territorial compensation on the east frontier.

3. Albania. Sovereign to be chosen by Great Britain and Austria-Hungary.

4. Limits as after the first Balkan war, inclusive Macedonia (exchange Kavalla against Valona with Greece?).

5. Greece. See clause 4.

6. Italy to abandon influence on east coast of the Adriatic. A rectification of the Austro-Italian frontier if desired by Austria-Hungary to be agreed to by Italy. No war contribution.

7. Turkey. Status quo ante. Signatory powers guarantee integrity of the Turkish Empire.

8. Belgium. Re-establishment against return German colonies to Germany.

9. France. Status quo ante.

10. Russia. Kingdom of Poland to be created as in existence between 1772–93. The King to be chosen by Great Britain out of three presented by Austria-Hungary. The Crown lands within the limits of the future kingdom of Poland to serve as security for the interest and principal of a loan of 25,000,000,000 marks in favour of Austria-Hungary. Great Britain will raise the full amount of the loan, i.e. 25,000,000,000 marks on behalf of Austria-Hungary, to whom the money is to be paid and who will settle all the expenses incurred in the arrangement for the preliminary conference mentioned in the first paragraph.

In the event of His Majesty the King of Spain declining two delegates as mentioned in the first paragraph the two governments will consider any further suggestion for the holding of the preliminary conference.

Amsterdam, 27 April 1916

In the course of conversation he gathered that the Austrians were not officials but directors of important shipping concerns who may have had some quiet official sanction for their errand. No money passed between them and Señor P—, but when Mr H— pointed out that he had come over on the understanding that he was not to be put to personal expense, they did give him £100 to cover his journey, which seemed to show that they thought his intervention was worth at least that amount.

It is to be feared that poor Señor P— did not enjoy his reception on his return to this country. His stay was extremely short and part of it was passed in a room without any of the amenities that he had been accustomed to in his suite at a first-class hotel. Since the Armistice he has again appeared as a man who can make fortunes. His fluent tongue, his moist eye and his extremely well-fed appearance were not given him for nothing.

Among the many queer people who graced my room was a certain Jugo-Slav lawyer-journalist who came I do not quite know why and left I do not quite know whither. He talked unceasingly about nothing in particular. He assured me that he was a frequent visitor to the Foreign Office and that he was a person to be reckoned with. I consulted a friend who knew him well and when I remarked that he did not quite seem to know what he wanted and that his discourse was sometimes incoherent, my friend assured me that all Jugo-Slav journalists are like that and that everything reasonable should be done to encourage him. And so when he called again and again I did not attempt to interrupt him: my time was a sacrifice laid on the altar of our international relations.

One day the awful news was received that the Jugo-Slav journalist was under arrest in Northumberland. In defiance of every prescription, human and divine, he had taken the train for Newcastle without complying with any of the police requirements and had gone straight off to the residence of Lord Grey of Fallodon. Lord Grey was away and his housekeeper, naturally disturbed, communicated with the police, when it was found that my Jugo-Slav friend had neglected to register his arrival. He was then contemplating a journey to Glasgow, Inverness and Edinburgh, but he was remitted under escort to London, where again he appeared before me. On this occasion incoherence would be a grave understatement of the nature of his discourse. I gathered that he had been grossly insulted, and that all Jugo-Slavia would rise as one man when they came to know of it. It was useless to point out that the law was no respecter of persons and that even the most distinguished foreigner was liable to indignities if he broke it, because my friend had no time for listening. He wanted to talk and talk he did. Still, he was no exception to the unbroken rule that no one who came into my room should leave it without thanking me and we patched up some kind of arrangement. I was shocked some few weeks later at learning that the poor man had died of general paralysis of the insane.

Among the detentions made at this period was that of an ex-naval officer, Commander von Rintelen. After leaving the German Navy he had embarked on international trade, chiefly in Mexico and had become a power in Central America. He had done many things that would have brought him within reach of the law in the United States. For some time he denied his identity, but the interrogation by the naval officers was conducted with remarkable skill and in the end he confessed. At subsequent interviews he became quite communicative, while of course he gave nothing away that would have injured his government. He was interned as an officer at Donington Hall.

The Americans would have been very glad to have him within their jurisdiction, but it was, of course, impossible to transfer a prisoner of war to the custody of a neutral. On the day when America entered the war on the side of the Allies the position changed. There seemed to be nothing to prevent a prisoner of war interned in one of the allied countries from being interned in another and it was decided to send von Rintelen over to America in British custody. A curious light is thrown upon the German mentality by an incident that took place just before he embarked. He stopped to make a solemn protest as a prisoner of war against his life being placed in jeopardy from German submarines if he were embarked upon a merchant vessel. His escort listened quite gravely to his protest and asked him to move on.

A good deal of latitude is allowed to prisoners on board steamers and one day von Rintelen found himself in company with a young South American who spoke German fluently. When he heard that he was going to South America he asked him to call upon the German minister in Venezuela and say to him the two words 'Rintelen *Meldet*' (Rintelen has arrived). That, he explained, would set certain machinery to work. He hinted darkly that there would be reprisals upon Colonel Napier, who was interned as a prisoner of war in Austria and he declared his intention of getting President Carranza to seize three prominent Americans in Mexico and make reprisals on them. His passion for reprisals knew no bounds. Some months later, while he was awaiting his trial in New York, he told this young man when he came to see him that he need not trouble further about delivering the message because Admiral von Hintze had passed through New York on his way from China and would see that the necessary steps were taken. I was glad to learn a little later that the British officer in question had been released and sent to England.

One early morning some fishermen who were walking under the cliff between Robin Hood's Bay and Filey saw two men wandering along the beach. They stopped them and, believing them to be Germans, took them to the nearest constable. Nothing very much could be got out of them except that they were German sailors and that they had buried some of their belongings in the sand. These were recovered and among them was a cheap watch which was still going. On the way to London they declared that they had swum ashore from a submarine in Robin Hood's Bay. It seemed impossible that a watch which had been immersed in sea water for perhaps twenty minutes should still be going and it was thought that they might have been landed intentionally. They proved to be a very interesting couple. The younger man was barely twenty-one. He had passed his examination for an officer's commission. The older man was a quartermaster of past forty. He could look for no further promotion. Both had been on night-watch on a German submarine lying in Robin Hood's Bay. The older man had suddenly shouted, 'Motorboat!' (Submarines were particularly nervous about our fast motorboats at that time.) At the same moment he clapped down the hatch, which was secured from inside and the submarine began to submerge. There was no escape for either man except by swimming. It was pretty obvious that the older man had had enough of cruising and intended to desert, for there had been ample time for both men to have passed through the hatch before it was secured.

And now they were marooned in the enemy country with nothing before them but internment as prisoners of war. I did not cover myself with glory during their examination. I asked the older man whether he would mind if I immersed his watch in a tumblerful of water during the interview. He made no objection and there that watch stayed under 3 inches of water for a full half-hour. When I took it out it was still going. If it had stopped, as any respectable watch would under such treatment, their story about swimming ashore would have been upset. It remained only to ask him where such a watch was made. He had bought it in Stettin for 5 marks!

During the last month in 1916 the Commissioner of Police was asked to furnish 800 trained police to serve in France, partly to regulate the traffic on the French roads behind the line. They were converted into military police for the purpose. I saw a few of them afterwards on this duty and very well they did it. There is a story, perhaps mythical, that during the retreat of the 5th Army in March 1918 a London policeman was seen standing at a corner where two roads converged. Down one was marching a body of British troops, down the other a body of Germans and he put out one arm mechanically to stop the Germans and with the other waved to the British to proceed as if, for all the world, he was controlling the traffic at Hyde Park Corner. With their innate obedience to authority, it is said that the Germans marked time. The story did not go on to say what became of the policeman, but there are not a few of my acquaintance whose calmness in moments of excitement would be quite equal to such an occasion.

One drawback to the submarine campaign against shipping was that we could no longer compel neutral ships to come in to Falmouth and Kirkwall for examination, since both these ports were in the danger zone: consequently the examinations were made in Halifax, Jamaica and Sierra Leone and no more suspicious travellers came to Scotland Yard.

In February 1917 drafts of civilian prisoners of war from the Isle of Man in exchange for an equal number of British from Ruhleben were shipped to Holland in the *Rjndam*. The representative of the Holland–America Line called at the American embassy to demand their passage money in advance. On being asked to collect it from the German government he replied that this was out of the question: they knew the German government too well.

It has always been a matter for wonder what led the Germans to adopt the suicidal policy of torpedoing hospital ships. The case is not made better by the reason given by themselves, namely, that an Austrian named Adalbert Messany had made a declaration that when he was repatriated in the 'hospital ship' *Britannic* there were 2,500 armed troops on board. A concert singer of that name, aged twenty-four and suffering from tuberculosis, had been deported from Egypt to Mudros in November 1916 and at Mudros he was embarked on the transport *Britannic* for repatriation. On such evidence as this the Germans sought to justify crimes as stupid as they were dastardly.

The long sojourn of the British Army in northern France was said to be causing uneasiness to some of the French, who viewed the erection of semi-permanent buildings as an indication that the British might delay demobilisation for years and be in virtual possession of all the Channel ports. One of them is said to have approached a certain eminent English official and to have asked how long he thought it would take the British to evacuate Calais at the end of the war. This Englishman, who is a cynic with a love for equivocal speech, replied, 'Well, I don't know. Last time it took them 200 years.'

CHAPTER 20

THE BOGUS PRINCESS

URING THE WAR bogus royalties and princesses sprang up like toadstools. Any young woman with a turn for private theatricals and a vivid imagination could burst forth as a high-born refugee and get someone to believe in her and, incidentally, to finance her until she found a husband from among the officers in one or other of the camps. The first I remember was a Russian princess who, while staying with a very influential lady in the Midlands, had become engaged to a certain temporary officer of large expectations. She was described to me as beautiful, with a peculiarly Russian type of loveliness, emotional, as all Russians are, with blue eyes that became easily suffused with tears and with a charming flow of broken English. I think it was the broken English that was her undoing, for she had the ill-fortune to come into contact with an Englishwoman who prided herself on her Russian and would insist upon showing it off to every Russian she met. Curious to relate, the princess had entirely forgotten her Russian and for some reason her parents had neglected to have her taught French, which is in the ordinary curriculum of well-born Russians. She accounted for this by vague allusions to the misfortunes of her family, who had had so troublous an existence that they appeared to have forgotten to teach her anything but English and this only broken English.

It was in the height of the spy mania and, not un-naturally, the Russian-speaking Englishwoman jumped to the conclusion that she had to deal with a German spy and, worse, a German spy who had got herself engaged to a British officer and so she came to me. I found that the princess's hostess was still ready to go bail for her and could not bear that her protégée should undergo the humiliation of being called to Scotland Yard, but I was adamant. Come the lady must. All I could promise was that she should not be dealt with harshly even if she proved to be a spy.

There walked into my room a beautifully dressed young woman with a full outfit of furs, because, I suppose, a Russian princess would not be Russian without them. Her broken English was certainly not the broken English of a Russian nor of a Frenchwoman nor of a German nor, indeed, of any nation that I had yet encountered. It was the broken English of the English stage; and when I came to look at the lady I was quite sure that whatever knowledge she had acquired of life had been acquired in the lower ranks of the profession.

I said: 'English does not come very easily to you. Shall we talk French?'

'I not speak French, sir.'

'But you are a Russian?'

'Yes, sir.'

'And your parents are now in Russia?'

'Yes, sir.'

'And yet you do not speak Russian?'

'No, sir. Russia I leave many years ago.'

'Can you describe to me your Russian home?'

'I leave, sir, when quite a leetle child.'

'Now,' I said, 'I want you to give me the address of your English mother. You see, in this room one has to drop all play-acting and tell the truth.'

Her blue eyes filled with tears, but at last, quite faintly, she gave me an address in London and retired to await the arrival of her mother.

There was no play-acting about this good lady when she arrived. She was a buxom woman of fifty, who earned her living as a housekeeper and had two daughters, one in a good situation and the other a young woman who had become stage-struck at eighteen and would from time to time fill the breasts of her mother and sister with silent indignation by flouncing in upon them in expensive clothes and attempting to patronise them. 'I always told her that she'd get herself into trouble if she went on as she did and now she has. You just let me see her for five minutes and talk to her.' I asked whether she had ever heard that her daughter was posing as a Russian. 'No,' she said, 'but I remember that one Christmas she got a part as a Russian princess in a pantomime and had to talk broken English.'

In fact, the war had broken out just in time to give this young lady an opportunity of continuing her part off the stage. She had had a glorious time. I was not present at the interview between mother and daughter, but at the end of it the mother informed me that she had promised to be a good girl and make a clean breast of it all to her patroness and also to the man whom she was about to marry and I heard that he, good fellow that he was, married her all the same.

Another young woman who appeared in 1915 aimed higher and, being better educated, played her part with more distinction. She was no less, according to the accounts that first came to me, than a daughter of Marie Vetsera, the heroine of the mysterious tragedy in which Prince Rudolf of Austria met his death and of course I need hardly say that Prince Rudolf was her father. She arrived from America and almost immediately became engaged to a British officer. She was invited to Scotland Yard for an interview. She did not talk broken English, but her accent was neither American nor English and, unlike the Russian princess, she was possessed of some means. Her story was full of mysteries and reticences. She could only tell me, she said, what she had herself been told. Her earliest recollections were of the convent in America in which she had been brought up. The Sisters would only tell her that a foreign-looking stranger had brought her there as a baby and that her parentage was very distinguished indeed. She must not ask too many questions. He had invested for her a large sum of money which she was to enjoy when she came of age. It had been placed in trust with a firm of lawyers who were under an obligation not to tell her whence it came. As the years went on there were hints about the Austrian royal family. Prince Rudolf had been mentioned and then one day the Mother Superior put her arm round her and whispered that her mother had been very unhappy, that the whole thing was very tragic and, again, that she must not ask too many questions. From this she inferred the rest – that she was the daughter of Marie Vetsera, born some time before the tragedy.

'I am sorry to interrupt you,' I said, 'but Marie Vetsera never had a daughter. The whole of her history is well known.'

Her eyes filled with tears and she replied that she could only tell me what she had been told. When she left the convent the lawyer had hinted at the same thing and had paid over to her the money that had been placed in trust.

'The lawyer's name?'

'Alas, sir, he is dead and the firm no longer exists.'

She then asked for advice as to how she should manage about her boy, then a child of about six. As far as I could gather, she had for some time been living on her capital, which must in due course come to an end. Asked what she would do when the inevitable happened, she shook her head and hinted that she would put an end to herself.

It transpired in the course of the interview that she could speak French and Polish fairly fluently and this may have accounted for the peculiarity of her accent. She had been taught these languages, she said, in the convent. She would not give the name of the convent and therefore all this part of the story may have been invented like the rest, but it was clear from inquiries that were subsequently made that by nationality she was American and that she was certainly not engaged in espionage.

But the most amazing of all the claimants was a certain soi-disant princess of a royal house who had succeeded in convincing a very large number of people that she was genuine. She was not in need of funds, nor had she any object in view except to gain the prestige which a royal parentage would confer upon her. It was therefore a quite harmless amusement and she must have got a great deal of fun out of it. Unfortunately for her, when she had first laid claim to her rank there was nothing to show that we were soon to be at war with the sovereign whom she claimed for father and when the spy mania was at its height he came, not unnaturally, under suspicion. It was still more unfortunate that her own brother was living in this country.

She had worked out the details of her claim with remarkable skill. Her mother was still living, as well as her two brothers and a sister. It was impossible to ignore them altogether and so she told a story of how she had been confided to the care of her own mother by an imperial lady who, for some unexplained reason, wished to keep her birth a secret. I commend this kind of story to any future claimant of royal parentage, because when sceptics begin to throw details of your early life in your face you can say, 'Quite so, all that happened, only you were never told the secret of my birth, which is known only to me and to one or two other people, who are dead.' All she had to do, in fact, was to read up all the movements of the court during the years of her infancy and childhood and retail them as a privileged eyewitness.

There sailed into my room one morning the most imperial-looking person I have ever seen. Even when sitting in my low armchair there was a calm and condescending dignity about her that would have impressed anybody. She had a husband who was on the way to make a fortune and who was in attendance to confirm everything she said and no one was ever more ready than she to help me over any difficult points, only I must tell her what they were. My first point was that her reputed mother did not and could not have had a child at the particular date when she said she was born. She smiled rather pityingly and said that no doubt I was not aware that her mother had spent some months alone at a watering-place in France at that time and that it was evident that I did not know how eccentric she was. As a matter of fact I did, but I also knew a good deal about the movements of the imperial lady immediately after the supposed birth and they did not at all tally with my visitor's story. I took her through her various statements and as I had no documentary evidence on the other side to confront her with she left with the honours of war, but she left me also quite unconvinced.

A few days later I discovered her brother, a composer of consid-erable ability and a very striking-looking man with a strong family likeness to his sister. He was in a state of great indignation against her, chiefly, I think, on account of the disparagement of his mother which was entailed by her story. He came fully armed with most convincing documents – family photographs from the time when they were all children together, letters written by the lady herself to her family and letters from his mother in Switzerland. Among the letters was one written when the claimant was a girl of seventeen. She and her sister were at a watering-place and she retails, with satisfaction, a remark she overheard about them, that they were *Kaiserlich mädchen*. This chance remark overheard in a hotel probably put the entire idea into her head. In appearance she was *Kaiserlich* to the finger-tips and it must have been balm to her soul to extend them to be kissed and to see the world curtsy to her. She was the daughter of a Jewish bank manager in a good position. She had been well educated and she knew a number of people who could tell her the gossip of the court. She could not have imposed on any one in her own country, but once abroad she began to expand and the story had given four or five years of intense pleasure.

Having satisfied myself that, whatever else the lady might be, she was not dangerous to the cause of the Allies, I dropped the case, thinking that if any exposure became necessary the brother would bring it about; but one day, to my great surprise, a friend who has a profound knowledge of Austria, told me that he was satisfied that she was genuine and thought it a great pity that she had been subjected to the indignity of interrogation. I made him a sporting offer. I said that the lady was probably expecting another interview, that I had documentary proofs in my possession and that if he liked I would invite her to see me again in his presence. He agreed and asked only that he might bring with him a personage who has since become very prominent in Europe.

The interview took place. The lady sailed in as imperially as before. My companions were presented to her and she acknowledged their bows with the slightest nod.

'Sit down, madam. Since I saw you last some very interesting documents have reached me and I want to put them to you. The first are some family photographs.'

I thought she flushed slightly.

'Oh, I can see what has happened. You have been in communication with Mr K—, who claims to be my brother. Poor man, it has become an obsession with him.'

I do not think that she was prepared for the family photographs, for at first she would not admit that the girl of fourteen in one of the groups was herself. A little later she seemed to think that this was a false move, for she said, 'I suppose that is my photograph, but you see at that time we should have been photographed together because I had been consigned to the care of Madame K—.' When she came to her own letters she was for the first time embarrassed and inclined to be angry, for she had at short notice to make up her mind whether she would deny the authorship altogether, or admit it and readjust her story. I was on pretty sure ground, because it happened that a relation of mine had been staying in the same house as her imperial 'mother' on an occasion when she claimed to have been present and that when her photograph was shown to this lady, she declared that the girl she saw there was quite a different-looking person. For the first time her imperial calm broke down. She became very pale and very angry. It was difficult to say whether fear or anger was the stronger of her emotions. She admitted the authorship of the letters and to all our further questions she would only reply that she was suffering for the malice of her brother.

For a time I think she dropped her royal pretensions. At any rate, she dropped the idea of writing a book, which was said to be nearly ready for publication.

Another case of impersonation was that of the man who called himself Count de Borch. He was a Polish Jew, well educated and well dressed and he seems to have had a curious fascination for persons with whom he came in contact. Any mysterious Pole was at that time an object of suspicion. This man had obtained employment carrying a small weekly wage with a firm of furniture dealers in London and yet he was able to cut a dash at London tea-tables and expensive restaurants. He had a large circle of hostesses from whom he would have been in a position to acquire a good deal of information useful to the enemy if he had tried to do so. He was brought down to Scotland Yard some weeks before the tragedy which brought his name before the public. The title of 'de Borch' was old and highly esteemed in Poland and I had been assured that whatever this man might be he was certainly not in any way connected with the family. He made a very bad impression upon me. He fell back upon the usual ruse of bogus claimants. He said that he knew nothing about his ancestry except what he had been told, that there had always been a mystery about his parentage because, owing to family differences, his father was anxious that his existence should be kept secret until the day when he could come into his own and so he had been supporting himself honourably with a firm in London until Poland was free. It was like a great many other cases at that time. Until some evidence was forthcoming that a man was engaged in espionage, he had to be left at liberty under surveillance. He was believed to be drawing sums of money from some of his hostesses to eke out his slender wages and it was his social side that was his undoing.

The tragedy in which he met his death was very fully reported at the time. Captain Malcolm had returned from the Front to find that this over-dressed and scented person had been trying to break up his home. He came to Scotland Yard to ascertain his address, but as it is not the custom to give addresses to callers no information was given. He found it out in another way, bought a horsewhip, with which to thrash the man and gained admittance to his room. In the scuffle that followed the use of the horsewhip, de Borch was shot dead, but as a loaded pistol was found in an opened drawer close to the bed it was held that de Borch intended to use it upon his unwelcome visitor and Captain Malcolm was acquitted.

CHAPTER 21

FOOTNOTES TO THE PEACE CONFERENCE

THREE DAYS BEFORE the Armistice was signed I went to Paris with representatives of the Office of Works and the Foreign Office to secure premises for the British delegation in the peace negotiations. I believe that Brussels and Geneva were both considered as meeting places, but for reasons, chiefly of lack of accommodation, were dismissed as unsuitable. The Majestic and the Astoria Hotels, the one for housing the people and the other for office accommodation, both near the Arc de Triomphe, seemed to be the only possible buildings available and in due course the British ambassador called on Monsieur Clemenceau to ask that they should be commandeered. He asked how many people had to be housed and was told that the number would be approximately 400, on which followed the quick comment, 'Ah, then the demobilisation of the British Army has already begun!'

We spent Sunday afternoon, 10 November, driving about Paris with M. Clemenceau's ADC to inspect premises for the accommodation of the Foreign Office printing staff. I noticed late in the afternoon that the Champs-Élysées was full of a holiday crowd carrying flags rolled tightly round the stick. All Paris was waiting for the news that the Germans had signed the Armistice. I had not seen the terms, but knowing that they were hard, I asked the French officer whether he thought that the Germans would accept them. He replied, '*Oui, les conditions sont dures, mais ils signeront.*' I was in Boulogne by 11 a.m. on Armistice morning and I had the news of the Armistice when I reached my daughter's hospital at Wimereux. The news had not then reached the French. At the entrance to the hospital I had to stand aside to let a party of German prisoner orderlies pass. They were laughing and singing, though the news had not actually reached the hospital by telephone at that time. No doubt they were banking upon the rumours of revolution in Germany. When our steamer sailed two hours later every whistle and siren was in full blast; the quays were lined with waving and cheering crowds; the sleepy old town was awake for once.

When the delegation was installed at the Hotel Majestic and the two subsidiary hotels, if one could believe the newspapers, the members spent their time in eating and drinking, in music, theatricals and dancing. But one could not believe the newspapers. No doubt in the early days of those protracted negotiations the staff was too big for the work and in the later stages the work was too big for the staff, but considering the enormous number of experts who had to be consulted on the whole range of human endeavour, political, naval, military, geographical, racial and industrial, it cannot be said that the staff was too numerous or that it did less than a day's work. Its recreations were certainly not excessive, seeing that for many dancing was the only possible exercise. It may well be asked what a police officer had to do with peace negotiations. He had nothing whatever to do with them. As Chief Security Officer, my function was to prevent if possible the leakages of information that took place during the Peace Conference in Vienna and for this purpose I took over with me a body of Special Branch officers to control the doors and see that no unauthorised person obtained access to the buildings. If occasionally they wounded susceptible feelings, they were of great use to visitors in the matter of passports and travelling facilities. There were arduous moments in their service. On one occasion I was asked to furnish the escort for a furniture van which was to be packed with papers of so secret a nature that the escort must remain with it night and day until it arrived in Paris. The van was packed and sealed in London and a very zealous young police officer left with it for Havre via Southampton. At Havre the French railway officials positively refused to attach the truck on which it was loaded to the express: it must proceed by the slow train. The escort telephoned this news quite cheerfully, though the rain was coming down in torrents. We made frequent inquiries at the Gare St Lazare, receiving conflicting accounts of the progress of the truck, until at last late on a Saturday afternoon we heard that it had arrived some hours before and had been shunted into a goods shed, where it would remain until the following Monday. Feeling sure that our zealous policeman had not deserted it, we sent the senior inspector to the station-master. He was adamant: the rules must be observed; even if an English policeman starved, the van must stay where it was till Monday. But the inspector was a man of resource: he was a Freemason and so, as it now appeared, was the station-master. So potent was this appeal that the shed was opened and there was our man, wet through, stiff and faint for want of food. We took him and his van to the hotel and under restoratives and a hot bath he soon recovered. So far I can vouch for the story. The sequel may be less authenticated. The seals were broken; the van was opened and lo! so the story ran, it contained nothing but the ninth edition of the *Encyclopaedia Britannica*. In London someone had blundered.

My principal duties being in London, I made flying visits of inspection to Paris at intervals of about a fortnight – flying in the literal sense occasionally – and it was curious to see how the amenities of the Hotel Majestic were modified as time went on. In the early days there was a full staff of House of Commons waiters and waitresses, who found so much to grumble at that they were soon sent home. Apart from the inevitable epidemic of influenza, the sick ward was always filled: at least two broken legs were being mended, besides minor accidents. Gradually the scale of entertainment became more Spartan, the edges began to wear off tempers, the spirit of criticism to rear its head and in my last visit the glory of the great Peace Conference had departed. Curious folk of every colour came as deputations from nearly every race under the sun to have their grievances redressed. They vanished as unobtrusively as they came, elated or disappointed according to their reception.

The Americans had established an excellent system of intelligence throughout Europe and, as we had been closely associated before, we agreed to pool our information. At that time there was not much happening in the underworld of Europe and America that we did not know. How admirably the Americans had profited by their experience probably few know so well as I.

It was very interesting to note the decline and fall of President Wilson's prestige among the French. At first he was expected to remedy all the evils from which Paris was suffering: he was to lower prices and raise the exchange; the maidservant thought that he would raise her wages. Week followed week and he did nothing sensational to justify these great expectations. When he announced the establishment of the League of Nations it was too late; his star was in eclipse and nothing he could say or do would ever bring him back to public favour. It is the fate of all mortals from whom too much is expected. I confess that his speech at the League of Nations plenary session disappointed me both in substance and delivery. When I said so to two of my American colleagues that evening one of them said: 'There are only two men at the Peace Conference who could have carried it off – Mr Balfour and Lord Reading.'

One of my friends, in whose cranium the bump of Veneration has been atrophied, wrote the following witty lines:

Hotel Majestic! Gaze in reverent awe
Upon the Fane of Peace – above whose door
It's clear to me the legend should appear
'Abandon Peace, all ye who enter here.'
Pass the gyrating door and, once within,
Detectives, hall-marked by their diamond pin,
Will put you through a strict interrogation –
Your birthmarks, age, religion and vocation:
Remembering that there's nothing like the truth
To rouse suspicion in your super-sleuth,
Answer at random – and they'll pass you through.
Proceed and Paradise is yours to view.
A stately hall, replete with every sign
Of true refinement (viz. Bosche-Argentine):
Luxurious straight-backed chairs: two spreading shrubs,
Two metres tall, in tasty Teuton tubs:
While the mere waving of some magic wand,
Either of Selfridge or, it may be, Mond,
Has given the final touch we else should lack,

That classic harmony, the Union Jack.
Here's where the Foreign Office wage their war,
And though the hours are, strictly, ten to four,
Even at five amid the tea-cups' clatter
Sit men who count discussing things that matter.
Birth, brains and beauty throng the crowded tables:
The typists, clad in silver fox and sables;
Second Division clerks, too proud by far
To go to work except by motorcar
(And Balham's happiness is incomplete
Without a bathroom and a first-floor suite):
Colonial Premiers, Rajahs, Plenipotentiaries,
True Britons, who have not been Jews for centuries,
Generals (but since they helped to win the war
No one can guess what they've been brought here for,
Unless some kindly soul leapt at the chance
Of letting soldiers sample life in France
And for the Navy thought it only fair
To give them ninety minutes' mal de mer):
Immaculate aesthetes, clad in perfect taste –
Unruffled voice and hair and such a waist
(The spelling's optional: I don't suggest
Any alternative – but you'll judge best);
Taking from tortoise spectacles and speed
(Who's seen them run – except, of course, to seed?);
Epitomising Foreign Office lore
In three short words – Ignore – Deplore – Encore.

At last the Peace Treaty was signed at Versailles. We know what contemporaries think of it; we can only guess at the verdict of posterity.

We see through a glass darkly that a rearrangement of frontiers which includes a corridor, a reduction of Austria to such proportions that she cannot feed herself, will not stand. The epigram ascribed to Herr Rathenau that the Treaty of Versailles set out to Europeanise the Balkans and has succeeded only in Balkanising Europe will gather truth with every month we live.

CHAPTER 22

THE ROYAL UNEMPLOYED

A GERMAN SUBJECT once irreverently described the Kaiser Wilhelm II as being half journalist, half actor-manager. Another German, even more irreverently, said he was a fool. Immediately after the Armistice we described him as a criminal who ought to be tried for his life. And thirty years ago *The Spectator*, when classifying the great men of the day, put him in a class by himself as the only genius of the first rank. Which out of all these is the real man?

A good deal of daylight has been let in during the last few months. It is now known that while the Kaiser most certainly did encourage the Austrians to send the ultimatum to Serbia and did approve of sending an ultimatum to Russia, he had not thought it possible for England to intervene in the war and he was not in favour of infringing the neutrality of Belgium. In fact, the Kaiser had not nearly so much actual power as he was supposed to have.

It is now known that it was the General Staff who decided upon invading Belgium; that for two whole days the Kaiser refused his approval and that at last, when the advance had already begun, von Moltke insisted upon an interview at two in the morning and in the Kaiser's bedroom told him plainly that the destiny of the German Empire was at stake and that if he, the Kaiser, stood in the way, the General Staff must take the responsibility. In other words, that he might either sign or abdicate. From that moment, as I believe, the Kaiser was allowed to play only a very secondary role. He was not consulted by the General Staff except when, for political reasons, they thought it prudent to be able to quote him. They kept him near them and pretended to obtain his sanction to important steps upon which they were already resolved and they found him useful as a sort of gramophone record that could make speeches in the hearing of reporters to stiffen the waning German morale. His life at Charleroi under these humiliating circumstances must have been hard to bear.

They tell a story of a painter who was commissioned to paint a portrait of the Kaiser in all his best clothes, mounted on his favourite horse, surrounded by hounds and crowned with a sort of Viking silver-plated casque, mounted with gold. The Kaiser asked him to paint in the corner of the picture two little angels carrying the Imperial Crown, after the manner of a famous classic Spanish painter.

'But, Your Majesty, I have never seen the Imperial Crown. I do not know what it looks like. May I see it?'

On this the Kaiser became nettled and said, 'You ought to know. The Imperial Crown is in Vienna. It ought to have come to Berlin in 1866.'

To a man with this kind of mind the dream of world empire must have come very easily. He had a sort of superficial interest in everything on which the German sun shone. He would talk not unintelligently to bankers about international finance, to motorcar manufacturers about the relative merits of new fuels, to painters about art, to writers about literature. All his opinions were strong and many of them were shallow or wrong-headed.

Undoubtedly he had a cult for England; a longing to be treated as an equal in the craft by English yachtsmen. English country life, with its accompaniments of hunting and shooting, was his ideal; the English tailor was superior to every tailor in the Fatherland. To him, therefore, it was a tragedy when he broke with England. And then how he hated us! He decorated Lissauer for writing the 'Hymn of Hate', and on this subject I remember a German telling me that the 'Hymn of Hate' was all a matter of policy. It was because the Germans were found not to be hating the British sufficiently that the government decided to mobilise its hate in order to strengthen the 'will to war'. But the Kaiser's hate was perfectly genuine because it was strongly mixed with fear. Some prescience must have told him that the fortunes of the Hohenzollerns hung in the balance and that their scale might kick the beam.

Probably no man, however well balanced, could pass through the fire of adulation, such as was the Kaiser's daily fare, and come out unscathed. When one year he was at Cowes he paid a visit with his staff to a country house in the neighbourhood without notice. His hostess invited him to sit down. He sat astride a chair and proceeded to address her as if she was a public meeting, with his staff grouped in a semicircle behind him. He said, apropos of the public health, that whenever he drove through Germany he would stop at the school, have all the scholars paraded before him and make them blow their noses, because he was convinced that the public health largely depended upon the blowing of noses – and much more in the same strain and at every remark uttered with intense seriousness, however foolish, the staff would gravely nod approval. If we all had to go through life with a claque to applaud every silly thing we said, the best of us would go under.

To such a mind as the Kaiser's the idea that Germany was being hemmed in came quite naturally. It was nothing to him that Germans were to be found working side by side with Englishmen in every part of the world, that her shipping and her international banking was gradually turning the world into a German possession in a way that actual possession by the hoisting of the German flag could never have achieved. What he wanted was the outward semblance of Empire and for this there were no waste places left. Gradually all the most unlovely features of the Teuton character began to blossom. Poisonous toadstools sprang up everywhere. Germany, that had been a sane, sober, thrifty and domestic country, became loud, vulgar, self-assertive, intolerant and altogether hateful to the world and even to its own citizens and the Kaiser made himself the embodiment of this spirit.

As Traill said of James II, 'Kings who fail in business undoubtedly owe it to their historical reputation to perish on the scaffold or the battlefield.' History demanded that the Kaiser should have gone forth at the head of his troops and been killed in battle. Then some heroic niche would have been found for him. He would have been a tragic embodiment of Frederick the Great and his past would have been forgotten. But he committed the one crime that can never be forgiven by Germans: he abandoned his people in their extremity and fled the country. But in sober fact this is what actually happened. During the last few days before the Armistice, von Ludendorff had practically broken down and the direction of affairs had passed into the hands of von Grunow. There came a day when it was necessary to tell plain truths to the Kaiser.

Von Grunow entered the room alone and told him that the war was irrevocably lost. The news did not appear to touch him very deeply.

Probably he had realised it already. Then von Grunow said, 'I have other bad news. A rebellion has broken out in Berlin.' The Kaiser started to his feet and said, 'Then I will lead the troops to Berlin in person. Please to give the necessary orders,' and on this von Grunow said, 'Sir, it is my duty to tell you that your life would not be safe with your own soldiers.' The Kaiser turned to the colour of ashes and fell back into his chair. Suddenly he had become a very old man without any power of decision or movement. The shock had been too much for him. After a hasty consultation it was decided that, with the growing spirit of rebellion that prevailed even among the troops connected with the General Staff, the Kaiser must be got into a place of safety at all hazards. A car was brought to the door and von Grunow himself helped him out of his chair and conducted him to the vehicle. The Kaiser was like a little child in his hands. The car then drove off and took him safely to Count Bentinck's house in Holland. It is a curious fact that the car was held up over three hours by a Dutch sentry. Just before this date the Dutch had decided to clothe their soldiers in the German field-grey and the sentry on the frontier was taken at first by the occupants of the car to be a German soldier in revolt. Probably no more unwelcome visitor ever applied for admission to Holland, but the asylum was granted and it was maintained. To do the Kaiser justice, he has never given the Dutch authorities any cause for complaint.

A still more unwelcome visitor was the Crown Prince, who followed his father. This young man was a joke even among his fellow German royalties as well as German commoners. One prince used to say to the Crown Princess, 'Why don't you get your husband to dress properly?'

'Why, what is wrong with his clothes?' she asked rather tartly.

'Well, his hat's wrong, his tunic's wrong and his boots are wrong.'

The Crown Prince was very vain about his clothes. He tried to lead the fashion by adopting a military cap made with a ridiculously wide crown, which he wore at the back of his head like a halo; a tunic absurdly tight at the waist and full in the skirts and boots tapered and pointed beyond all reason. He had one quality in common with Frederick the Great – an envy of French lightness and wit and a desire to be accepted by the French as a kindred spirit. In pretending to conduct the siege of Verdun he was certainly dissembling his love, but he tried to make up for it at Charleroi by clumsy civilities to the French residents and a real love-affair with a French girl, to the scandal of Germans and Frenchmen alike. If the Kaiser's life was not safe with his own soldiers still less was the Crown Prince's and if the young gentleman has not been credited with respect for the serious things in life, no one has yet affirmed that he lacks respect for his own skin. So he, too, fled for Holland and thereby he forfeited any slender chance he may have had to ascend the throne of the Hohenzollerns. He has one redeeming virtue – his love of approbation and his craving for affection and so within the narrow limits of his island home in Holland he goes about with pockets full of chocolates and a troop of village children at his heels. He knows the family history of every villager and loves nothing better than to take part in every village fete, showering favours on all alike. His popularity in this narrow circle has given him more pleasure than he ever had as heir-apparent to the German Empire. Perhaps the bumptious qualities that were remarked when he visited England are now a little toned down.

Another exiled sovereign seems to have disappeared altogether from the newspapers. Ferdinand of Bulgaria has an intellect. He is a fine musician, a noted ornithologist, a considerable engineer. Politically, he is cunning, unscrupulous and incurably frivolous, but no doubt he took care to make ample financial provision for himself outside Bulgaria before the crash came. He crept out of obscurity to ascend the throne and now the darkness has swallowed him up again. He had no lust for power, no illusions about the risks run by Balkan sovereigns, but he had made a special study of the art of making oneself comfortable and at the moment a throne – even a Balkan one – seemed to be the best thing that offered.

But Providence had denied him one gift – personal courage – and his life was poisoned by the fear of assassination. How he contrived to escape it for so many years speaks volumes for the qualities that earned him his nickname of 'The Fox'. For, as he used himself to say, assassination is so easy, especially in the Balkans. The assassin who means business has only to aim from a window or take a sporting shot at you from the thickest of the crowd and the trick is done. And it comes naturally from a Bulgarian. Just before Bulgaria entered the war a Bulgarian diplomat came to take leave of a certain British Under-Secretary. 'Mind,' he said, 'I have nothing to say against this plan of yours to assassinate King Ferdinand, but unless I'm much mistaken you will find Ferdinand far more useful to you alive than he can ever be when dead!'

When Ferdinand came to take leave of Sir Arthur Nicholson, our ambassador in Russia, in reply to an earnest expression of hope that he would use all his influence to prevent disturbances in the Balkans, he waved a fat forefinger in the ambassador's face and said, 'Have no fear at all. I will be like a leetle lamb.' Within two months he had the whole place by the ears. He had learned the wrong part in the tragi-comedy: instead of the 'leetle lamb' he had cast himself for the part of the ravening wolf.

There is no form of unemployment so deadly as that of the continental monarch who has 'lost his job'. It is the last post on earth that any man of sense would care to take in these days, because there is no privacy and no retiring age; moreover, it is hard and distasteful work nearly all the time. But the daily life of a king in exile is so ghastly that I blame none of them for trying to get back again. As a rule they are poor and they have to support a number of court functionaries as poor as themselves. And with the daily struggle to make both ends meet goes the uneasy feeling that they are neither fish, flesh, nor fowl. Some of their acquaintances treat them as royal, others do not. There are continual difficulties with the authorities of the country of their exile. If only they could begin life afresh on a lower plane they could, like the rest of us, scratch up a living in honest trade. As it is, they see stretching out interminably before them a life devoted to attending concerts and opening charity bazaars, to which only death will bring surcease, unless, indeed, some endless chain of dreary functions is reserved for them in the place of torment.

The ex-Emperor Karl was a gallant gentleman who refused to sit down tamely under these conditions, but was ready to dare everything to regain a throne. He was not endowed with brains, but the most successful kings have often been those who have their thinking done for them by other people. He had what is far more useful – a good presence, amiability and a very clever wife. She was a Bourbon and it has always been believed that her brother, Prince Sixte, who lives in Paris, was cognisant of the two attempts at restoration to the throne of Hungary which miscarried. Prince Sixte was said at the time to have sent a message to his brother-in-law from Paris to the effect that unless he did something to recover his throne his opportunity might never come again; but that once let his reinstatement become an accomplished fact and he would have, perforce, to be recognised by the Allies. How near the second attempt came to being successful few people know. The majority of the Hungarians were ready to welcome him and, but for the fatal delay of twenty-four hours while conferences were being held and dinners were being cooked and eaten, he might have been proclaimed in Buda Pesth instead of being an exile in that land of bad hotels, Madeira. It is said that when one of his followers produced a priceless tapestry which he had cut down from the walls of one of the imperial palaces and suggested that it should be sold in order that the ex-Emperor should live upon the proceeds, Karl sent it back to the Republican government.

There can be little doubt that some of these dethroned monarchs will return. The greater part of Bavaria is royalist at heart and any day within the next two years we may open our morning paper to find that Prince Rupprecht is king. Baden may not impossibly follow suit. Europe may even come round to the belief that a hereditary president, which is the real position in a limited monarchy, is cheaper than the American form of elected autocrat. Russia herself is awake to the fact that the Red Czar, whom she did not even elect, is a worse form of autocracy than any they knew under the White.

CHAPTER 23

UNREST AT HOME

I N ORDER TO understand the revolutionary movement in England it is necessary shortly to review the movements of the past ten years.

Apart from the Independent Labour Party, which was formed in 1893 by the late Mr Keir Hardie to introduce socialists into the trade unions and to procure their nomination for the House of Commons, it may be said that there were no formidable extremist bodies in Great Britain before 1911; for the British section of the Industrial Workers of the World, the Socialist Party of Great Britain and the Socialist Labour Party were insignificant in numbers and in influence. In the summer of 1911 there was a great wave of industrial unrest, involving strikes of dockers and transport workers in Manchester, Liverpool and London, followed by a railway strike in August. In three days, with one or two exceptions, most of the lines ceased working and troops were called upon to guard the railways and vital points. The men's grievances were submitted to a Royal Commission and in the debate in the House of Commons initiated by the Labour Members, for the first time political action began to attract trade union leaders. The Trade Union Act passed in 1913 gave the unions power to add political action to the objects covered by their rules.

In 1912 the coal-miners came into the field with a strike for a minimum wage and the government conceded some of their demands in the Coal Mines Minimum Wage Act. In south Wales the coal strike was attended with disorders that called for measures of protection by the military.

In 1913 the Dublin Transport Workers went on strike and the solidarity achieved by this body during the strike made the rebellion of 1916 possible.

In April 1914 the Miners, Transport Workers and Railwaymen appointed a committee to work out a scheme for a Triple Alliance which was to brood over the community as a threat of paralysis whenever one section of the Alliance formulated demands which the employers were not disposed to concede. It was never more than a threat foredoomed to be ineffective, because the component parts were so unwieldy and their interests were so diverse, that they could never be got to work as parts of a single machine. But as a threat it was held *in terrorem* over the nation for seven years. It was believed that the new Alliance would try its strength in support of the railwaymen, who were said to be meditating another strike, but however that may have been, the war, that great composer of petty disputes, intervened to prevent it.

There were two cross-currents in this rapid development of the Labour movement: on the one side a tendency towards the amalgamation of unions, as in the case of the National Transport Workers' Federation and the Triple Alliance and on the other, the tendency of the rank and file in the unions to break away from their leaders.

The declaration of war shattered all the hopes of the International at a blow. Its promoters had forgotten human nature. In 1907 the Second International had passed a resolution binding the workers of all countries to compel their governments to make peace even if war were declared, and as late as 1 August 1914 Messrs Arthur Henderson and Keir Hardie issued a 'Manifesto to the British People' in the sense of the resolution of 1907. On 2 August there was a demonstration in Trafalgar Square to support it. So little knew the leaders the temper of the people they had been chosen to represent! On 6 August the war Emergency Workers' National Committee was formed and within three weeks the great mass of Labour was taking part in the recruiting campaign. In September the Trade Union Congress endorsed their patriotic attitude.

There followed an industrial truce; strikes were abandoned and the railwaymen dropped their national programme; the Triple Alliance was suspended. This situation might have lasted throughout the war but for the rise in the cost of living and certain flagrant examples of profiteering. Conscription gave a great impetus to the revolutionary Pacifists and the Workers' Committees, under the name of the Shop Stewards' Movement, seized upon their opportunity.

The International was, in fact, trampled to death by the rapid march of events. On 31 July 1914 Jean Jaurès had been assassinated in Paris and the French socialists had lost their most trusted leader. This was rapidly followed by the invasion of Belgium and by the voting of the war credits by German socialists. What was now to become of the doctrine, 'Should war break out it is the duty of socialists to intervene to bring it promptly to an end ... to rouse the populace and hasten the fall of the capitalist domination'?

The conversion of British Labour leaders was very rapid. On 7 August Messrs W. C. Anderson and Arthur Henderson, for the

Executive Committee of the Labour Party, stated that while the party condemned the diplomacy which had made war possible, it advised all its members to relieve the destitution and suffering which must inevitably ensue, but on that very day the Labour Party allowed the vote of credit to pass and Mr Ramsay MacDonald resigned in consequence. The left wing, which followed Mr MacDonald, issued a manifesto on 13 August, in which it sent 'Sympathy and greeting to German socialists across the roar of the guns … They are no enemies of ours, but faithful friends,' but on 20 August the Labour Party definitely joined in the campaign to strengthen the British Army and even Mr Keir Hardie wrote, 'Any war of oppression against the rights and liberties of my country I will persist against to the last drop of my blood.'

We are inclined now to imagine that open violence began only at the beginning of the war. We have forgotten the part played by foreign anarchists three or four years before – the Houndsditch murders, the siege of Sydney Street, the outrages of Tottenham. There has been nothing like these since the Armistice.

We date most of our social troubles from August 1914, as if politically England was Utopia before the war. I was reminded by a friend the other day that during the summer of 1913, in a conversation about Labour unrest, I had said that unless there were a European war to divert the current, we were heading for something very like revolution. That was before the railway strike of 1913. I suppose that the dock strike, the growth of bodies like the Anarchists and the Industrial Workers of the World and the unrest that had set in even among disciplined bodies like the police and prison warders, in all civilised countries, had induced this unwonted pessimism. Yet there was a section among our own people who talked glibly about European war producing revolution and therefore one cannot blame the Germans for counting us out of the war. Even during the war itself I can remember several periods when the outlook among our own people was darker than it is now.

With the Independent Labour Party stood the Union of Democratic Control and Pacifist Societies, such as the No-Conscription Fellowship, the Fellowship of Reconciliation and the National Council for Civil Liberties, began to spring up like toadstools. Internal dissensions increased to such an extent that at last the loyal Labour and socialist group formed themselves, in April 1915, into a body known as the Socialist Nationalist Defence Committee, to defend themselves from internal persecution. This committee contributed largely to the patriotic reception of the Conscription Act. As the time went on the committee became the British Workers' League and by July 1918, the League had over 220 branches. Patriotic Labour leaders suffered acutely at this time. Through pressure exerted by his trade union one after another was forced to resign from the League.

There is a rapid evolution in political unrest. Subversive societies are like the geysers in a volcanic field. After preliminary gurgling they spout forth masses of boiling mud and then subside, while another chasm forms at a distance and becomes suddenly active. I have described how the Militant Suffragettes subsided on the day war was declared. The country was so much preoccupied with the war during 1915 that no new geyser had a chance of boiling up. It was not until 1916 that the Pacifist became active.

The Union of Democratic Control was founded in the early days of the war by a small group, of which Mr E. D. Morel, Mr Charles Trevelyan, Mr J. Ramsay MacDonald, Mr Arthur Ponsonby and Mr Ralph Norman Angell Lane, generally known as Norman Angell, were the most prominent. Its four cardinal points of policy were that no province should be transferred without the consent of the population, that Parliament should control all Treaties, that our foreign policy should be directed towards the setting up of a League of Nations, then called an International Council and that England should propose a reduction of armaments. The public mind was to be permeated with the idea that war was a criminal absurdity and of course the union had strong things to say about the Foreign Office. The Diplomatic Service was to be completely reformed, Treaties were to be periodically submitted to a Foreign Affairs Committee in the House of Commons and a 'real European partnership' was to be substituted for 'groupings and alliances and a precarious equipoise'. In 1916 the Union of Democratic Control added to the articles of its programme, 'to prevent the humiliation of the defeated nation', from which it may be inferred that the members of the executive already felt confident that the Allies would win the war. It will be seen that the main points for which the union stood are in process of realisation.

The Union of Democratic Control grew rapidly and within less than a year it had founded sixty-one branches. A branch was also in process of being formed in Paris. Naturally, the union became the rallying point for most of the Pacifists in the country and though the union itself disclaimed any desire to hinder the prosecution of the war, it could not be said to have done anything to support it. One rather prominent member set himself to palliate the German disregard for treaties and international usages. But while the union included people whose attitude is always pro-anybody except pro-British, there were others who would have deeply resented any imputation of a lack of patriotism. Its speakers encountered a good deal of opposition by bodies such as the No-Conscription Fellowship and the Fellowship of Reconciliation. The Union of Democratic Control was an academic body: the No-Conscription Fellowship speedily came within the reach of the law. Compulsory service was bound to provoke resistance and, as all those who have sat on tribunals are aware, the conscientious objectors included men of very different character. Perhaps the smallest class had real conscientious scruples. Many of the others mistook for conscience a natural bent for resisting any kind of compulsion and there was, besides, the class of young man whose personal vanity was hypertrophied and who courted martyrdom for the sake of its advertisement. One would have said he was peculiar to England if the same type had not appeared in Holland and America. Looking back on this period, I am very doubtful whether conscription could have been safely introduced at an earlier date. The country had been drained of its best men and the pity of it was that the finest material for the officers who were so badly needed later in the war was sacrificed in the trenches. But it was this very sacrifice that prepared men's minds for conscription and neutralised the strong opposition to compulsion. As seemed to be inevitable, the Germans were our best friends in this matter. By the outrages in Belgium, by the callousness of submarine commanders, by the sinking of the *Lusitania* and hospital ships, the Germans kept up our own war spirit and themselves neutralised the danger of pacifism.

The pacifist societies had marshalled quite a respectable little army of conscientious objectors. These, while they gave great trouble to government officials, from the tribunals down to the prison warders, were really of very little importance while such tremendous events were proceeding. Public opinion ran strongly against them and even in Princetown, Dartmoor, where the population had been accustomed to see nothing but the worst class of felon, murmurs were heard that it was time to send back the old convicts who knew how to behave themselves instead of the dreadful people with long hair and curious clothing who infested the single street.

All through 1916 the Ministry of Munitions had a separate little branch for keeping themselves informed about labour unrest that was likely to interfere with the output of munitions. In December 1916 they came to the conclusion that the work would be more efficiently and more cheaply done by professionals and I was called upon to take over the service with my own trained men. Pacifism, anticonscription and revolution were now inseparably mixed. The same individuals took part in all three movements. The real object of most of these people, though it may have been subconscious, appeared to be the ruin of their own country. This is no new thing in English history. There were pro-Bonapartists in the Waterloo time and pro-Boers eighty-five years later and though this modern brand were not perhaps strictly pro-enemy in sentiment, they acted as if they were. Does not Maitland record how, when Napoleon Bonaparte was leaving Plymouth on his last voyage to St Helena, an attempt was made by his friends in London to serve a subpoena on him in the hope of delaying his departure?

The Unofficial Reform movement was first heard of in south Wales in 1911, where it opposed the policy of conciliation of the South Wales Miners' Federation. Probably it resulted from Mr Tom Mann's Syndicalist campaign in 1910. *The Miners' Next Step*, published in 1912, set forth its programme, which was the first attempt on the part of declared revolutionaries to attack trade unionism. This book demanded one union to cover all mines and quarries in order to be in a position to call a simultaneous strike throughout the country.

Out of this grew the Rank and File Movement, which covered that extreme body, the Clyde Workers' Committee and, in common with the British Socialist Party and the Socialist Labour Party, it had sympathetic relations with the Industrial Workers of the World. It had a definite policy of the Russian Bolshevik type, arrived at quite independently, which was, through the Workers' Committee, to overthrow trade unions and reorganise all workers in a single union with a committee vested with full power to seize all workshops and factories and thus bring about the Social Revolution. There were special reasons in 1916 why the Rank and File Movement should become popular. The industrial truce of the trade unions, arrived at for the successful prosecution of the war, had weakened the influence of the executives. Most of the agitators were strong pacifists and it was easy for them to represent the trade union leaders as having betrayed the cause of the workers by abandoning their hard-won rights in order to support a capitalist war. Any improvement in working conditions which tended to allay discontent was opposed by the Workers' Committees because it set back the day when any ill-feeling between capital and labour would make it impossible for employers to carry on their business. A better understanding between employers and employed was to them a propping up of the capitalist system of society. While the Rank and File Movement was not identical with the Shop Stewards' Movement, the revolutionary element secured so many posts as shop stewards that the two became confused. Gradually the shop stewards developed into a useful institution. As the elected representatives of labour in our factories they could make the views of the workmen clear to the foreman and the employer and so save a great deal of friction. Unfortunately, at first, the movement had fallen into the hands of persons with revolutionary views, who decided to use the shop stewards as a means of ousting the regular trade union leaders. It was to be a 'Rank and File' Movement and the power to call a strike, vested nominally in the rank and file, was really to be exercised by an Association of Shop Stewards, all of revolutionary views. What they wanted was an excuse for sudden action and the excuse came with dilution and with conscription.

On 5 May 1917 began the most serious strike of the war. It broke out at Rochdale on a pottery dispute in which the employer was in the wrong. He had applied the dilution scheme to civilian work that had nothing to do with the war. The shop stewards among the engineers at once held a secret meeting at Manchester and determined to call a national strike. Two days later the Rochdale men went back to work, but by that time the engineers were out at Manchester, Coventry and Sheffield and within a week a bus strike was preventing munitions workers from getting to Woolwich. The excuse given was the proposal to 'comb out' the young unskilled men and it was curious to find south Wales, the Clyde and Leeds standing firm at a moment when a national strike was in the air. On 16 May the strike spread to Southampton, Ipswich and Chelmsford. Important work on large howitzer shells and range-finders, all urgently needed, was held up and the country was faced with the gravest danger that it had had to meet since the beginning of the war. We knew all the men who had brought about the strike and the only question was whether they should be prosecuted. There was, of course, the risk that their arrest might precipitate a general strike, but as that seemed likely to come in any case, the risk seemed worth while taking. I felt pretty sure that as soon as a few arrests were made the strike would collapse.

The government had always said that it was ready to meet the strikers with their official executive, but the official leaders hitherto had declined to deal with men who had flouted their authority. They consented only after several arrests had been made and on 19 May the strike was called off on condition that there should be no more arrests but that the prosecution of the men already arrested should be proceeded with. The bus strike had collapsed on the previous day. Nine men appeared at Bow Street and gave an undertaking that they would not again do anything to obstruct the output of munitions and as the strike was at an end they were released.

It must not be judged from the extent of the Labour disturbances of 1916 that the Workers' Committees of Shop Stewards had really captured the body of Labour. It must be remembered that the people at home, as well as the soldiers in the trenches, were suffering from war strain. Probably at no time have men ever so much needed a holiday. This was shown by the behaviour of those who went on strike. So far from collecting at street corners and listening to pacifist harangues, the Lancashire men took advantage of the fine weather at Blackpool, or were found quietly working in their allotments.

All the cherished trade union principles had been surrendered one by one. The men had submitted to dilution and even to dilution with women, to an increase in hours of labour and in output and to the exposure of their pet fallacy that engineering is so highly skilled a trade that an apprenticeship of several years is necessary before even a moderate efficiency is acquired.

The damage caused by industrial disturbances to our national prosperity was enormous. In 1918 there were 1,252 strikes, involving a loss of 6,237,000 working days. In 1919 there were 1,413 strikes, involving a loss of 34,483,000 working days and the persons involved in these disputes numbered 2,581,000.

I suppose that England has always been divided between the unreasoning optimists and the unreasoning pessimists and that public opinion oscillates between the two. In 1919 the word 'revolution' was on every lip, as it was in 1793, 1830 and 1848: in 1922 you will hear that the British working man is too staid and sensible a person ever to think of revolution except through the ballot-box. And in a few months the pendulum will have swung the other way and people will again be in a flutter. The optimists of 1922 are right, but they forget what determined minorities can do with an irresolute mass. A single fox will clear out a hen-roost while it is cackling its indignation to the skies. If Louis XVI had mounted his horse and charged the mob there might have been no Thermidor: if Louis Philippe had spoken two words to his soldiers there would have been no 1830. In Paris a street riot became a revolution and street riots unchecked were formidable affairs in those days. Who now remembers what happened in London in 1780? Yet William Beckford writes from Antwerp on Midsummer Day, 1780:

> *This characteristic stillness was the more pleasing when I looked back upon those scenes of outcry and horror which filled London but a week or two ago when danger haunted our streets at mid-day. Here I could wander – without beholding a sky red and portentous with the light of houses on fire, or hearing the confusion of shouts and groans mingled with the reports of artillery.*

Until six months after the Armistice there were several independent organisations for furnishing information. Every new ministry created during the war almost inevitably formed an 'Intelligence Section'. It is true that nearly all these co-operated closely with one another, but there was overlapping and waste of energy, to say nothing of the inevitable waste of money. Moreover, it was nobody's business to act upon the information with reasonable dispatch. By the time it reached a particular minister it was generally too late for action. This applied particularly to civil intelligence at a time when the Russian government was financing subversive organisations in this country. It was decided, therefore, to co-ordinate all this kind of information under a single head who would be responsible to a minister for any action that ought to be taken.

On 1 May 1919 this new arrangement came into force. A most admirable and efficient little staff was organised at a very low cost to the country. The revolutionary press tried to spread the belief among its readers that enormous sums were being lavished, that I went about with bulging pockets corrupting honest working men; whereas, in fact, all the most useful and trustworthy information was furnished gratuitously and the corruption was all on the other side. Many of the communist leaders and organisers were receiving salaries from Russia and, as a communist said feelingly a few months ago, 'These men are all out for money and they would sell their own grandmothers.' I have a shocking confession to make: I numbered among my friends communists who, while quite honestly entertaining communist views, disapproved very strongly of the manner in which the movement was being exploited.

There are a number of virtuous people who think it highly improper for a government to keep itself quietly informed of what is going on in its own and other countries. They forget that they themselves, in the lobby of the House of Commons, in their clubs and at their dinner-tables, are collecting and dispensing intelligence all the time. That is how public opinion is formed. The duties of an intelligence officer are very like those of a journalist, the difference being that in the case of the intelligence officer he tries to sift out the truth and to give it all to his superiors, whereas the journalist has first to consider what it is good for the public to know and what will contribute to the popularity of his newspaper. I have tried hard to put myself into the mental attitude of the good people who think intelligence 'immoral', and I cannot help feeling that their real objection is that it is inconvenient.

However this may be, it was certainly the case in 1920 and 1921 that while our expenditure had decreased there was not much of subversive activity in any part of the world that was unknown to us and whether we liked it or not, we were forced into the position of becoming a sort of clearing-house for foreign countries. The great art of acquiring information is to have friends in every grade of society in as many countries as possible.

During the first three months of 1919 unrest touched its high-water mark. I do not think that at any time in history since the Bristol Riots we have been so near revolution. The Workers' Committees had acquired the chief power in London, Sheffield, Coventry, Wales and on the Clyde and the cry for shorter hours was seized upon eagerly by the revolutionaries. On 27 January there were extensive strikes on the Clyde of a revolutionary rather than an economic character. There was great restlessness also among the electrical engineers and a general strike at the power stations had been fixed for 5 February. This was stopped by a new regulation which made strikes at power stations and similar vital undertakings illegal. The authorities had made arrangements for taking over the service if the strike occurred and no doubt some rumours about the arrangements had leaked out among the electricians. I remember waiting at the telephone at 11 p.m. one night. If the strike had taken place the leaders would probably have been brought to trial. I counted on a certain number of men coming out without the strike becoming general and in this event we should not have taken any action. The messages began to come in. No one had answered the call to strike except in one power station, where twelve men walked out into the street. Consequently, no action was taken.

Late in January the 'Hands Off Russia' movement had been started and at a meeting at the Albert Hall on 8 February every section of the revolutionary movement was represented on the platform. The speeches were probably the most startling that had ever been made in that somnolent and respectable edifice. The workers were urged to arm themselves and people who had not been following the movement were in a flutter. To one whose business it is to know individuals and to watch the formation of subversive bodies this inflammatory oratory does not quicken the pulse by a single beat. It is all as hollow as the declamation of a tragedian in a stage rehearsal. One knows so well that if the drum did beat these fiery orators would take good care not to be among the first casualties. A retrospect is very instructive, for one sees how a movement which creates public consternation for a few weeks boils up, cools and evaporates. It was so with the People's Russian Information Bureau, to which no fewer than a hundred societies affiliated themselves; it was so with the Sailors', Soldiers' and Airmen's Union and, later, with the Councils of Action and it will be so with the 'Hands Off Russia' movement, with the Union of Democratic Control and with many other more sinister movements that will shake the nerve of future generations. All, all will pass into the lumber room, where the dust is already accumulating over the Union of Democratic Control and its sisters, the Pacifist Societies.

In April 1919 we learned that a conspiracy was on foot to induce serving soldiers who enlisted under the Derby Scheme and under conscription to 'demobilise themselves' on 11 May on the ground that they enlisted for the period of the war and six months after. They were to strip off their badges and march out of barracks, not only in Kempton Park, Winchester, Salisbury and Oswestry, but in Rouen, Havre, Boulogne and Calais. In a speech delivered on May Day a member of this league who, during 1917, was employed in the Adjutant-General's department, War Office, urged a general strike to enforce demobilisation on 11 May and about the same time a leaflet headed 'To British Sailors' incited naval ratings to seize the ports and invite soldiers and policemen to join them.

The *Daily Herald* of 7 and 8 May published paragraphs supporting the view that the men were entitled to leave the colours on 11 May. The unrest among serving soldiers, especially the technical services, such as mechanics, drivers and other trades, many of whom were members of trade unions and had or thought they had jobs waiting for them which might be snapped up by others, was such that very serious disturbances might have resulted from this insidious form of incitement. But the Army Council issued a statement explaining the conditions of enlistment, which appealed to the good sense of the men, and 11 May passed off without disturbance.

CHAPTER 24

OUR COMMUNISTS

KERENSKY'S REVOLUTION DID not take the official world by surprise: it was, in fact, inevitable. The Revolution was hailed by uninstructed public opinion in England as a fulfilment of long-deferred hope and some statesmen who ought to have had more prescience joined in the acclamation. The worst of revolutions is that they never know where to stop and when in the middle of a war they befall one of the Allies upon whom the rest are counting, they are a disaster of the first magnitude. Kerensky was not fashioned by nature to ride the whirlwind: a mountain-top, whence he could indulge his gift of impassioned oratory, would have been a safer steed for him. His nerveless fingers never gripped the reins: he could not even bring himself to execute mutineers and deserters in the field. It was inevitable that a stronger hand should thrust him aside. Strange that we should ever have talked of Russia as the 'Steam Roller!' All that is left of it now is the red flag.

Of all the stupidities committed by the Germans during the war I think that the locked train was the most inexcusable because, as

Ludendorff has since admitted, it was fraught with grave danger primarily for Germany herself. There had congregated in Switzerland a little band of revolutionaries who had fled after the disturbances of 1905. There, year in and year out, they frequented cafés and smoked and talked as only Russians can talk until the whole world became unreal and danced before them through a haze of cigarette smoke. For them revolution meant no half measures. They had drunk in the fatuities of Karl Marx until there was no room left in their minds for sober reasoning and here in their own country was their opportunity. In Russia a torch was to be put to dry thatch and presently the Red conflagration should spread until it consumed the world. The workers with sickle and hammer should unite over the whole world to wipe out the bourgeoisie. That was the measure of their intelligence.

All this the Germans knew. They would not have such inflammatory material loose in their own country, but as a means of paralysing the army of their ancient Muscovite enemy it should be used at once, for Kerensky was reported to be preparing a new offensive. It is not quite clear from whom the proposal first came; whether the Bolsheviks asked for a 'safe-conduct' across Germany, or whether some German diplomatic agent invited the request; but it is known that the exiles packed themselves into a train which was sealed at the German frontier and kept so until it crossed into Russia. Had Kerensky and his advisers been wise and strong they would have hitched a locomotive to the other end of the train and sent it back, but they were neither wise nor strong. It is said that when Ulianov, otherwise Lenin, was making inflammatory speeches Kerensky was implored to take action against him and that he said, 'Let him talk: he will talk himself out.'

I remember speaking about this time to a diplomatist with a knowledge of Russia and asking him whether he thought that the Czar, who was then a prisoner in his own palace under Kerensky, was in any personal danger. He shook his head and said that he doubted whether the Czar would come out of the welter alive.

With the second Revolution in November 1917, the Bolsheviks came into power. They included Nihilists, Anarchists and extreme Social Revolutionaries, who were all soon to be enrolled in a single body as communists and followers of Karl Marx. Lenin has never swerved from his plan of making Russia merely the seed-bed for a general revolution in Europe on a class basis. He hoped for it in Germany, Austria and Italy; he was certain of it in the Ukraine and Poland, but he admitted that his chances of success in England and America were small because in England he held the working class to be too ignorant and in America there had been no preparation. For the moment the Bolsheviks showed a frenzied energy in striking terror into their political opponents. There were mass executions and the horrors attending some of them, especially at Kronstadt, were not exaggerated. Even Tchitcherin, usually the mildest of men, wrote on 11 September 1918 to the head of the American Red Cross:

Our adversaries are not executed, as you affirm, for holding other political views than ours, but for taking part in the most terrible battles, in which no weapon is left untouched against us, no crime is left aside and no atrocities are considered too great when the power belongs to them ... 300 have been selected already (for execution) as belonging to the vanguard of the counter-revolutionary movement. In the passionate struggle tearing our whole people do you not see the sufferings, untold during generations, of all the unknown millions who were dumb during centuries, whose concentrated despair and rage have at last burst into the passionate longing for a new life, for the sake of which they have the whole existing fabric to remove?

In the great battles of mankind, hatred and fury are unavoidable as in every battle and in every struggle.

If he had said simply that they were executing their opponents in order to save their own skins he would have been nearer the truth, for fear is always more fertile in violent outrage than the spirit of revenge.

There was something providential in the sequence of events. The Bolshevik Revolution came at a time when the entire people in England except a few defeatists and pacifists had gritted its teeth and was determined to see the war through. If it had come eighteen months later, when demobilisation was in the air and people were looking for a new world, it might have gone hardly with us. As it was, the ordinary Englishman felt that he had been 'let down' by the Russian Bolsheviks and he resented the treachery.

The second Russian Revolution turned the heads of the pacifists and defeatists in England. They had failed in every enterprise: the country had declined to endorse their scheme for obtaining peace by negotiation with the Germans and here at last was a great people ready to put the doctrines of Karl Marx into practice. They had a great deal to explain away: it was impossible altogether to deny the atrocities of the Bolsheviks, but they could attack their own government on the score of the Allied intervention, which they represented as an attempt on the part of the capitalists to strangle an infant socialist state at birth and to excuse the excesses of the torch-bearers of revolutionary socialism. This, they thought, would be a more popular cry than 'Peace by Negotiation'.

On 3 June 1917 they called a National Conference at Leeds, which was attended by over 1,900 people. It was said at the time to have cost £5,000 and to have been held at the expense of the Union of Democratic Control. Mr Ramsay MacDonald described this conference as the most active gathering he had ever attended; Mr Sexton as 'the most bogus, the most dishonest and the most corrupt conference ever created by the mind of man'. It was resolved to divide Great Britain into Soviets to the ominous number of thirteen, with headquarters in Duke Street, Adelphi. These Soviets existed for a few weeks and then expired. At Tunbridge Wells some attempt was made among soldiers awaiting demobilisation to organise support for a local Soviet among the troops, but there was little response. The Provisional Council, nominated presumably with their own consent, were also to be thirteen – a number which seemed to exercise a fascination on the Conference. They included Messrs Robert Smillie, Philip Snowden, Ramsay MacDonald, Robert Williams, George Lansbury and Joseph Fineberg, the Russian-Jewish secretary to Litvinoff. It is believed that this council never met, though manifestoes were issued by Mr Albert Inkpin in its name.

The Russian Revolution dug Karl Marx out of the grave in which he had been lying uneasily since 1883. Karl Marx was a Prussian Jew born in 1818. He was driven successively from Prussia and from France and he found an asylum in London. He was not a working man, nor had he any business experience and his theories about capital and Labour were purely academic. His philosophy was really an attempt to reconcile the doctrine of the Brotherhood of Man, expounded by Rousseau, to modern economic conditions. In his time Rousseau's theories were a little fly-blown. Marx attempted to rehabilitate them by pointing out that the industrial revolution had lowered the status of the workmen while immensely increasing their economic value; that it had deprived them of all real interest in their expanding industry and had converted them into 'wage-slaves'. He called upon them to take arms in the class war throughout the industrial world. His manifesto, used by the Russian Bolsheviks and the British extreme socialists, was, 'Workers of all lands, unite!

You have a world to win; you have nothing to lose but your chains,' and in another passage, 'We make war against all the prevailing ideals of the state, of country, of patriotism.' As Burke once said of the Jacobins: 'This sort of people are so taken up by their theories of the rights of man that they have totally forgotten his nature.'

Between 1848 and 1860 the idea of international solidarity of classes was popular, but after 1860 the lines of cleavage tended to become vertical rather than horizontal, for from that date Europe became increasingly nationalist. Moreover, Marx himself, owing to his long residence in England, had begun to waver in his opinion. The mid-Victorian trade unionist believed in constitutional action. Marx, who had formed a Communist League in London in 1847, had seen it collapse in 1852. It had been re-formed in 1862 as a result of the cosmopolitan feeling created by the Great Exhibition, but after a few meetings, generally held in Switzerland, it languished and died. The only power that seemed to be growing was that of the constitutional trade unionist and before his death Marx was himself inclining in that direction.

Some months before the Bolsheviks came into power a curious document which has since received much attention in England was brought to the notice of the State Department in Washington. *The Protocols of the Wise Men of Zion*, first published in Russian in 1897 by a Russian named Nilus, purported to set forth the details of a secret Jewish conspiracy for the domination of the world. A committee of Americans were preparing a report upon the document and I was asked unofficially to give my opinion upon its authenticity. Besides the internal evidence there was very little to go upon, but I reported that the 'protocols' were almost certainly fabricated by some anti-Semitic organisation and I heard afterwards that the American Committee had reported in the same sense.

It was quite natural that when the Bolsheviks came into power and it was seen that nearly all the people's commissaries were Jews, so obvious a fulfilment of the *Protocols* should not pass unnoticed. It was useless to point out that, 'protocols or no protocols', it was inevitable in a country like Russia: people would have it that the first part of this sinister programme had been realised and that worse was still to come. No doubt, the famous *Protocols* did faithfully reflect the kind of talk that has been current among fanatically nationalist Jews among themselves for more than a century.

How the Russians themselves regard their Jewish masters is shown by a popular story now current in Russia. At a Soviet meeting the list of elected delegates was read over. The secretary came to the name 'Ivan Ivanowitch Petroff'.

'But what's his real name?' asked a delegate.

'Ivan Ivanowitch Petroff. He has no other name.'

'Bah!' said the Jewish delegate. 'These Russians will push in everywhere.'

In Bela Kun's regime in Hungary, as well as in Russia, nearly all the commissaries and especially those who were guilty of atrocious acts of cruelty, were Jews.

There is one and one only virtue in the Russian Bolshevik – that he knows what he wants and allows no weak scruples or respect for public opinion to prevent him from getting it. Fancy a government of this country that knew its own mind and had no scruples and cared nothing for public opinion! It is conceivable that it might really bring about 'a country fit for heroes to live in' instead of a country in which only heroes can live.

At this time even the professional moulders of our opinions failed us. I remember saying to a great newspaper owner in 1917 that he might devote his papers to a denunciation of Bolshevism and he replied, 'Who's afraid of Bolshevism? I tell you there will be so much employment in England after the war and the people will be earning such high wages, that they will have no time to think of Bolshevism.'

Well, the truth, as usual, lies midway. We had the fever mildly and now our temperature is a little below normal and so the world will go on in impulse and reaction to the end, always making a little progress in the long run unless the great catastrophe that has overtaken civilisation in Russia should overtake the civilisation of the globe. There have been Nineveh, Babylon, Egypt, Carthage and Rome and the fate that overtook those great empires may overtake empires again, on so slender a thread hangs all human stability.

The Soviet ideal never got beyond its paper stage in England. Perhaps the nearest approach to it was the Rank and File Movement, which Lenin afterwards declared to be the nucleus of an organisation which embodies his ideas; but by the time the Russians were ready to subsidise the Rank and File Movement, workmen had realised the advantage of electing moderate men and women to represent them and the Rank and File Movement was dead.

One revolutionary paper, *The Call*, printed an article, 'Learn to speak Russian!' and said that the working class must 'assert its will in Russian accents ... It would be anti-Parliament, as the great Chartist Conventions were. Then we shall soon see how easily Russian can be spoken even in these islands without the knowledge of grammar or vocabulary'; but *The Call* had few readers at that time and there was a general distrust of anyone who held up Russian institutions for imitation.

For some months we were concerned with the antics of Maxim Litvinoff, whom the Bolsheviks had appointed their representative in England. On 18 February 1918 he addressed a meeting in Westminster at which the late Mr Anderson MP presided; 2,000 tickets were issued. Litvinoff's reception on this occasion seems to have turned his head. He had taken an office in Victoria Street, at which he received visits from Russians serving in the British Army, from the crews of Russian ships of war lying in British harbours and from a vast number of persons of Bolshevik sympathy. Indeed, the number and the quality of the visitors became so embarrassing to the other tenants that the landlord evicted him. He had already appointed Mr John M'Lean, of the British Socialist Party, to be Bolshevik Consul in Glasgow and he himself called at the Russian embassy and demanded that it should be handed over to him.

Litvinoff is said to be a native of Baisk, a town in the Baltic Provinces. Both his parents were Jewish and his father's name was Mordecai Finkelstein, a shopkeeper who used to give private lessons in Russian and Hebrew. Having associated himself with the revolutionary movement he left Russia and after some vicissitudes he came to London and obtained work at a stationer's shop under the name of David Finkelstein. Later he changed his name to Harrison and became secretary to a Russian group of political refugees. He married a lady of Jewish descent, a British subject, though of foreign extraction. When the Russian Government Committee was formed for the purchase of war supplies he obtained work in the Agricultural Department and he kept his post for some months after the second Revolution and left it only in July 1917. He took this post under the name of Maxim Maximovitch Litvinoff. While Kerensky was in power he showed no Bolshevik leanings, but these appeared very soon after the subsidy from the Russian provisional government was stopped. He then left the committee and joined the Russian Delegates Committee with Tchitcherin at Finsbury House.

Soon after his appointment as Bolshevik representative he began to associate with English pacifists. He wrote and circulated a manifesto which appeared in the *Woolwich Pioneer* and he was accused of urging the soldiers who visited his offices to engage in propaganda in their regiments. As soon as the deputation from the Russian patrol vessel *Poryv* returned from seeing him a mutiny broke out on that vessel and on her sister ship, the *Razsvet*, both lying in Liverpool, and voices were heard crying, 'Shoot the officers!' A British naval officer came on board and saved their lives. The crews were taken on shore to the police cells and some of them made statements affecting Litvinoff. Deportation orders were made against them and they were sent back to Russia.

Litvinoff's cup was full. It was decided, none too soon, that he should leave the country and not return to it. For a man of so humble a position and so lofty an ambition it was a severe blow. No doubt he had lain awake at nights dreaming of himself in uniform and decorations among the Corps Diplomatique at St James's and it was not surprising that his disappointment should vent itself in bitter antagonism to this country. We had not quite done with him. The Russians had taken many British prisoners of war and they nominated Litvinoff to represent them in the negotiations for their release.

The high cost of living had provoked an outcry against profiteering and was causing very serious unrest. The London docks were choked with frozen meat that nobody wanted, but flour and other food-stuffs were deficient. A number of ill-informed people believed that there were large stores of corn in the granaries of south Russia and that if the cost of living was to be reduced in England this corn ought to be got out even at the cost of entering into quasi-diplomatic relations with the oligarchy in power in Moscow. An officer of the Ministry of Food made himself a laughing-stock by writing a grave essay to that effect, but it was no laughing matter, for there ensued from it the phrase, 'the bulging corn-bins,' though it was well known at the time that if the corn-bins bulged it was because there was nothing in them to support the walls.

At the beginning of 1920 the Soviet government was holding a number of British officers and soldiers as prisoners of war, although we were not at war with Russia, nor at the time were there any military preparations against her.

The pressing need was to rescue these prisoners and Mr O'Grady MP was sent to Reval to confer with Litvinoff, as representative of the Soviet government. Now Litvinoff had never concealed his strong desire to return to England in any capacity which might result eventually in his recognition as Russian ambassador. These negotiations were dilatory and ambiguous, being designed to bring the maximum of pressure to bear on the British government through the unfortunate prisoners.

Out of this conference, which did at last result in the release of the prisoners, grew the Russian Trade Agreement with England. The trade that has resulted is negligible. We have sold the Russians very little, we have got from them practically nothing that we wanted, but a great deal that we did not want at all. In May 1920 Kameneff and Krassin arrived in London to arrange the Agreement. A Jewish journalist of ability and experience named Theodore Rothstein at once attached himself to their delegation. During the war he had been employed in the press section of one of the government departments, where his known communist sympathies were thought unlikely to be dangerous to the country. He had never lost his Russian nationality, though his son, who shared his father's views, having been born in England, was a British subject. Mr Rothstein immediately threw all his energies into a campaign in favour of communism in this country. He was the intermediary for subsidies to revolutionary organisations and his secret activities were far-reaching. Fortunately, in August 1920, he was selected to accompany Monsieur Miliutin to Russia and from that country he was not allowed to return. A year later he became the Bolshevik representative in Teheran.

This was not Kameneff's first visit to England. Not very long after the Armistice he arrived in this country with another communist on his way to Paris and Berne, where they were respectively to become the permanent Bolshevik representatives. They brought with them a cheque for a large sum of money and a mass of propaganda literature in leather trunks, rove with steel chains, which they said had been used by the imperial Russian couriers for conveying documents of a specially secret nature: they chuckled over the manifest impossibility of the British police examining the contents without leaving their mark behind them. It was tempting Providence! As it was clear that the French government would not admit them and that they could not stay in this country they were both sent back to Russia with all their luggage and the cheque was handed to them on embarkation. There was a good deal of difficulty in inducing them to go, for one of them declined to get out of bed and a gigantic Cossack in physical charge of the party could speak no language but his own. But a display of tactful firmness by the Special Branch inspectors got them to King's Cross just in time to catch the boat-train.

Under these circumstances it was scarcely to be expected that Kameneff would be friendly to this country and he soon began to show his hand. There were several counts against him. He had deliberately falsified a dispatch on the question of the Polish War at a time when the Councils of Action were ready to swallow any false information if it came from a Russian source and he had been foremost in arranging a Russian subsidy for the revolutionary press in England. He was plainly informed that the British government was aware what he had done and that they did not regard him as a proper representative of the Russian government. He departed to Moscow on the understanding that he would not return.

He was succeeded by Krassin as the head of the present Russian Trade Delegation. Every member of it gave an undertaking in writing not to interfere in the internal affairs of this country, or to be interviewed by representatives of the press: Monsieur Krassin gave a verbal undertaking to the same effect. While he tried loyally to carry out this undertaking and to confine himself to the non-political business for which he was admitted to this country, it was not so with many members of his staff and, as propaganda is considered to be the first duty of every communist, it was scarcely to be expected that they would keep any such promise. They had private conferences with members of the Council of Action and they supplied the *Daily Herald* regularly with 'news' from Russia.

Bolshevism has been described as an infectious disease rather than a political creed – a disease which spreads like a cancer, eating away the tissue of society until the whole mass disintegrates and falls into corruption. It has other attributes of disease. Captain McCullough has given an excellent description of its first febrile stage, when a young Russian bluejacket named Mekarov, who was certified to be Bolshevik-proof, returned from a Bolshevik meeting mad drunk on Bolshevik oratory and bad alcohol and went roaring up and down the corridor with a revolver threatening to murder the British officers. It is not recorded whether the same symptoms were observed in Paris during the Terror, but a German who had been through the recent revolution in Germany told me that he had noticed the eyes lighted by dull fire from within. I noticed the same symptoms in a young policeman who was shouting, 'Let's have a revolution!' during the police strike. The Russians, the most amiable and the most docile of people, took the malady in its severest form; but while there were outbursts unknown to western Europe all over the country, the propagandist was displaying almost superhuman industry in Petrograd and Moscow. Leaflets were poured out from the press by the ton and the Russian revolutionaries living in foreign countries were at once mobilised to preach the Red doctrine.

In July 1918 Miss Sylvia Pankhurst, who had long been working on revolutionary lines in opposition to the rest of her family, joined with Mr W. F. Watson, of the Rank and File Movement, to found the People's Russian Information Bureau on funds provided by the Russians for the dissemination of Bolshevik literature and the preaching of revolution.

On 30 August the police strike filled the extremists with renewed hope. For the Londoner the bottom seemed to have fallen out of the world. That a body so trusted and so patriotic should refuse duty in the last stages of a war in which so many of their comrades were fighting, implied that there was none of our settled institutions in which one could trust any more. There was no real cause for anxiety: the strike was economic, not revolutionary. For many months an agitation fostered by an ex-inspector who had left the Metropolitan Police with a grievance had been carried on and a Police and Prison Officers' Union had secretly been formed. It had gained few adherents until the rise in the cost of living without a corresponding rise in pay swelled the membership to several hundreds. The Commissioner, Sir Edward Henry, was fully alive to this just grievance and had put forward proposals which had been approved. If the approval had been made public perhaps there would have been no strike, but unfortunately part of the scheme was an endowment for the widows of policemen and the actuarial calculations that were involved were holding up the whole scheme. For some days before the strike there had been a vigorous campaign of recruiting for the union and word had secretly been passed round that all members were to be ready. The great mass of the older men knew nothing of these plans. When they came on duty on the morning of 30 August a strong picket ordered them back and as they encountered the picket singly most of them obeyed. A number, however, refused to be intimidated and some of these were made afterwards to pay for their loyalty. Sir Edward Henry was on leave; Scotland Yard was filled with excited demonstrators in plain clothes. There were marches to Tower Hill, where the extremist members of the London Trades Council addressed the men. Special Constables were hustled and abused, but as might have been expected of the London driver, the traffic managed itself with surprisingly few accidents.

As soon as their grievances were remedied the great body of the men returned to duty. Sir Edward Henry retired, receiving a baronetcy for his services, and Sir Nevil Macready, the Adjutant-General, was appointed in his place. The Police Union, with the support of many Labour leaders, was now pressing for recognition and as a union in a disciplined force would have been unworkable, representative boards forming a direct channel from the men to the Commissioner were instituted and accepted by the Force. All this was skilfully managed by Sir Nevil Macready.

The officials of the Police Union, encouraged by revolutionary Labour, now began to organise a second police strike for the 'full and frank recognition' of the Police Union. The authorities were aware of their plans and were also aware that the higher pay granted on the recommendation of Lord Desborough's Committee had satisfied the great majority of the men. In August 1919 when the strike was called, barely 1,000 men responded in London. At Liverpool the number was much larger and many of the warders at Wormwood

Scrubs Prison also came out. All were dismissed. Among them, no doubt, were many thoughtless men who had done good service in the war, but had lacked the backbone to stand out against the revolutionary agitator. Their places were filled by demobilised soldiers, among whom were a few demobilised officers. Many of the police strikers joined the extremists in a campaign for reinstatement, but on this point the government has remained firm.

At this time the great body of Englishmen had only one preoccupation – the last phases of the war. There were distractions abroad as well as at home. In Finland the Red Terror had broken out and the Finnish right, for self-defence as they said, called in German troops for their protection. Many of the outrages during the Red Terror were committed not by Finns but by the Russian Bolsheviks who had poured into the country. There followed a reaction, which Finnish socialists describe as a White Terror, though in fact it seems to have been greatly exaggerated.

While the whole world was watching Marshal Foch's counterstrokes with bated breath it had no time to think of revolution and even now it is not generally known that revolutions on the Russian plan actually broke out on Armistice Day, 1918, in Switzerland and Holland. They failed because the Swiss and the Dutch are not Russians. Immediately, the stable populations of these countries determined to take no further risk. In Switzerland military lorries drove up to the door of the Soviet representatives and the whole gang, men and women, with their belongings were packed into the vehicles and conducted to the frontier under a military escort. In Holland the orderly people formed a *Burgerwacht*, a sort of volunteer special constabulary recruited from all classes down to the humblest workman and for the moment the revolutionary movement was stifled. In Hungary Bela Kun, acting under the orders of Lenin, produced a revolution on the Russian model and that unspeakable ruffian, Szamueli, who 'committed suicide' and so escaped the penalty for his crimes, ravaged the country for five months and brought it to ruin.

Our first troubles in England arose out of demobilisation. As long as hostilities continued no soldier minded going back to France, but men did not at all see the necessity of going back when there was no more fighting to do. On 10 January 1919 there were military riots at Folkestone and shortly afterwards at Calais and there was a feeling throughout the army that the system of demobilisation in liberating first the key industry men, irrespective of their length of service, was an injustice.

During the first month of 1919 there were minor disturbances at several of the camps, chiefly among the technical services, in which a large proportion of the men belonged to trade unions.

In the months following the Armistice some of the societies of ex-servicemen began to give anxiety. The most dangerous at the moment seemed to be the Sailors', Soldiers' and Airmen's Union, which had wholeheartedly accepted the Soviet idea and was in touch with the police strikers who had been dismissed, with the more revolutionary members of the London Trades Councils and with the Herald League. The 'Comrades of the Great War' never gave any cause for anxiety, nor, on the whole, did the National Federation of Ex-Servicemen, though some of its branches were swayed by a few of the more extreme members.

During February 1919 a young Russian Bolshevik violinist was touring the country and drawing large audiences of working men and women not so much to listen to his playing as to the revolutionary speeches with which he interspersed his performances. His was a typical case of the epidemic in its febrile stage, a stage from which the British appear to be immune. In the disturbed state of the public mind it was decided that Soermus would be better in his own country and his triumphant tour was interrupted in order that he might be put on board a boat which was about to sail for Norway. This happened to be fixed for the day before the 'Hands off Russia' meeting at the Albert Hall, at which every section of the revolutionary movement was represented on the platform. Soermus was to have been on the platform at this meeting. There was a large strike on the Clyde at the moment and many of the speakers really believed that it was the beginning of the General Strike which was to merge into revolution. At that moment we were probably nearer to very serious disturbances than we have been at any time since the Bristol Riots of 1831. A few days later the reaction began. On 12 February the Clyde strikers resumed work and a few weeks' later the National Industrial Conference met.

In March the storm centre moved from the engineering industries to the Triple Alliance and there were signs of co-operation between ex-servicemen and the extreme Labour organisations. The Sailors', Soldiers' and Airmen's Union exacted a pledge from its members that they would take no part against strikers and certain branches of the National Federation of Ex-Servicemen were for supporting the miners on strike in south Wales. This attitude was perfectly natural. The men had been led by public speeches to imagine that they were coming home to find things much easier for them than they had been before the war: they found a shortage not only of houses but of many other comforts, such as beer. But there were hopeful signs: the Workers' Committees were losing power; the propaganda in favour of shorter hours had failed; the ballot of the Electrical Trade Union on the question of striking to secure a forty-four-hour week had left the extremists in the minority and the report of the Joint Committee on the Industrial Conference was a step towards a better understanding between capital and Labour. All this illustrated a fact too little realised in England – namely, that the great body of Labour opinion is not and never has been in favour of violence. Unfortunately, the older men prefer the quiet of their homes in the evening to attending stormy branch meetings at which a number of hot-headed youths make speeches about the class-war without knowing about the interests of their trade and howl down any moderate speaker who talks common sense. Consequently, the extremists have things entirely their own way. They pass resolutions which are sent to headquarters as representing the real views of the branch and it is not until the time comes for a ballot that the real weakness of their position is made evident.

During April there was a wide extension of craft unionism. Agricultural labourers, shop assistants, policemen and actors became trade unionists. Ex-servicemen had become persuaded that employers were attempting to re-engage men on pre-war rates and there were frequent demonstrations. As long as the international movement was concerned only with the general interests of Labour it was a more or less academic matter, but now for the first time we had in Europe a revolutionary government amply supplied with funds, which was prepared to finance and instruct the revolutionary agitators in every civilised country in the hope of producing a world revolution, without which its own tenure of office was recognised to be precarious. For the first time in history, the revolutionary agitator need not be a fanatic, for his profession had now become lucrative and a loud voice and a glib tongue became worth anything from £6 to £10 a week. The Soviet government, or rather, the Council of the Third International, under which it chose to screen its activities, had been told by its representative in England that a revolution was certain within six months. In France and Italy it was to come even sooner and in Germany the pressure of the extreme left would soon force the majority socialists out of power. Then the effigy of Karl Marx would be worshipped in every capital and the world would have entered into the Millennium.

One result of all this was to augment the little band of intellectual revolutionaries who have always bloomed among us modest and unseen. Most of these are men who see in a future Labour government a short cut to power. They think that it is easy to be a Triton among minnows. Not a few of them are ex-officers in the navy and army; and even among the undergraduates at Oxford and Cambridge and in one or two of the public schools, there are little cliques of 'Parlour Bolsheviks'.

At the Municipal Elections in November 1919 the Labour candidates had a sweeping victory. Many had declared themselves revolutionary and were determined to convert the municipal organisations into municipal Soviets, but responsibility soon began to dim these fiery spirits and it was maliciously reported that many of them were more concerned with the social status of their wives and with the question of payment for their municipal work than they were with revolution.

Then began the great propaganda campaign for nationalisation of the mines. More than a million leaflets were printed, countless speeches were delivered and for a moment it seemed as if a passion for nationalisation was to sweep the country. Soon, however, it became evident that nobody quite knew what nationalisation meant. Many miners thought they were to own the mines themselves and work the number of hours that happened to suit them at a scale of pay laid down by themselves. When these were told that the government was to own the mines and that they were to have civil servants as their bosses they became grave. The moulders' strike was gradually paralysing many industries and swelling the ranks of the unemployed. In December there were rumours of lightning strikes among the dockers, as well as the railwaymen and the abolition of the unemployment donation was causing widespread discontent. Ex-soldiers began to claim that the National Relief and the Canteen Funds should be used for their benefit. The year 1919 closed with the uneasy feeling that, though we might be readjusting ourselves more smoothly than any other nation, we must be prepared for serious disturbances.

Forecasts in political matters are proverbially wrong. By the end of the year the great question of nationalisation was in a state of suspended animation, scarcely to be distinguished from dissolution. The Councils of Action which in August had almost threatened to become Soviets were now derisively termed in Labour circles 'Councils of Inaction', and little more was to be heard of them. Of the really great menace to civilisation that was so soon to fall upon the world nobody seemed to be thinking at all.

About this time I remember having a long conversation with the late Dr Rathenau before he accepted office in Germany. He said:

> *Hitherto we have always considered the consumer as a constant factor and concerned ourselves with over- and under-production. Before the war we never thought that the consumer could cease to consume. That is the real cause of the trade depression and unemployment.*

The trade depression, dark as it is, has had a sobering effect on the wilder spirits in revolutionary labour. Trade unions had blundered into the political field and had tried to coerce the government on matters of foreign policy which they did not understand. Many working men were under the delusion that the Councils of Action had prevented the government from going to war with Russia and they were considering what they should do about the Irish, the Japanese and the Indian questions. The effect of all this had been temporarily to impair the influence of Parliament, but the British working man never really takes much interest in foreign affairs and this insular tendency has been the great stumbling-block of revolutionary agitation.

It was possible about this time to make an estimate of the number of class-conscious communists who would be prepared to lay down their lives for their ideals. The membership of the communist parties was then put at 20,000, but after a close study of individuals, extended over many months, I was inclined to put the number of would-be martyrs at well under twenty. The communists were quite aware that, though minorities could make revolutions, when one embarks upon revolution by bloodshed it is well to have the support of numbers. Otherwise, martyrdom may loom a little too near. It was all very well for Mr Tom Mann to boast that in Russia 60,000 communists were in control of more than 80,000,000 Russians, but where would 20,000 British communists, largely diluted with aliens and Jews, be when they tried to hold down 45,000,000 in this country? The Russians had devised a recruiting system of their own. In every union a 'cell' was to be established which would grow unseen, as in the incipient stage of cancer, until the heart of the union was eaten out. They counted upon the behaviour of some of the leaders of British trade unionism, who seemed to favour the dictatorship of the proletariat, not knowing that the more sober had been driven into the Councils of Action by the fear of being left out in the cold.

CHAPTER 25

THE RETURN TO SANITY

A S I HAVE said, publicity has been the best weapon of defence against the forces of disorder. The fact is that there is little love lost between revolutionary leaders and an atmosphere of cold suspicion broods over their conspiracies. At one period German communism was rent in twain by excessive subsidies from Moscow, because those who did not get what they held to be their fair share turned upon their leaders.

I suppose that few men in England have had to read so many revolutionary speeches and revolutionary pamphlets and leaflets as I have. All display the same ignorance of elementary economics – an ignorance so childish that it cannot be assumed. They seemed to think that capital was gold kept in a box, perhaps under the capitalist's bed, perhaps in the vaults of a bank and that when the 'proletariat' became dictators they had only to dip into the box to get all the capital they needed for running a communist state. If the capital ran short they could always raise money by taxation. It had never dawned upon them that there is comparatively very little gold; that under the communist state there will be nobody to tax and that as soon as private credit is destroyed capital goes up in smoke, as the Marxists in Russia have found out for themselves.

Another of their fallacies is the belief, quite honestly entertained, that the proletariat is 90 per cent of the population, whereas, in fact, the people who work with their hands and their families form, in a country with a large middle class such as England, actually little more than half the population, and that the other half would not sit down tamely under the forcible rule of the least educated moiety of the community. Under the stress of unemployment they are beginning to understand that these islands cannot support a population of 45,000,000 except by foreign trade, but they do not even now know how much capital the people of this country have invested in undertakings abroad.

The Statist gives the value of our foreign investments as follows:

India and Colonies – £481,529,927

Argentina – £118,339,585

Brazil – £88,227,036

Chile – £27,563,340

Cuba – £14,563,385

Mexico – £33,822,322

Peru – £6,988,691

United States – £164,201,850

Rest of America – £11,128,188

Austria – £6,247,896

Bulgaria – £3,819,499

Denmark – £6,844,600

Egypt – £6,427,577

Finland – £3,441,450

Greece – £3,301,644

Hungary – £2,077,240

Norway – £4,833,250

Romania – £4,429,875

Russia – £46,214,906

Siberia – £994,993

Sweden – £4,556,000

Turkey – £4,745,869

Other European countries – £9,280,176

China – £27,805,737

Dutch colonies – £12,236,971

Japan – £22,447,240

Persia – £2,706,250

Philippines – £2,238,283

Siam – £1,102,500

Rest of Asia – £175,000

Africa – £2,702,603

Others – £2,436,146

Total – £1,127,431,129

It has never been explained why the political phenomena in one country appear simultaneously in practically all civilised countries. The general wave of unrest among Labour in 1912 was not a local phenomenon; it was like the wave that ran through Europe in 1848, though of course it was less marked. From Norway to Italy, from Siberia to Portugal, the same phenomenon was to be noticed.

As I said in an earlier chapter, on Armistice Day there were simultaneous attempts at revolution in Switzerland and Holland, countries which had suffered severely from the war though they took no part in it.

Italy and Spain were unstable and in the United States and Canada the spread of Bolshevik ideas had begun to cause serious alarm. The Americans and the Canadians had passed legislation making it a penal offence to advocate a change in the form of government by force or violence, or even to carry the Red Flag in processions. In America they proceeded to apply the new law so drastically that there was some reaction. As long as the much abused 'DORA', by which the Defence of the Realm Act had come popularly to be known, was in force, there was no need for fresh legislation in England, but when the Act lapsed on 1 September 1921, the defects in the English laws against sedition began acutely to be felt. There was, it is true, an Act which gave power to the government to declare a state of emergency, when certain powers made under the Emergency Powers Act would come into force, but until a state of emergency is declared the authorities have to rely upon the old Sedition Laws, which entail indictment for seditious libel or seditious conspiracy, or for incitement to injure persons or property.

Now procedure by indictment is a slow process and generally out of proportion to the offence: the offender is given what he most desires – an exaggerated importance and advertisement. If there happens to be on the jury one person who sympathises with his views or is terrorised by an Anarchist society, he will escape altogether and even if he is convicted and sentenced he must be treated as a first-class misdemeanant with privileges which, to persons of his stamp, reduces imprisonment to the level of a rather amusing experience. Moreover, the delay between the offence and the conviction deprives the sentence of its value as a deterrent. In the provinces a seditious speaker may have to wait four or five months for his trial. By that time the emergency which made it necessary for the government to proceed against him has gone and the prosecution is then accused of vindictiveness in continuing the proceedings when the need for a warning has lapsed.

What is wanted is summary procedure, where the offender can receive a short deterrent sentence. It is true that he may now be summoned to be bound over to be of good behaviour, but this penalty is ludicrously inadequate. As it stands, the law punishes a subordinate who does some violent act at the instigation of another and leaves practically untouched the organiser of a campaign of violence and outrage. After the lapse of DORA there was a very marked recrudescence of incitement to violence. It is quite true that most of the inflammatory speeches and writings of irresponsible agitators may be treated with contempt, but from time to time cases do occur in which such incitement cannot safely be left unchecked. It has always been noticed that a timely prosecution and conviction of one or two persons has a very sobering effect on the rest and that when an agitator is sent to prison for two or three months he never regains his old ascendency.

At present it is not an offence to introduce money or valuables from abroad for the purpose of inciting people to violent revolution in this country. Any bill prepared for the House of Commons should make it an offence to import any document of which the publication would be an offence in the United Kingdom, except for purposes of study and any money or valuables brought in with the above-mentioned object.

It is curious now to look back upon our purblind extravagance during the two years following the war. We were far more alive in the early part of 1918 to the need for rigid economy after the war than we were in those boisterous days of rejoicing. The banks were full of money. There were strikes, but everyone felt that as soon as the moulders' strike was liquidated there would be a boom in all industries. We continued feasting and dancing for many months. As far as unemployment is concerned, if people had been as careful about expenditure as they are now, they would have money free for purchasing what they need.

Disastrous as it was economically, the coal strike which began on 18 August 1920 let light into many dark corners. It was the last chance of the Triple Alliance. It must be confessed that the coal-owners might have smoothed away many difficulties if they had issued at an earlier stage a statement of their case in simple terms and plain figures. As it was, not only the miners but the public failed to understand what their offer really was. Many of the steadier miners abstained from voting in the ballot and the extremists had things all their own way. There was an overwhelming majority for rejecting the owners' terms.

This brought matters to a head and there were few people who did not think that we were in for what amounted to a general strike. Knowing that if the other unions called out their men a minority only would respond, I felt certain that some pretext would be found at the eleventh hour for withdrawing from the false position. At the historic meeting in one of the committee rooms at the House of Commons, when certain members sought enlightenment, it cannot be said that the spokesman for the owners made matters much clearer, whereas Mr Frank Hodges conducted his case with the greatest ability. It was by accident that he happened to be in the lobby at all, but many crises are resolved by accident. He spoke the absolute truth when he said that the miners were less concerned about the National Pool than they were about their wages. Comparatively few miners understood what a National Pool really was; they did understand what a cut in wages meant and there were many wild stories about cuts of 9s. a week. The surrender of the National Pool was the turning-point. The strike had been called for midnight on 15 April and still I felt sure that the hard facts, which must be known to the railway and transport leaders, would prevail.

The government was right in taking no chances. The organisation for feeding the large cities was even better than it was in the railway strike of 1919 and as a means of coercing the public the strike must have failed in any case. Everything turned upon the meeting of the other two unions. It was a stormy meeting and the leaders were glad to have the excuse of the surrender of the National Pool for calling the strike off.

When the dust and the shouting had died down and the great captains were denouncing one another in private, it was possible to see what 15 April, 'Black Friday', which the *Daily Herald* hoped to be able to refer to as 'Red Friday', really meant. 'Yesterday,' said its editorial, 'was the heaviest defeat that has befallen the Labour movement within the memory of man.' If for 'Labour movement' the writer had said 'communist movement', the statement would have been accurate.

Men were becoming weary of the incessant patter about class consciousness and were beginning to understand that in the economic crisis which has involved the entire world only the nations who can pull together can hope to weather the storm.

The coal strike was economic and not revolutionary until the communists tried to exploit it as a 'Jumping-Off Place' for 'the Day'.

But the *Herald* should have worn a black border for the Triple Alliance. Like other alliances known to history, it was all right as long as it was never asked to function. In fact, it lay in the sky like a cloud no bigger than a man's hand. Every now and then it blew itself out portentously and obscured the sun. The clouds were big with thunder and men trembled and then, as sometimes happens in the firmament, they dispersed without a storm. It had been so in the railway strike. We went about with bowed heads for quite a week. The day was fixed when we were to wear out our shoe-leather by tramping about our business, because the streets were to be silent and grass-grown and the rails of the Underground were to rust in their chairs, but at the ninth or tenth hour there appeared a Conciliation Committee, consisting of the two component bodies of the Triple Alliance who had not come out and wanted to hold back by the coat-tails those who had. It was not, let it be understood, out of pure philanthropy, but for that very cogent reason that if they did call a strike among their own men the strike would be abortive because a very large percentage of them would stay at work.

This time it was not the tenth but the eleventh hour. It was not the government preparations, the trains of lorries, the gathering Reserves, the stirring recruiting of the Defence Force, but the fact, which was borne in upon the delegates at their secret meeting late on Friday afternoon, that they might call a strike at 10 p.m. but that nobody would be a penny the worse, that all the essential services would be maintained, not by volunteers but by the professionals themselves and – and this was the most important point – that the leaders would be left out in the cold and might very well lose their jobs.

It would not be right to say that the Triple Alliance is dead and lies upon its bier unwept, but rather that it never existed, except as a figment of the brain and that it never can exist where so many diverse interests are concerned and as long as human nature, the one immutable thing in this world of ours, remains unchanged.

Towards the middle of 1921 it became known that the supply of gold in Moscow was running short. This was borne out by a growing disinclination on the part of the Third International to subsidise revolutionary movements abroad; but at the same time the Third International awoke to the possibilities of turning the great masses of unemployed in all countries to account. A document that had been circulated in Norway showed how this was to be done. The unemployed were to organise themselves into bodies with a Central Executive Committee. They were to go down to the relieving officer and demand a rate of relief equal to the trade union rate of wages. The local authority would then be compelled to draw upon the national exchequer and in a short time the country would be involved in bankruptcy. As the Third International put it:

> *By uniting the unemployed with the proletarian vanguards in the struggle for the social revolution, the Communist Party will restrain the most rebellious and impatient elements among the unemployed from individual desperate acts and enable the entire mass actively to support under favourable circumstances the struggle of the proletariat ... In a word, this entire mass, from a reserve army of industry, will be transferred into an active army of the revolution.*

And, in another place:

> *As Municipalities are more likely to yield to demands, the first attacks of this kind should be made upon Municipalities and made in such a way as to exclude any possibility of tracing them back to a general scheme. The demands should appear to be local, having no apparent connection with similar attempts in the same country.*

These instructions were acted upon in London and other places. Most of the agitators among the unemployed were communists with headquarters at the International Socialist Club, which had received a subsidy of £1,000. It is unnecessary to add that they were drawing salaries.

The unemployed leaders did not find the guardians as pliable as they had hoped. Even when they engaged in a system of bullying individuals, as in the case of a certain chairman of a London board who was a beneficed clergyman and whose church was visited with the express intention of disturbing the service, they could not extort grants approaching what they demanded and the boards which were controlled by Labour members had no balance in their banks and could not obtain an overdraft without the consent of the Ministry of Health, which, of course, laid down a reasonable scale beyond which they could not go. I do not know that the fear of being surcharged personally would have deterred them, for most of these gentlemen, having few possessions, would welcome the advertisement of an attempt at distraint upon their goods, but the impossibility of getting money from the bank was a difficulty not to be got over. The real unemployed took no part in these demonstrations. They were orderly and reasonable folk who had begun to realise that unemployment was a condition far beyond the control of the government of a single country, but a world phenomenon which had to be lived through as patiently as possible, and consequently the revolutionary agitators failed again.

The famine in Russia brought a new factor into the situation. Russia is so huge a country that there have been always periodical famines in one part of it or another. As long as there was an efficient central government it was possible to relieve the want in one province by the superfluities in another, but under the communists the entire railway system had broken down and it was no longer possible to carry supplies to the Volga. So the communists began to appeal to foreign countries. They represented the famine as having been caused by the intervention of capitalist states and when this argument was found unconvincing they accused first Denikin and Kolchak and then the weather. The central government did not seem to care how many of the wretched peasants perished, but they did want to convince the distant provinces that it was only to the communists that they could look for relief. Their great dread was that someone else would take the credit from them.

Strange stories reached us from time to time. In some provinces the Bolsheviks had made a clean sweep of the priests and churches and in many of the villages there had been no religious teaching for four years. In a few of these it was alleged that people had reverted to paganism and had hoisted the head of a bull into a tree and made offerings to it. These stories were never confirmed, but they are consistent with the religious aspect of the Russian peasant character.

About the middle of 1921 the communists realised that it was impossible longer to maintain the pretence that communism was an economic success. They had spent their gold reserve lavishly and they had got very little in return for it and now they saw the day approaching when there would be nothing left. Faced with these prospects, there was nothing for it but to agree with their enemies, the capitalists, quickly. True, they could continue to hold the reins of power because they had been careful to disarm all the Red Army except a few trusted battalions, but inevitably a government which cannot pay its way, is bankrupt as a concern and has made it impossible for its subjects to pay any taxes, must fall and so the Lenin Party announced publicly that it intended to veer to the right. This announcement was hailed by all the people who wanted to begin trading with Russia as a genuine conversion. It was bitterly opposed in Russia by the 'die-hard' communists, who argued quite reasonably that the admission of the foreign capitalist or, indeed, of any foreigner at all, would sound the death-knell of the Soviet. And then M. Krassin took upon himself to explain what the moderates really meant by reversion to capitalistic principles. They would die sooner than surrender the railways or big industries, or land or mines, to private ownership: all they intended was to grant leases to concessionaires, who would be permitted to work their concessions under Soviet control, giving a share of their profits to the Soviet government, who would provide them with the necessary labour. The communists would not listen to a suggestion that they should recognise their debts to foreigners until the foreign governments had agreed fully to recognise them as a sovereign state. He seemed to have a childlike belief that political recognition would immediately result in financial advances to the Russian government. He, too, appeared to believe that the British government keeps vast hoards of gold in its vaults and that all it has to do when it makes an advance is to scoop up so many millions and hand them over to M. Krassin himself. After all, his own government, as long as it had gold to play with, financed people in just this way. But credits are provided ultimately by the man in the street, who has outlets for his savings in nearly every part of the world among honest men who pay their debts, and why should he, therefore, adventure his money among people who make a boast of their contempt for monetary obligations and who have proved that even when they had money they lacked the ordinary business ability for turning it to account?

All those who have had to do with Russia realise that it is useless to talk of reconstructing the country until the communist power has become as it did in Hungary – a nightmare of the past. All this talk of conferences extending from Prinkipo to Genoa is merely putting off that inevitable day.

The fixed idea that without exports from Russia prices cannot fall in England is a very curious obsession not only of Labour but of some of those who have access to the trade returns. In 1900 Russia exported very little to foreign countries at all and the world got on. In the next decade the exports gradually increased until in the record year, 1913, they amounted to £28,000,000, but this was a small proportion of the £600,000,000 of our foreign imports. In that year we exported £17,000,000 to Russia. The bulk of the Russian exports was cereals, of which nearly all was produced by the large landowners, who have ceased to exist. The peasants, who then had manure from their beasts, exported very little: their surplus went to the large towns. But now the beasts, like the landowners, are gone. On the Soviet figures, the horses have been reduced from 28,000,000 to 3,000,000, of which only half are fit for agricultural work. Think what this means in a country like Russia, where every pound of produce has to be taken an average of 30 miles to the nearest railway and where ploughing is the first essential! What the Soviet government thinks of it is shown by a curious little incident. Early in the year M. Krassin sent to a firm of agricultural machine-makers the working drawings of a human tractor which had been prepared in Moscow by a Russian engineer. It was to be made on the principle of the trolleys used by platelayers on the railway. It was to have two levers, each operated by three men – forced labour, of course – and the seventh man was to steer. A plough was to be attached to it. The firm refused the order for the twofold reason that the machine would scarcely be powerful enough to carry the seven men without the plough and that it was inhuman to employ men to do the work of animals under such conditions.

If trade with Russia is essential to a low cost of living in this country, why have prices continued to fall? The reason is given in the Board of Trade returns. The world, having done without Russian exports for eight years, has readjusted itself. The cereals, butter, eggs, timber and flax, which we formerly had from Russia, are now being produced in Canada, the Argentine and other countries. Half the flax-producing provinces of Russia now lie outside her frontiers. The world can do without Russia until such time as she recovers her sanity. As long as she continues to tolerate the form of government that has brought her to economic ruin she is beyond help.

Trade with Russia has been opened for the past eighteen months and there has been no trade. This has not been for lack of enterprise on the part of traders. It is due to the fact that Russia now has practically nothing to give in exchange, but there is the further factor that one cannot trade with people of bad faith. Two or three vessels carried goods to Odessa last winter. They were not allowed to sell them except at prices fixed by the Moscow Soviet and these prices were below cost.

A Belgian firm undertook to repair and run the Odessa tramways. They had to pay a large deposit for the concession. As soon as the tramways were running the local Soviet stepped in and sequestrated the tramway as Soviet property and when the syndicate protested it was threatened with arrest by the Tcheka. It then demanded the return of the deposit, which at first was refused: in the end half only of the deposit was repaid.

It is difficult for those who do not know the communists to understand this policy of suicide. The fact is that only 10 per cent of the communists in Russia are men of education; the remaining 90 per cent are illiterate workmen, peasants and jailbirds, who have achieved by the Revolution a position of power and comparative affluence which they never dreamed of under the old regime. They have just sense enough to know that, if foreign capital is admitted into the country and the Russians are freed from the Terror, their day will be done. Lenin and his colleagues may propose; they, the majority, dispose; and while Lenin may quite honestly mean what he says about a change of heart he is powerless to carry out his promises.

One of the most curious of the obsessions is the fear of anarchy if the Reds fall. There is anarchy already. Russia is the last country in the world to fall into the sort of anarchy feared by our statesmen. For centuries she has been accustomed to village councils, with which the Czarist government interfered very little. She has them now and all that will happen when the communists fall, as fall they must, is that the country will break up into these little entities, each stretching out hands to its neighbours. In such conditions the last state of Russia will be better than the first.

Meanwhile, the real government, so far as there is a central government at all, is the Tcheka, the Extraordinary Commission, which has changed its name but not its nature. It is now called a political committee under the Commissary of the Interior and in due course, when its new name becomes as much hated as its old name, it will change it again. Even Lenin himself would not be exempt from its attentions and he knows it. This terror that walks by day and night is the real government of Russia.

The conviction, honestly held by all classes of Germans, that the war was forced upon them by an inexorable ring of steel that hemmed them in, is not to be dismissed lightly as the figment of their military party. It was a subconscious impulse like that of a hive of bees before they swarm and, like the bees, they were armed with stings. It is even now idle to point out to them that their surplus population was as free as air; the sparsely populated regions of the earth lay open to it; it could do as so many thousands of Germans had done and form German-speaking communities, not in German tropical colonies, which have never been successful, but in temperate zones where men can reap the fruits of their own labour; that was not their vision of a place in the sun. Nor is their conviction shaken by the argument that by their industry and their commercial enterprise abroad they were already beginning to inherit the earth. Perhaps the Great War was the first premonition of what is to be the destiny of poor humanity. Far back in the ages the millions of Asia, driven out of their own lands by drought and famine, swarmed westward and swept away the Roman Empire, but then there was land enough for all and as a torrent pouring down a mountain canyon comes to rest in the broad waters of the lake, so the irruptions from the East spent themselves and subsided. But when there is no longer any lake, what then? In the time of Elizabeth the population of England and Wales was 5,000,000, as late as 1750 it was only 6,500,000 and in 1801, the year of the first census, under 9,000,000. Up to that date these islands were self-supporting. During the last century it has increased at a rate of more than 2,000,000 every ten years, in spite of emigration, and if we were cut off from supplies from abroad we should be starving in a few weeks. The population of the earth is now estimated at something over 1,500,000,000: at the present rate of increase it may be 3,000,000,000 in less than a century. The empty spaces of the world are rapidly filling and when all those in which men can support themselves are filled up, posterity will have to look to itself. Nature's old remedy, plague and the early death of the weakly and the ailing, have been subdued and unless the birth-rate is artificially regulated the subconscious swarming instinct, having no outlet, must behave as it does in the hive and whole nations and classes will fall upon one another for the right to live. Beside such a vital struggle the Great War will seem as insignificant as the Crimea. The generation upon which this catastrophe falls will find plenty of reasons to justify the breach of peace and it will remain ignorant of the root cause to the end.

Therefore it is idle to think that the world has seen the last of war: conferences on disarmament and the revival of world trade are mere temporary palliatives which can do nothing for any generation but our own, for the one unchanging thing in the world is human nature and the strongest instinct in human nature is self-preservation. This terror will not come in our time nor in that of our children, but come it will.

Subconscious impulse is manifested in little things as well as in great. The dress of women is passing through a period of décolletage as it did immediately after the Napoleonic campaigns and after all the great wars of modern times. There was always a marked deterioration of public morals in every country after visitations of plague, as if the race were unconsciously obeying an instinct to quicken up the process of replacement. Fashion is supposed to be controlled by the dressmakers: is it not more likely that the dressmakers are merely quick to interpret the inclinations of those whom their clothes are to adorn? A whole generation of young women have lost the mates of their own ages; another generation who were in the schoolroom during those tremendous years are treading hard upon their heels. Are they to lose their birthright of wifehood and motherhood and tamely be laid upon the shelf? Their subconscious instinct impels them to attract; their dressmaker divines the impulse and obeys it. The dress shrinks to its narrowest dimensions.

We have lived through war: we have yet to live through peace with the economic fabric of civilisation shaken if not shattered. Let those who feel it difficult to face the lean years read the intimate records of the ten years after Waterloo and take heart again.

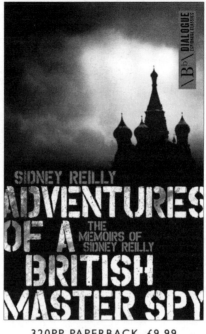

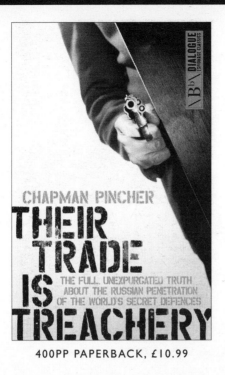